Palgrave Studies in the History of Economic Thought

Palgrave Studies in the History of Economic Thought publishes contributions by leading scholars, illuminating key events, theories and individuals that have had a lasting impact on the development of modern-day economics. The topics covered include the development of economies, institutions and theories.

The series aims to highlight the academic importance of the history of economic thought, linking it with wider discussions within economics and society more generally. It contains a broad range of titles that illustrate the breath of discussions — from influential economists and schools of thought, through to historical and modern social trends and challenges — within the discipline.

All books in the series undergo a single-blind peer review at both the proposal and manuscript submission stages.

For further information on the series and to submit a proposal for consideration, please contact Wyndham Hacket Pain, Economics Editor (wyndham.hacketpain@palgrave.com).

The series is dedicated to the memory of former editor and distinguished economist Geoff Harcourt.

Fernando Collantes

Consumer Society and the Economists

Consumption and Well-Being in the History of Economic Thought

palgrave
macmillan

Fernando Collantes
Department of Economics
University of Oviedo
Oviedo, Spain

ISSN 2662-6578 ISSN 2662-6586 (electronic)
Palgrave Studies in the History of Economic Thought
ISBN 978-3-031-96644-6 ISBN 978-3-031-96645-3 (eBook)
https://doi.org/10.1007/978-3-031-96645-3

Cover credit: Doug Armand | Getty Images

This Palgrave Macmillan imprint is published by the registered company Springer Nature Switzerland AG.
The registered company address is: Gewerbestrasse 11, 6330 Cham, Switzerland

Competing Interests

The author has no competing interests to declare that are relevant to the content of this manuscript.

About the Book

Is consumer society a vehicle for progress? Or, on the contrary, a detour leading us away from the path to the good life? To what extent is consumer society a relevant object of analysis, after all? Today, these questions are central to the debate on capitalism, its dynamics, and its consequences. Yet they are by no means exclusive to our time. This book traces the history of economic thought on consumer society from the late eighteenth century to the present day. Some economists viewed consumption as an opportunity for progress, others as a dangerous deviation, while some sought to reconcile both perspectives. Whereas some attributed great significance to the triumph of a consumption pattern featuring abundance and diversity, others remained sceptical about the value of consumer society as an object of study.

This is the story of how economists debated consumer society and, underlying that debate, another fundamental discussion: how economists should conduct their research and what kind of relationships they should (or should not) maintain with other social sciences and the humanities. Engaging with this second debate is essential to addressing the challenge that the story recounted here poses for the future: incorporating the world of consumption into the great debates about capitalism and doing so in a manner that captures the complexity of its links with human well-being and social progress.

Praise for *Consumer Society and the Economists*

"This book challenges the ideas of consumption as progress and the hegemony of growth, studying theories that have proposed consumption as deviation. The author revitalizes the debate on consumer society and reinforces in a very compelling way the relevance of history, sociology and philosophy. By doing so, he opens the path to achieving a synthesis that could lead us to seeking the good life that we deserve to live."

—Estrella Trincado Aznar, *Complutense University of Madrid*

"This book provides an insightful and important contrast between two visions of the economy: one in which human preferences, expressed in consumption patterns, is a key driver of economic progress; and another one where consumption patterns are a manifestation of more fundamental forces, often expressed in the pursuit of social status through consumption. It convincingly shows that, while most mainstream economic theory has sided with the first vision, a critical assessment of the broader impacts of the economy in our lives can only be achieved through the second vision. This excellent book deserves a wide readership by all those interested in achieving a broader understanding of such an alternative and important vision which, despite its relative neglect today, has a long and distinct tradition in economics."

—Nuno Ornelas Martins, *Universidade Católica Portuguesa*

"Collantes delivers a concise history of economic thought on consumer society from the 18th century onward. The project is ambitious, but the gamble pays off! Centered around the dialectic between the progressive thesis, the deviationist antithesis, and the attempts at synthesis, the narrative is compelling."

—Alexandre Chirat, *Université Paris-Nanterre*

Contents

About the Author

Fernando Collantes (Torrelavega, 1976) is Professor of History and Political Economy at the University of Oviedo (Spain). His previous books include *Milk in Spain and the History of Diet Change: The Political Economy of Dairy Consumption Since 1950*; *The Political Economy of the Common Agricultural Policy: Coordinated Capitalism or Bureaucratic Monster?*; and *Peaceful Surrender: The Depopulation of Rural Spain During the Twentieth Century*. See https://www.fernandocollantes.es/english-version for more details.

List of Figures

CHAPTER 1

Introduction

The process of writing this book began long before I became aware of it. When I was in my final year of studying Economics at the University of Cantabria, back in 1998, my academic vocation was awakened by the History of Economic Thought course taught by Rafael Domínguez. It was fascinating to have access to a pluralistic framework where the education I had received throughout my degree coexisted with other ways of viewing and practising economics. Two moments were particularly memorable. One occurred near the beginning of the course when I was introduced to Aristotle's economic thought. So, the famous philosopher had argued—contrary to what we had been taught in both letter and spirit for four years—that the unlimited pursuit of material wealth could be a mistake? The other moment came near the end of the course, with a certain Thorstein Veblen, whom I had never heard of before. So, there was an economist who, when he looked at consumers, did not see the utility maximisers who had filled our textbooks until then but rather individuals driven by an instinct of emulation and a taste for "conspicuous consumption"?

I did not pursue these topics during my early years as a researcher, but their echo continued to resonate. I immersed myself in the field of economic history, where the prevailing spirit could be summarised in these words: "the more, the better". The dominant narrative was one in which nations participated in a race towards material abundance, with some

F. Collantes, *Consumer Society and the Economists*, Palgrave Studies in the History of Economic Thought,
https://doi.org/10.1007/978-3-031-96645-3_1

achieving greater success than others. I found this very relevant but also incomplete. After all, what happens to the prince and the princess after the end of the story, once the narrator assures us that they lived happily ever after? What happens to the economies and societies we call "developed" once they reach that point? I dedicated the first part of my research career to studying depopulation and development in rural areas, a problem that could be seen as a kind of collateral damage caused by the march towards progress. Later, I became interested in changes in food consumption, focusing on the dietary problems of developed societies.

The empirical side of this latter study always evolved well. I took a small case—the consumption of dairy products in Spain from 1950 to the present—and ensured that I explored the various quantitative and qualitative sources in detail. The result generated a reasonable level of interest among my colleagues, both in economic history and in related fields. However, something was missing. Article after article, presentation after presentation, I could not shake the feeling that the theoretical concern that had motivated the study, which went beyond food studies to encompass consumer society and affluence, never quite came to the surface. Finally, I attempted to write a text in which this theoretical interest would frame my empirical study on dairy consumption, but then something became clear—something I had been suspecting (and denying): the gap between the theoretical debate on consumer society and the historical analysis of my small case study was too wide, jarring even.

I owe it to Laurent Herment, who read that text, for pointing it out to me with both clarity and delicacy. Laurent suggested that perhaps these theoretical reflections on consumer society needed more space than I could give them in the first section of a twenty-page text. Could they perhaps be material for the opening chapter of that book on the history of Spanish dairy consumption that Laurent knew I was beginning to write? I thought Laurent was right and started working on that chapter immediately. The writing was fluid, and soon authors and readings that had accumulated over the years—without ever quite finding their way into my writing—began to surface. But over time, the writing became too fluid, so to speak. If only because of the sheer number of pages that began to pile up, it was clear that this could no longer be the introductory chapter of a book. It seemed more like the germ of a different book, one that reconstructed the history of economic thought on consumer society. I had been preparing for years to write that book, and I had not noticed.

An Overview of the Book

Is consumer society a vehicle for progress? Or, on the contrary, a detour leading us away from the path to the good life? And to what extent is consumer society a relevant object of analysis, after all? Today, these questions are central to the debate on capitalism, its dynamics, and its consequences. Yet they are by no means exclusive to our time. This book traces the history of economic thought on consumer society from the late eighteenth century to the present day. Some economists viewed consumption as an opportunity for progress, others as a dangerous deviation, while some sought to reconcile both perspectives. Whereas some attributed great significance to the triumph of a consumption pattern featuring abundance and diversity, others remained sceptical about the value of consumer society as an object of study. This is the story of how economists debated consumer society and, underlying that debate, another fundamental discussion: how economists should conduct their research and what kind of relationships they should (or should not) maintain with other social sciences and the humanities.

The second chapter presents the terms of the debate and the conceptual framework that will be used throughout the book. One of the most striking features of the history of capitalism is the formation of consumer societies across the globe. In embryonic form from around 1870 and more fully after 1945, market societies have witnessed an unprecedented expansion in the scale and scope of consumer expenditure. This development has given rise to two rival perspectives. The first is the progress thesis, according to which consumer society brings material prosperity and expands people's opportunities to lead a good life. The second is the deviation thesis, which holds that the emphasis on growing material wealth ultimately hinders individuals' capacity to make progress in other dimensions of the good life, such as interpersonal relationships and the cultivation of existential meaning. Alongside these two opposing views, a third stance must also be considered—one that rejects both by denying the significance of consumer society as an object of study altogether. Our interest in this book will be on reconstructing the evolution of these perspectives during the last 250 years, from Adam Smith to the present. Our approach is influenced by the work of Albert Hirschman and Joseph Schumpeter. We take inspiration from Hirschman's use of ideal types as a starting point for identifying intellectual genealogies and their points of interaction. This includes the possibility of discovering "synthesis views", which in the particular case of consumer society would be in line with the analysis provided by today's historians. From Schumpeter, we take an interest in exploring the relationships economics maintains with other social sciences and the humanities, as well as a preference for long-term periods in the reconstruction of the history of economic thought.

The third chapter is devoted to the period between 1770 and 1870: the era of the industrial revolution and the intellectual cycle of classical political economy. The industrial revolution changed the world by freeing economies from their tendency towards stagnation, yet it initially had little effect on the consumption patterns of the masses. It is therefore unsurprising that, in an era still heavily marked by scarcity and deprivation, political economists from Adam Smith to Karl Marx lacked a coherent vision of consumer society. What these economists did possess, however, was a set of intuitions concerning the world of consumption and its impact on human well-being. The most striking feature of these intuitions was their ambivalence. Material abundance was at times perceived as a vector of progress—valuable in itself and for its potential effects on the non-material dimensions of the good life. Yet, in other instances, certain patterns of consumption were portrayed as forms of materialistic deviation. The most consistent articulation of these rival perspectives was offered by John Stuart Mill, through his use of the concepts of productive and unproductive consumption. The adoption of an analytical framework grounded in the notions of surplus and reproduction was significant in enabling the economists of this period to bequeath an intellectual map with the potential to evolve into a form of "synthesis view". Just as important as these questions of what might be termed "pure" economics, however, was the fact that political economy remained open to the incorporation of historical, sociological, and philosophical elements.

The fourth chapter shows how the economic debate on consumer society began to take shape during the period 1870–1945. This was a time in which early forms of consumer society began to emerge in North America and Western Europe. There was also a transition from the tradition of political economy to an increasingly institutionalised discipline of economics. Yet the economics of the period remained pluralistic, and this pluralism is reflected in the diversity of perspectives that economists began to develop concerning the nascent consumer society. The marginalist school focused on the figure of the rational, utility-maximising consumer, who derived pleasure through well-informed consumption decisions—a formulation broadly aligned with the progress thesis. Complementing this, the Austrian school advanced the notion of the sovereign consumer, whose preferences served as the *primum mobile* of capitalism and whose freedom of choice was a cornerstone of non-authoritarian political order. In contrast, within the institutionalist tradition, Thorstein Veblen emphasised the role of consumption as a marker of social status. In doing so, he offered a powerful formulation of the deviation thesis, highlighting the socially corrosive effects of conspicuous consumption. Some economists sought a synthesis of these perspectives. Alfred Marshall and John Maynard Keynes, in particular, intuited that the progress thesis might hold true during a long historical phase marked by material privation for most of the population, while the deviation thesis could become increasingly relevant in a later stage of affluence. The deviation thesis—and the broader synthesis view to which it could contribute—flourished within intellectual traditions that treated economics as an open discipline, receptive to insights from history, sociology, and philosophy. However, in the final decades of this period, this open conception of economics came under serious threat from the rise of the neoclassical paradigm as envisioned by Lionel Robbins. Lines of confrontation began to take shape—lines that would later define the major clash of views on consumer society that would erupt after 1945.

The fifth chapter deals with the period 1945–1990, during which the battlefield that had begun to take shape during the period 1870–1945 became the scene of direct confrontation between rival views of consumer society. This was the period during which fully developed versions of consumer society emerged—first in the United States and later in Western Europe and Japan. It also marked the consolidation of the neoclassical school's hegemony within the discipline of economics. Consumer society came under critical scrutiny from the institutional economist John Kenneth Galbraith, who, at this point, was joined by some Marxists as well as by internal dissenters within the mainstream. Galbraith elaborated a kind of "synthesis view" that echoed the earlier formulations of Marshall and Keynes, combining the progress and deviation theses in a diachronic manner. However, the deviation thesis was met with strong opposition from the core of the profession, increasingly united around the kind of neoclassical economics championed by the Chicago school. Under the eventual leadership of Milton Friedman, most economists aligned themselves with the progress thesis. Contributing to this alignment was their particular understanding of economics both as a theoretical framework—centred on the notions of equilibrium and scarcity—and as a social science that had little to gain from engagement with history, sociology, or philosophy.

Equally significant was the fact that, in the turbulent context of the Cold War, many economists adopted a political discourse—inspired by the tradition of Austrian economics—that cast the sovereign consumer as a bulwark of democracy and a safeguard against authoritarianism. The ascendancy of these perspectives led, by the final years of the period, to the disappearance of consumer society from the analytical horizon of new generations of economists, who were educated within an intellectual milieu that left little room to explore combinations of the progress and deviation theses.

Our historical route ends in Chap. 6, devoted to the study of the period since 1990. The conversation of the last thirty years has been heavily shaped by the outcome of the major confrontation that took place during the Cold War. While a new wave of expansion in consumer society unfolded, a mainstream current rooted in neoclassical economics was consolidating within academia, albeit now characterised by a significant degree of internal pluralism and theoretical fragmentation. In this context, consumer society has largely remained outside the field of vision of most economists. Among those who have engaged with the topic, heterodox and dissident economists have revisited the deviation thesis, experimenting with different ways of articulating it with the progress thesis. Alongside continuators of earlier intellectual traditions, ecological economists and happiness economists have stood out in this regard. Most economists, however, have continued to align themselves with the progress thesis. This reflects the extent to which the Cold War-era trajectories remain operative. Except in its growing connection with psychology, economics has largely sustained its intellectual isolation from other social sciences and the humanities. This has reduced the space in which the deviation thesis might emerge, and by extension, where a synthesis view might be developed. Moreover, most economists—including many aligned with social democratic political agendas—have continued to adhere to the doctrine of the sovereign consumer as a cornerstone of market democracies. Nevertheless, these path dependencies remain open-ended, and the question of consumer society continues to resonate in our time.

We close the book with a final chapter of conclusions. The historical journey undertaken in this book reveals that economists have struggled to develop a synthesis view of consumer society. Naturally, one must be cautious about overgeneralisation: it is possible to distinguish two distinct intellectual genealogies. The first—chronologically speaking—comprises economists who have shown a willingness to consider (at least as a theoretical possibility) the deviation thesis. These figures are found across a wide range of schools, including classical political economy, Marxism, institutionalism, ecological economics, and even strands of neoclassical economics. The second genealogy aligns strongly with the progress thesis and is associated with the type of neoclassical economics that rose to dominance during the mid-twentieth century and, to a significant extent, continues to shape mainstream economic thinking today. The difficulties encountered by the deviation thesis within this second genealogy stem in part from matters of economic theory, but also from a specific conception of economics as a social science, as well as from the political success of the doctrine of consumer sovereignty. The deviation thesis emerged more naturally among economists of the first genealogy, yet the path towards a synthesis view has faced significant obstacles. Some of these relate to the theoretical integration of the world of consumption. Others stem from persistent challenges in forging meaningful connections with history, sociology, and philosophy. Meanwhile, consumer society has maintained only an intermittent presence in the field of vision of economists across various schools and tendencies—something that has further limited the profession's capacity to elaborate a synthesis view. The history traced in this book presents us with a challenge: to bring the world of consumption into the heart of the great debates on capitalism, in a way that acknowledges the complexity of its ties to human well-being and social progress.

Notice

Throughout the book, I use a conventional author–year system for bibliographic references. In some cases, I have worked with editions that are not the originals, including Spanish-language editions. I have cited then the original year of publication, while the page numbers refer to the edition I actually used. Full details are provided in the list of references at the end of each chapter. When I have not used an English edition, I have tried to reproduce direct quotations as they appear in the English version. When this has not been possible, I have provided my own translation.

Acknowledgements The gestation of this book has been so prolonged that listing all those to whom I am indebted becomes even more difficult than usual. I have already noted the fundamental—albeit unintended—role played by Laurent Herment in making it possible for readers to have this book in their hands today. Once I had a preliminary version of the manuscript, several people were kind enough to read it, in whole or in part. These were Alexandre Chirat, Rafael Domínguez, Domingo Gallego, and Patricia Suárez. Their insightful comments helped me to identify which parts of the manuscript required more direct argumentation and which ones needed greater nuance. During the long period in which this book was taking shape (even if I did not know it), I also benefited from many conversations on the subject with Ernesto Clar. The anonymous reviewers not only provided constructive suggestions but also, to my surprise and delight, encouraged me to write a more ambitious book than I had originally envisioned.

I had the opportunity to present parts of this book at various conferences: those of the European Society for the History of Economic Thought (twice, in Padua and Graz), the European Association for Evolutionary Political Economy (in Bilbao), and the Spanish Association for Economic History (also in Bilbao). I am grateful to the participants, whose feedback helped me to refine my arguments and open them up to alternative perspectives. I am particularly thankful to Angela Ambrosino, Jonathan Andreas, Maria Bach, Michele Bee, Katia Caldari, Mario Cedrini, Oliver Kessler, Estrella Trincado, and Louise Villeneuve. I would like to offer special thanks to Steven Medema, who acted as a meticulous discussant of my work at one of these conferences. In his case, even more than in the others, the usual caveat applies: any shortcomings in the text are solely the result of the author's own ignorance and stubbornness. I would also like to extend my thanks to the members of the committee that assessed my application for a professorship at the University of Oviedo and commented on a synthesis of this book during the second part of the evaluation process: Rosa Congost, Vicente Pinilla, and Nuria Puig, in addition to the aforementioned Rafael Domínguez.

I owe a special debt to those who generously took the time to respond to queries from someone who, to them, was a perfect stranger. I was fortunate enough to receive comments from James K. Galbraith and Juliet Schor on passages related to them—passages about which I felt especially unsure. There was also one such passage related to Albert Hirschman, and Jeremy Adelman kindly responded to my questions with warmth and diligence.

Over the years, my research on consumer society in the history of economic thought has benefited from funding provided by two projects supported by the Spanish Ministry of Science and Innovation (PGC2018-095529-B-I00 and PID2022-138886NB-I00) and two research groups funded by the Government of Aragon (S55_20R and S55_23R). I am grateful to Vicente Pinilla—already mentioned above—who led these projects and groups and who generously regarded this research as a natural extension of the work we were conducting in the field of agri-food economic history.

I am also thankful to the Palgrave team. Wyndham Hacket Pain was a fantastic editor. He was the first to see the potential for one of my conference papers to become the starting point for a book in this series. He also accepted the very extended timeline I proposed and, when the moment came, was open to working with me to find a title that was better than the provisional one we had agreed upon.

I will end with the usual suspects: Elena and our children, Diego, Ana, and Álvaro. I cannot resort to any of the clichés: they played no part in drafting the manuscript, contributed no brilliant ideas, and read no early drafts. Nor did they have to endure a husband or father who spent most of his time with his head in the clouds (or at least, I believe they didn't!). But I owe them thanks for something important—something Elena always understood, and our children are gradually coming to grasp: that writing books like this, or teaching courses on these subjects, is my vocation. Would this book have come into being without that understanding? I believe not. It would likely have faded away somewhere along the many miles of motorway that have always separated our home from the universities where I have taught and continue to teach. Thank you so much for understanding.

Santander
May 2025

CHAPTER 2

The B-Side of Capitalism

Albert Hirschman concludes his book *The Passions and the Interests*, a study on political thought regarding capitalism in the eighteenth century, by asserting that

> both critics and defenders of capitalism could improve upon their arguments through knowledge of the episode in intellectual history that has been recounted here. This is probably all one can ask of history, and of the history of ideas in particular: not to resolve issues, but to raise the level of the debate. (Hirschman, 1977, p. 135)

The premise of this book is that among the many things that can certainly be done to "raise the level of the debate", one of them is to incorporate consumers into a picture that already includes entrepreneurs, workers, or policymakers: the overarching picture of economic life that, in the absence of a better term, we call capitalism. For a long time, this was a cursed word, but in recent years, following the Great Recession that began in 2007, it has made a strong return to academic conversation and public debate (Hodgson, 2015; Kocka, 2016; Milberg, 2019). When capitalism reemerged, however, it did so primarily to focus on what we might call the "A-side" of the system: the production and distribution circuits on which crucial variables such as economic growth and social inequality depend. The "B-side", the world of consumption where individuals and societies

F. Collantes, *Consumer Society and the Economists*, Palgrave Studies in the History of Economic Thought,
https://doi.org/10.1007/978-3-031-96645-3_2

use the resources generated and distributed in the A-side, has received much less attention.

The motivation of this book is to incorporate the world of consumption into the set of topics that inform the conversation about capitalism. To this end, we offer a reconstruction of what economists have thought about consumer society. The title of the book is a nod to *Capitalism and the Historians*, the work developed within the Mont Pelerin Society and coordinated by Friedrich Hayek in 1954, but its spirit is quite different. Hayek introduced the reader to historians who held an essentially positive view of what the birth of capitalism had meant for the standard of living of the common people. His goal was for the general public, whose political opinions were inevitably shaped by a certain awareness of historical experience, to "learn the truth" from historians deemed appropriate (Hayek, 1954, p. 3). Our goal, in contrast, is to reconstruct what economists from different schools and trends have thought about consumer society. Our ambition is not to reveal some definitive truth, but in the spirit evoked by Hirschman at the beginning, to improve the terms of the debate.

This chapter presents our approach. We begin by defining consumer society and narrating its triumphant rise throughout the modern and contemporary eras. We then engage with the debate generated around it, identifying two rival views: what we will call the progress thesis and the deviation thesis. A later section motivates the adoption of a historical approach to reconstruct and analyse the debate. Finally, the section preceding the conclusion presents the conceptual framework for the rest of the book.

The Global Triumph of Consumer Society

In his address to the nation on the afternoon on 11 September 2001, US President George W. Bush explained that "today, our fellow citizens, our way of life, our very freedom came under attack in a series of deliberate and deadly terrorist acts". What did this "way of life" consist of? Among other things, the maintenance of high levels of consumer spending. A few weeks later, Bush called on Americans to "take your families and enjoy life, the way we want it to be enjoyed". An example? "Get down to Disney World in Florida".[1] The emphasis on consumption as the highest expression of the American way of life was in no way a partisan choice. On the Democratic side of the political spectrum, Robert Reich, who had been

[1] https://georgewbush-whitehouse.archives.gov (accessed 11 November 2024).

Secretary of Labour during Bill Clinton's presidency, also wrote at the end of September 2001:

> The theory is that we demonstrate our resolve to the rest of the world by investing and consuming at least as much as we did before, preferably more. The terrorists tried to strike at the heart of American capitalism. We show that American capitalism is alive and well by giving it as much of our credit card as possible. (Stewart, 2021)

What a stark contrast to what political leaders had asked citizens to do in past emergency situations! Instead of calls for moderation, instead of exhortations to accept personal sacrifices in the name of the national interest, a form of "patriotic consumerism" emerged (Stewart, 2021).

Such a thing could only occur in a consumer society. By the turn of the millennium, the three conditions had long been in place in the United States that, in our opinion, best help identify this often-elusive reality. The first condition, not very demanding but necessary as a starting point, is that this was a market society (Polanyi, 1944; Hirschman, 1986). Household consumption practices were embedded in an economic system in which markets played a central role in coordinating individual behaviour. The world of consumption can, in fact, be seen as the primary outlet of the production and distribution circuits that constitute what might be called the "A-side" of the system.

Once this context is established, our two other conditions have to do with the "B-side", with the world of consumption. These conditions are expansion and diversification, and both convey the image of a continuous revolution in what Fernand Braudel (1979) calls "material life". Expansion is a general trend towards growth in consumption, so that a large portion of the population has access to ever more goods and services. Diversification is an increasing variety in the consumer basket. A good indicator of this variety is the transformation in the composition of consumer expenditure by product types, and more specifically, the declining share of products that satisfy basic needs. Thus, for example, the share of food in household budgets tends to decrease, while that of (say) vacation tourism tends to increase. A related feature is an increasing variety within each of these categories of expenditure.

Readers familiar with the work of Simon Kuznets (1966) will have perceived that our focus on expansion and diversification resembles his focus on economic growth and structural change. We shall not enter here into a discussion of Kuznets' role in the construction of the system of national accounts and the early debate over the extent to which it should have been oriented towards the measurement of welfare (Mitra-Kahn, 2011). We simply wish to emphasise that, in a manner analogous to Kuznets in his later empirical work, our intention is to focus not only on the expansion of consumer spending or the shopping basket but also on their composition. The basic idea is that consumer society involves a change in the consumption patterns of most people: to consume more, certainly; but also to consume differently.

This definition of consumer society may seem insufficient in the eyes of some readers. After all, consumer society is more than just an economic phenomenon. It is also a political phenomenon: in this type of society, consumption becomes a key component of the social contract upon which political systems are based. And it is, of course, a cultural phenomenon: in this type of society, consumption acts as a vehicle for the expression of personal identity, as a space for sociability, and as a material basis for the formulation of various intersubjective representations of reality (Cross, 2000; Glickman, 2009; Trentmann, 2016). Nevertheless, we will maintain our definition within the economic sphere, as it is within this sphere that the debate of interest to us throughout the book takes place: the debate on consumer society, human well-being, and social progress. And even then, it must be acknowledged that the focus will remain on private household consumption, while the consumption of public goods and services will feature only tangentially in the analysis.

Defined this way, consumer society is a recent historical phenomenon; more recent than capitalism itself. By 1870, capitalism was widely spread across Europe and North America as a result of institutional reforms and revolutions that had accumulated over the preceding decades and (in some cases) centuries. However, even in the most advanced economies, the other two conditions we established to identify consumer society were not present. The material life of most people continued to be marked by deprivation and scarcity. Basic needs such as food, clothing, and housing consumed most household resources, and even then, they were met in a precarious and often problematic manner. Only among a narrow social elite could a more affluent consumption pattern and a more diversified spending be found.

This does not exclude the possibility that, like any other historical process of this kind, the formation of consumer societies may have had its antecedents in earlier periods. For example, historians have found evidence of relevant changes in consumption patterns taking place in the early modern period. Ever broader segments of European society were exposed to new goods from the overseas colonies (sugar, coffee, spices), which attracted their attention. There was also increasing interest among the middle-high classes in goods aimed at improving their personal appearance and equipping their homes. These changes were so significant that some historians have identified this as the factor that motivated Europeans to work harder and longer and produce an "industrious revolution" that would have paved the way for the subsequent development of the industrial revolution (de Vries, 2008).

Nevertheless, the social and territorial limits of this renewal of the world of consumption were evident. The process was largely driven by a small number of societies in northwestern Europe, such as the Netherlands and England, as well as by an emerging middle-upper class of merchants, artisans, and prosperous farmers. It is not that these dynamics were absent in other territories and social classes, but in general, in most countries and for most families, the precariousness of material life was evident. Moreover, this precariousness continued to be widespread even during the early stages of European industrialisation, a period for which a mountain of evidence has accumulated, alerting to a disconnect between macroeconomic improvement and living conditions. The persistence of famines and subsistence crises well into the nineteenth century is a good testament to how far the notions of abundance and comfort that we associate with consumer society continued to be alien to the experience of the European populations of the time (Martínez Carrión, 2012; Pamuk & van Zanden, 2010; Shammas, 2012; Vanhaute et al., 2007). The situation was probably even worse in the vast fraction of the world that was still immersed in a pre-industrial dynamic and thus began to suffer what Kenneth Pomeranz (2000) has called "the great divergence".

The economic conditions we have associated with consumer society began to be realised during the period between 1870 and 1945. It was during this time that the consumption pattern began to become more abundant and, in part related to this, the shopping basket became more diverse. These were changes that also reached a notable degree of social generalisation. However, this was still an embryo of consumer society, rather than a fully developed version of it. To begin with, both its scale and its reach advanced in a frankly irregular manner over time. The trend towards new consumption patterns was blurred at critical moments such as the two World Wars and the Great Depression. Each of these moments, although they were relatively short-lived pauses, had a profound impact on the material life of millions of people and, consequently, left a deep mark. Furthermore, even in the phases when the underlying trend towards a consumer society unfolded more or less smoothly, it was evident that it did so alongside remarkable inequalities. It was not the same (for instance) in the United States as in Spain, and within each of these two countries, it was not the same for the higher class of industrial magnates as it was for the lower class of agricultural day labourers. It would be a mistake to think that peripheral countries or the lower classes were completely excluded from the dynamics of consumer society, but there is no doubt that the latter faced notable territorial and social limits (Bairoch, 1997; Deaton, 1975; Francks, 2009; Gordon, 2017; Rodríguez, 2021; Trentmann, 2016).

It was during the decades following the Second World War that these limits faded away. While capitalism experienced an unprecedented period of expansion, a fully formed version of consumer society flourished in more and more countries. Replicating the kind of pattern that is sometimes described as "great acceleration" (McNeill & Engelke, 2014), consumer spending grew at an unprecedented rate after 1945 (Fig. 2.1). Not only was there expansion, but also much diversification. A drastic reorganisation of the shopping basket took place, as food and other basic needs gave way to cars, household appliances, tourism, and leisure, to name but

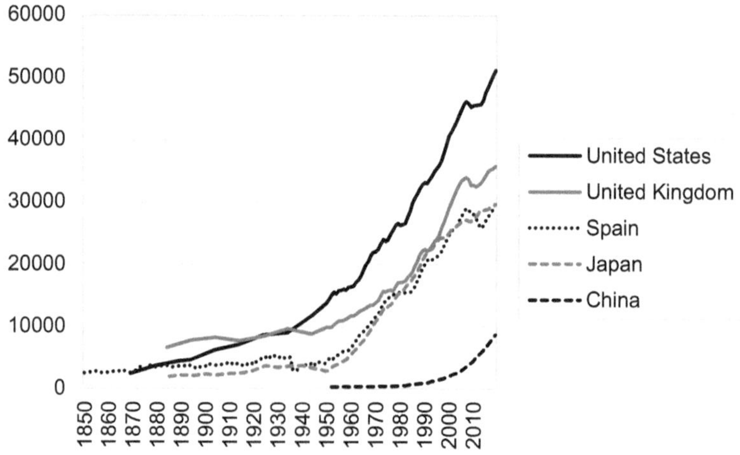

Fig. 2.1 Consumption expenditure per capita in five countries (2017 US dollars). *Sources:* 1850–1950: Francks (2009, p. 224), Kuznets (1962, pp. 80–81 and 86–89), Maddison Project Database (www.rug.nl/ggdc, accessed 13 February 2025), and Prados de la Escosura (2017, updated series); 1950–2019: Penn World Tables 10.01 (www.rug.nl/ggdc, accessed 13 February 2025). The data before 1950 have been scaled back according to the 1950 figure in the Penn World Tables

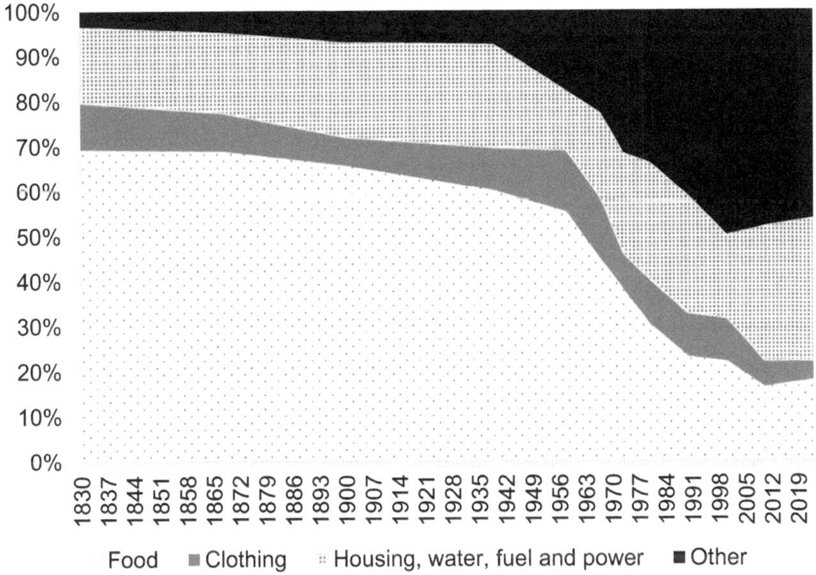

Fig. 2.2 Composition of private consumer expenditure in Spain, 1830–2023. *Sources:* 1830–2000: Maluquer de Motes (2005, p. 1297); 2010–2023: Instituto Nacional de Estadística (2025)

a few (Fig. 2.2). Of course, substantial differences continued to exist between the upper and lower classes, but even the latter had clearly escaped their traditional basic deprivations and were now firmly incorporated into a dynamic of greater abundance and variety. The United States continued to be the epicentre of this revolution in material life, but it was soon joined by other countries: first, Northwestern Europe and Japan; later, Southern Europe. A good illustration of the depth of these changes is the fact that it was during this period that the expression "consumer society" began to spread across the different affected countries, sometimes accompanied by a significant addition: "mass" consumer society (Cross, 2000; de Grazia, 2005; Francks, 2009; Levy, 2021; Offer, 2006, 2014).

With this, we do not intend to abstract away from the national variants through which the underlying dynamics of consumer society manifested themselves. These variants even affected the very trajectory of the concept. In Anglo-Saxon countries, the term *consumer society* is still used to this day. In languages more closely related to Latin, however, the focus is not on the consumers but on consumption; not on the people, but on the activity. Thus, we speak of *société de consommation* in French, *società dei consumi* in Italian, or *sociedad de consumo* in Spanish. Some readers may have rightly suspected that the conditions we have established for speaking of a consumer society fit slightly better with the versions of the term used in Latin-based languages, but this does not mean its utility is restricted to such a geographical context. What is more significant is the much starker contrast between the terms used in each language to construct an "-ism" from consumption: the English *consumerism*, the Spanish and Italian *consumismo*. Here we find such a distance that, throughout the book, we will avoid using the term. *Consumismo* in the Latin-based languages is unequivocally used to criticise materialism, whereas English-language *consumerism* is often also used to refer to the organised defence of consumer rights. Having made this distinction, we believe that beneath the national nuances, the conceptual and material history of the consumer society is based on compelling unifying features.

During the Cold War, the main limit on the advance of consumer society was of a territorial nature. It is true that consumers in the Soviet Union and its Eastern European satellites had access to a more abundant and diversified basket than before, but they did so within a different institutional order. Nor can we speak of fully formed consumer societies, or even embryonic ones, in the countries that during the Cold War made up the so-called Third World. In these low-income countries, the scope for consumer expenditure in anything other than food, clothing, and housing remained limited (Table 2.1).

However, in both cases in recent decades there has been a clear convergence towards the type of consumer society that triumphed in the West and Japan during the decades following the Second World War. The

Table 2.1 Composition of private consumer expenditure in four groups of countries in the 1950s

	High income	*Middle-high income*	*Middle-low income*	*Low income*
Food	36.4	45.4	50.4	56.4
Clothing	14.6	10.4	10.1	10.6
Housing	11.6	14.2	11.3	11.1
Other	37.4	30.0	28.2	21.9
Total	100.0	100.0	100.0	100.0

Source: Kuznets (1962, p. 24). Housing includes water, fuel, and light

process is slow, and there is no doubt that it remains incomplete today. However, its manifestations are evident. The "shock therapy" with which Russia returned to capitalism made possible a striking burst of exuberance in consumption, at least among the elites who were most able to benefit from regime change. And, above all, more and more developing countries have witnessed the rise of a new class of high- and middle-status consumers, generally located in large cities, who are channelling ever-increasing resources to access a deeply renewed consumption pattern and lifestyle (Trentmann, 2016). China, for instance, remains well behind the West in terms of consumer expenditure, but it cannot be denied that this variable has truly taken off in the last few decades (Fig. 2.1).

We must also add the development of a new wave of consumer society in its original home of North America and Western Europe. Here, except during exceptional circumstances like the Great Recession after 2007, household expenditure has continued to increase rapidly, thus feeding a new cycle of expansion and diversification of the consumer basket. Historians have spoken of this as an era of "hyper-consumerism" (de Grazia, 2016). Whatever the labels used, few would doubt that the dynamics of consumer society have continued to thrive in our time.

Rival Views of Consumer Society

The personal testimony of South Korean sociologist John Lie, born in South Korea in 1959, vividly illustrates the revolution in material life brought about by the formation of consumer societies worldwide. His starting point is a childhood straddling between Seoul and Tokyo:

> Seoul in the early 1960s was my childhood conception of backwardness. While I marveled at traffic jams in Tokyo, I was horrified by the oxcarts tottering along on Seoul's dusty roads. Tokyo seemed indisputably modern, with its international-style high-rises, electronic toys, flush toilets, air conditioners, and refrigerators. Seoul, in contrast, appeared unmodern with its Japanese colonial-period architecture, wooden toys, non-flush toilets without toilet paper, and, at best, electric fans and ice blocks. Tokyo was dynamic—new buildings popping up everywhere, store shelves overflowing with new products; Seoul was stationary, trapped in tradition. In Tokyo, I gorged on caramels and chocolates sold in tidy stores; in Seoul, I gagged on grilled grasshoppers peddled on the street. (Lie, 1998, p. 1)

But what did Lie find when he returned to his home country a quarter of a century later, in the 1980s?

> I encountered upper-middle-class housewives sporting *haute couture* and affluent youths leading lives of invidious distinction and dissolution. Clean and well-lit coffee shops had replaced the dark and dingy cafés; McDonald's and Pizza Hut, the noodle shops and cheap eateries. (Lie, 1998, p. 4)

In other words, Seoul had become Tokyo. The permanent revolution in material life had begun.

Lie's testimony is interesting not only as a historical description but also for what it suggests from an analytical perspective. When South Korean bathrooms lack toilet paper, consumer society is perceived as a desirable destination, as the overcoming of the very "conception of backwardness". However, once that destination is reached, Lie cannot help but comment on the "invidious distinction and dissolution" of the lifestyles of a younger generation. In the space of just a few lines, consumer society is first praised and then problematised.

The main theme of this book is the tension that has existed throughout the history of economic thought between these two rival views of consumer society. Each of them remains alive today, and it is precisely for this reason that we will start from there to illustrate them. Moreover, as each of them remains alive beyond the walls of academia, we will begin with prominent public intellectuals to establish an initial contact with them.

The first view is what we will call the progress thesis. According to this view, consumer society represents a spectacular advance in terms of material prosperity compared to previous societies marked by poverty, deprivation, and difficulty in meeting basic needs with any degree of comfort. Psychologist Steven Pinker is one of the public intellectuals who has vigorously defended this thesis in recent times. In an ambitious book about the state of the world, Pinker tells us:

> An American in 2015, compared with his or her counterpart a half-century earlier, will live nine years longer, have had three more years of education, earn an additional $ 33,000 a year per family member (only a third of which, rather than half, will go to necessities), and have an additional eight hours a week of leisure. He or she can spend that leisure time reading on the Web, listening to music on a smartphone, streaming movies on high-definition TV, Skyping with friends and relatives, or dining on Thai food instead of Spam fritters. (Pinker, 2018, p. 327)

Pinker admits that these possibilities may not always be used in the best possible ways, and that some people's tastes lead them to prefer, for example, watching television and playing video games rather than enjoying works of art and nature. But the balance is clear: "a wide self-service of opportunities to enjoy the aesthetic, intellectual, social, cultural, and natural pleasures of the world, regardless of what each person places on their tray, is the supreme form of progress" (Pinker, 2018, pp. 310–311).

Even with the frictions logically associated with the concerns and emotions inherent in any adult life, the translation of this social progress into terms of individual well-being seems clear:

> Developed countries are actually quite happy, most countries have increased their happiness, and to the extent that countries become wealthier, they should become even happier. (Pinker, 2018, p. 352)

The humanism that Pinker (2018, p. 499) advocates consists of "maximizing human prosperity and flourishing" in a broad sense to include "life, health, happiness, freedom, knowledge, love, the richness of experience". However, he soon points out that "[a]lthough it is easy to dismiss national income as a superficial and materialistic measure, it corresponds with all indicators of prosperity". In fact, according to Pinker, "material well-being" has improved even more than monetary indicators suggest, because these fail to capture the impact of the emergence of new and better products. The exponential increase in material well-being would have been accompanied by parallel progress in non-materialistic pursuits, such as contact with loved ones and access to the richness of the natural and cultural worlds (Pinker, 2018, chaps. 8 and 17).

But is it enough to simply have these possibilities? In contrast to the progressive view of consumer society, there emerges what we shall refer to as the deviation thesis. According to this thesis, more is not always better, and consequently, affluence can divert us from the path that leads to the good life. An illustration of this possibility is given by Miguel de Cervantes through the voice of his ingenious knight, Don Quixote of La Mancha. In Chapter VI of the second part of the novel, when Don Quixote seems determined to venture out into the world again in search of new adventures, his niece attempts to convince him otherwise, ultimately accusing him of being blind: he aims to be a knight when he is actually a poor man for whom such a rank is denied. Don Quixote then embarks on a lengthy discourse regarding the different types of lineages that populate the world and the true meaning of grandeur and poverty. After having presented the main types of lineage, Don Quixote concludes:

> There is great confusion regarding lineages, and only those who appear great and illustrious demonstrate it through the virtue, wealth, and liberality of their possessors. I said virtues, wealth, and liberality, because the great man who is vicious will be a great vicious man, and the rich man who is not liberal will be a miserly beggar. For it is not the possession of wealth that makes one happy, *but the spending of it*, and not just spending it as one pleases, but *knowing how to spend it well.* (Cervantes, 1605, p. 396; emphasis added)

Is it then possible that we get the horn of plenty and squander it?

One of the most vivid presentations of this thesis is provided by psychiatrist Iain McGilchrist (2009), when he speaks of a "sleepwalker whistling a happy tune as he ambles towards the abyss". McGilchrist's argument, which has had a notable influence beyond academia, is structured around the contrast established by neuroscience between the left and right hemispheres of the human brain. For McGilchrist, contemporary changes typically labelled as progress have generated a problem that may be subtle but has monumental consequences: an imbalance in favour of the left hemisphere of the brain, which is oriented towards representation, abstraction, and problem-solving, and against the right hemisphere, which is attuned to meaning, experience, and participation in the flow of life. The industrial revolution would have created a world increasingly similar to that of the left hemisphere, but at the cost of weakening the capacities and values associated with the right hemisphere.

As a result, we are much less happy than one might expect:

> No two ways about it: We are making ourselves wretched. We are more affluent than ever, but riches—and power, the only point in having riches—do not make people happy. [...] No, affluent as we are, we are also more anxious, depressed, lonely, isolated, and lacking in purpose than ever. (McGilchrist, 2024)

For McGilchrist, the left hemisphere fails on its own terms by being incapable of solving the problem of maximising life satisfaction. The latter does not lend itself well to the type of direct, focused maximisation typical of the left hemisphere. It does not result from narrowly concentrating on acquiring and using, but it rather emerges more indirectly from the deployment of an empathic integration into the social and natural world of which we are a part. Affluence has, thus, had a by-product with fatal consequences:

> Capitalism and consumerism, ways of conceiving human relationships based on little more than utility, greed, and competition, came to supplant those based on felt connection and cultural continuity. (McGilchrist, 2009, p. 390)

Hence, beyond a certain threshold, the increase in material wealth and comfort ceases to contribute to our life satisfaction and may even begin to deteriorate it.

The tension between these two opposing views, the progress thesis and the deviation thesis, is the main theme of this book, but it will be accompanied by a parallel theme to which we will also give considerable importance. The theses of progress and deviation are obviously contradictory, but they share something in common: both convey the sense that consumer society is a relevant object of analysis. But what if not everyone agreed? Let us consider Joseph Schumpeter's concept of "vision":

> In any scientific venture, the thing that comes first is Vision. That is to say, before embarking upon analytic work of any kind we must first single out the set of phenomena we wish to investigate, and acquire "intuitively" a preliminary notion of how they hang together. (Schumpeter, 1954, p. 626)

Consequently, every analysis is preceded by a "preanalytic cognitive act that supplies the raw material for the analytic effort". In this case, the usual suspects of scientific practice, such as "observation, experimentation, and orderly logic", are not involved, but rather something that is more akin to "artistic creation" (Schumpeter, 1954, pp. 78 and 153). What if not everyone, or even a majority of researchers, had a vision (in Schumpeter's sense) of consumer society to begin with?

Alongside the substance of the debate, which concerns the nature of the arguments involved, we will also be interested in its profile, which refers to its position within the broader conversation. Vigorous debates attain a high profile because they attract a large number of participants and are followed with interest by those who, despite not directly participating in the debate, position their results within a wider discourse. At the other extreme, there are low-profile debates: less attended, self-contained within niches, and largely invisible to those who do not participate in them directly. While there may certainly be connections between the substance of the debate and the higher or lower profile it attains, we are dealing with essentially different dimensions of intellectual life and we will study them accordingly.

Our first encounter with assigning a low profile to the debate about consumer society will also come from outside the field of economics. In this case, it is historians we will consider. In his tetralogy on modern world history, Eric Hobsbawm provides a vibrant portrait of the transformation of the economy, society, politics, culture, and science across four eras: the age of revolution (1789–1848), the age of capital (1848–1875), the age of empire (1875–1914), and the age of extremes (1914–1991). Although the Marxist inspiration of his approach ensures that economic and social changes play a significant role, there are not any references to the making and development of consumer society, let alone its potential consequences for well-being and progress. In a particularly striking manner, the rise of mass consumer society in the decades following the Second World War is not even mentioned in the chapter of *The Age of Extremes* devoted to what Hobsbawm (1994) calls the "social revolution" of the period.

A similar situation occurs with another work of unusual scope: the economic and social history of the modern world by Paul Bairoch (1997). It spans over 2000 pages, in which Bairoch gives himself the opportunity to explore in detail a variety of themes, geographic spaces, and time periods. However, except for three pages devoted to the relative decline of food in consumer expenditure in developed countries during the twentieth century, changes in consumption are strikingly absent.

Of course, in the thirty years since the classic works of Hobsbawm and Bairoch, many historians have turned to the study of consumption. Perhaps the flagship of this historiographical cycle is Frank Trentmann's (2016) *tour de force* on consumer cultures, but quickly other names come to mind (Berg, 2005; de Grazia, 2005; de Vries, 2008; Glickman, 2009). Nonetheless, the capacity of this research to establish a place in general historical narratives has been much stronger for the 1500–1800 period than for the post-1800 period. Consumer society, in the sense we have given to this term in the previous section, remains largely invisible to most historians.

Even a growing interest in living standards among economic historians has not yet firmly positioned changes in consumption within the broader conversation. Take, for example, the best synthesis of the historical evolution of living standards: the compilation *How Was Life?*, where a group of researchers coordinated by Jan Luiten van Zanden seeks to project backwards in time the type of report that the OECD has been producing under the title *How's Life?* (van Zanden et al., 2014). Here we find a wide range of variables, including everything from education to life expectancy, income distribution to environmental sustainability, gender gaps to political freedom. The reconstruction of long statistical series for these multiple variables is of obvious value, but in vain will we search for consumer society in this research programme. Not a single chapter is dedicated to the world of consumption, and the only reflection we find on the subject is an invitation to dilute it within what we already know about the evolution of GDP per capita (Bolt et al., 2014, pp. 70–71). Except for specialists in historical anthropometry, who consider food consumption in their accounts of heights and other biological indicators of well-being (Medina-Albaladejo et al., 2023), the growing interest in living standards has had surprisingly limited spillover effects on the world of consumption.

This digression on historians illustrates the difference between the two dimensions we identified earlier. One thing is how the substance of a debate evolves, or in this case, how the substance of research in a field evolves; another is how the profile of that debate evolves, or in this case, the profile of that research within the broader framework of the profession. Hence, alongside the central theme of a tension between the theses of progress and deviation, this book will also pay attention to the parallel theme of the greater or lesser presence of consumer society in more general conversations.

Revisiting the History of Economic Thought

Most readers will probably agree that a historical approach is needed to reflect on rival views of consumer society. If, as is the case with this and many other topics, today's conversation is part of a conversation that actually began yesterday, we need to understand the past in order to engage meaningfully with the present. But how should we frame this historical research?

Our focus will be on economics and political economy. The choice is less obvious than it might seem, given the fragmentation of today's social science. A process with as many and varied implications as the formation and reproduction of consumer societies has sparked lively discussions across different academic disciplines. As could be inferred from the rival views presented in the previous section, this book will focus on the conversation about human well-being and social progress. Other equally interesting conversations will therefore fall outside the scope of our study. Does consumer society lead to the lethargy of civic virtues? Is the shift from a society of producers to one of consumers a factor that conspires to deteriorate citizen participation in the political life of democracies? Or, on the contrary, does it strengthen the very notion of citizenship that serves as a premise for democracy? And what about the impact of consumer society on culture? Does it open up a fantastic variety of options, allowing more and more people to enjoy art and culture? Or, on the contrary, does the combined result of massification and narcissism crowd out all sorts of valuable cultural traditions and possibilities?

In no way do we intend, therefore, to produce what (again following Braudel) we would call a "total" intellectual history of consumer society. Our interest in the conversation surrounding human well-being and social progress will lead us to focus on the history of economic thought, as it is there that we will find the intellectual genealogies that have shaped this debate. This does not exclude some consideration of authors who have formally belonged to disciplines other than economics, nor those who wrote before economics became institutionalised as a discipline. It simply conditions their inclusion to the fact that they participated in the type of conversation we are interested in here.

A more significant dilemma is how to choose our time frame. If our premise is that we need to understand the conversation of yesterday in order to participate competently in the conversation of today, it would be foolish to erect a large dam around a specific historical date and pretend that it is from that point onwards, and not before, that the truly valuable part of the conversation takes place. After all, is this not precisely what those who dismiss the history of economic thought, and somewhat myopically focus on the conversation of the day, do? Whatever starting point we choose, one can always go further back in time and identify antecedents and connections. With this caution in mind, the present study will take the final stretch of the eighteenth century as its starting point.

This decision is partly linked to the chronology of the events that inspire the ideas we are going to examine. As we pointed out in the first section of this chapter, the three conditions we have set for identifying consumer society (market order, sustained growth of consumption, and diversification of the consumer basket) only began to come together with some clarity in the second half of the nineteenth century. It even seemed prudent not to lose sight of the dividing line drawn by the Second World War:

it was particularly in the decades following this conflict that consumer societies with outstanding scale and reach were consolidated. Consequently, attempting to reconstruct in detail economic thought on consumer society in contexts such as Ancient Greece or medieval Europe would be a somewhat anachronistic undertaking.

However, there is one case in which it is worth exposing oneself to the danger of anachronism and rescuing the thinkers from a period prior to the birth of consumer society. This is the period immediately preceding it: the intellectual cycle that opens with Adam Smith witnesses the unfolding of what was later called classical political economy, and closes with Karl Marx. The reason lies in the fact that, by the time consumer society was born, the reflections of economists could not help but be heavily conditioned by the intellectual map created by preceding generations. In particular, the enormous influence of classical economists and Marx in defining a working field and some relevant arguments cannot be ignored. Whether to confirm, refute, or modify these arguments, later generations of economists were profoundly influenced. We will approach the intellectual cycle of the classics and Marx through an exercise in what Axel Leijonhufvud (2006) calls backtracking. We will search for answers in them to a question that was not actually posed at the time, but in doing so, we will listen to powerful voices that help trace the outlines of later debates.

Thus, the focus on the last two hundred and fifty years leads us, in a rather unoriginal manner, to the time frame that historians of economic thought have most thoroughly reconstructed. And yet, consumer society has not featured prominently in such reconstructions. It is fair to acknowledge that this partly reflects the need to reconstruct what can most properly be considered central to the evolution of successive authors and schools of economic thought, leaving other aspects aside. In an effective synthesis in which he distinguishes as many as nine such schools, Ha-Joon Chang (2014, pp. 155–158) proposes that only one of them, the neoclassical school, takes trade and consumption as a priority area of analysis. The other schools, in contrast, would prioritise production and distribution. There is some simplification in this approach, especially regarding the institutionalist school. After all, the moments when the great reconstructions of the history of economic thought come closest to consumer society are those in which institutionalists such as Thorstein Veblen or John Kenneth Galbraith come into the picture. Nonetheless, it is also true that the institutionalist school has not fared too well in these reconstructions.

Schumpeter (1954) never wrote his chapter on institutionalism. Mark Blaug (1968) did, but he gave it a truly secondary role. Alessandro Roncaglia (2005, 2019) devotes so much attention to the dichotomy between the genealogy of the classics and Keynes, on the one hand, and the neoclassical genealogy, on the other, that he admits there is little room for exploring institutionalist and evolutionary theories. The result is that, whether due to the nature of the economic thought being reconstructed or the conceptual framework used for such reconstruction, the world of consumption has had a modest presence in the broader conversation on the history of economic thought.

A different issue is that, undoubtedly, there are many works in the history of economic thought that can help us reconstruct the debate on consumer society. Throughout the book, the reader will have the opportunity to identify some of the most representative works as we rely on them to analyse specific authors. An illustrative case, which we mention both for its intrinsic value and for its paradigmatic nature, is the extraordinary monograph by Alexandre Chirat (2021) on the economic thought of John Kenneth Galbraith between 1933 and 1983. Over more than 800 pages, Chirat immerses us in the universe of this important economist: he identifies his underlying analytical frameworks, positions Galbraith's work in relation to his academic background and the historical context of his time, and examines in detail both his major published works and his lesser-known manuscripts and personal correspondence. At the end of the journey, we learn a great deal about Galbraith's thought on consumer society, as this topic naturally becomes an attractor for Chirat: how could it be otherwise in a book about the author of *The Affluent Society* and *The New Industrial State*?

But what we cannot expect from Chirat or other authors engaged in such research is that, in addition to the fantastic work that they already do, they should also bear the burden of constructing a long-term narrative that ultimately shifts the focus away from the individual economists who are their primary objects of study. It is the task of more specific investigations, such as the one we propose here, to identify the connections, comparisons, and contrasts that can reconstruct long-term intellectual genealogies and put them at the centre of the stage. The reader needs to be warned from the outset that this undertaking only stands a chance of success if it is the ideas, rather than their proponents, that are allowed to play the leading roles.

We do not aim to uncover an alternative Galbraith, although someone may do so in the future. At most, we hope that making Chirat's Galbraith one of the vehicles for our history can help establish connections that move forward the analysis of his work in a later step. What has been said about Galbraith and Chirat applies to the other economists and historians of economic thought who will appear in these pages. Our ambition is not to engage with those parallel historiographies, but to construct a broad framework on the conversation surrounding consumer society. In this respect, the book aligns with Cosimo Perrotta's (2004, 2018) reconstruction of economic thought on consumption. The principal difference lies in the fact that, as he moves into the post-Smithian era (precisely the period of interest in this book), Perrotta gradually shifts the focus of his analysis from consumption to the related—but fundamentally distinct—issue of unproductive labour. This shift prevents consumer society from becoming the central axis of his reconstruction of the modern period.

If I have one request for the readers, it is that they pay more attention to the merits of the whole that is going to be presented than to the defects that, no doubt, can be attributed to each of its parts individually. It is precisely to facilitate this kind of reading that we now present the conceptual framework that will be employed throughout the book.

Of *Petites Idées* and *Tours De Force*

The conceptual framework of this research is inspired by Albert Hirschman and Joseph Schumpeter. These are two authors with markedly different approaches and results. One need only think of the contrast between Hirschman's preference for *petites idées*, condensed into brief essays, and Schumpeter's propensity to intellectual *tours de force*, embodied in colossal works. It will be important to clarify what we take from each of them and how these different contributions can be reasonably combined. In several cases, it will also be necessary to go beyond Hirschman and Schumpeter to pursue their suggestions with the help of other authors.

Our starting point has been the identification of two rival views of consumer society, the progress thesis and the deviation thesis, which will serve as ideal types with which to identify, classify, and analyse a succession of authors and approaches. In this, we have followed Hirschman's (1986) classic study on what he calls rival views of market society. In this essay, Hirschman constructs a *tableau idéologique* in which four theses emerge: the thesis of *doux commerce*, according to which the development of capitalism strengthens civic and political life; the thesis of self-destruction, according to which the opposite occurs; the thesis of feudal shackles, according to which conflicts seemingly caused by capitalism reflect its inability to destroy pre-existing feudal inertia; and the thesis of feudal blessings, according to which these persistent inertias could actually be a factor of political cohesion. It must be stressed that our object of study, as has already become clear, is different: while Hirschman is concerned with the effects of capitalism and the market order on civil society and political life, our interest is in consumer society and its effects on human well-being and social progress.

That said, the approach is similar. We will share with Hirschman a preference for the use of ideal types as centres of gravity around which to identify trends, schools, and authors. Our protagonists will be the ideas, rather than their proponents or disseminators. We will also share with Hirschman an interest in going beyond the identification of ideal types and exploring possible interactions between them. Hirschman, in particular, concludes his essay by suggesting that perhaps, after all, each of his four rival views of market society may be valid. It may be that each of them is valid within a certain historical context, so that part of the tension between them dissipates when we stop considering them as grand narratives that are valid at all times and places. Hirschman (1986, pp. 136–137) goes one step further:

> It is conceivable that, even at the same point in space and time, a simple thesis may contain only a portion of the whole truth and may need to be complemented by one or more of the others, no matter how incompatible they may seem at first glance.

For example, if the development of capitalism has not prevented the persistence of feudal elements in politics, society, and culture, would it not seem reasonable to deduce that this could lead to benign effects in some respects and pernicious effects in others? Subsequent essays by Hirschman (1991, p. 153, 1994, p. 211) propose some labels to shape this type of message: rival views operate from an "exalted level of generality", while seeking ways to combine them would be akin to adopting a "mature position".

We will not retain this latter term, which we find problematic, but will use the term "synthesis view" to refer to attempts to combine the theses of progress and deviation. As Hirschman, we will distinguish between weak and strong forms of synthesis: weak, when each of the rival views receives a period or a context in which it reigns supreme; strong, when the possibility arises that the rival views coexist within the same period or context. The former would be a diachronic synthesis; the latter, a synchronic one.

This "synthesis view" is not to be taken as a canon that necessarily entails intellectual progress simply by virtue of its existence. Although Hirschman seems to understand it this way in his case study, it is evident that there will be other cases where intellectual progress consists of embracing one (correct) thesis and rejecting its (incorrect) opposite. As Roncaglia (2005) reminds us, it is one thing to reject the "cumulative" view of the history of economic thought, which sees it as a triumphant movement from weaker to stronger approaches, and another thing to assume that all approaches are equally valid: that the difficulties in the commensurability of research programmes, central to the "competitive" view of the history of economic thought, should lead to attributing similar validity to each of them. What happens in our case is that we have a compelling reason to retain the Hirschman-style "synthesis view" as a guiding reference: it closely mirrors the image offered by historians who study consumer society from the perspective of human well-being.

From the outset, even those historians who saw consumer society as a desirable endpoint in modernisation processes, such as Walt Rostow (1960), did not fail to pepper their narratives with ambivalent notes. Rostow regarded the "era of mass consumption" as the fifth of five "stages of economic growth" that, according to him, had been followed by Western countries, and which served as a comprehensible reference for the countries then known as the "Third World". However, for Rostow (1960, p. 64), it was an era of "not unequivocal joys". It was likely that consumption was beginning to be subject to diminishing returns as a driver of well-being. Excess in certain consumptions, such as food, could even threaten well-being. One could even speculate whether the line between comfort and boredom was not becoming disturbingly thin.

Rostow's intuition about "not unequivocal joys" now shines brightly in subsequent generations of researchers. When we read historians such as Avner Offer (2006, 2012) or Emanuele Felice (2020), we find a carefully ambivalent appraisal of consumer society. On the one hand, their approach accommodates the narrative that has dominated the conversation among economic historians for decades: a narrative about how Western economies (and later others) moved from stagnation, with mediocre living standards, to sustained growth, with living standards that eventually became much higher, thanks in part to the possibility of accessing a much more abundant and varied basket of consumer goods.

But, on the other hand, it seems that consumer society also entails threats and challenges to the quality of life. For Offer, affluence created, from 1945 onwards in the United States and Britain, not only a world full of consumer goods but also a world saturated with the promise of instant gratification. This is something that eroded individuals' capacity to make those stable commitments that could do the most for their long-term psychological well-being. The compulsion to consume could thus become an obstacle to well-being, in which variables such as social connection, reciprocity, and approval were central. Felice, for his part, suggests that the triumph of consumer society and the hedonism associated with it has resulted in a clear improvement in freedom from material deprivation but has done little to improve performance in the other two dimensions that Felice considers constitutive of happiness: the quality of personal relationships and commitment to activities that give life its meaning. Only an "ethical revolution" could correct the deviation that has led us towards a "dystopia based on passions and egocentric impulses" (Felice, 2020, pp. 235 and 280). In an echo of the type of synchronic synthesis suggested by Hirschman, Offer even cautiously expresses optimism regarding the capacity of affluent societies to develop new social and cultural structures to replace those that have been undermined by the unforeseen negative effects of consumer society.

Through these or other paths, ambivalent images abound among historians of capitalism and consumption. Jonathan Levy (2021) speaks about an improvement in the standard of living of the US population throughout much of the twentieth century but finds problems in the fact that material abundance fostered the consolidation of a consumerist culture. Some of those who have most advocated for a de-problematization of consumer cultures, such as Frank Trentmann (2016), end up problematizing the environmental implications of consumer societies around the world in recent decades. And specialists in specific areas, such as food, quickly convey the historical irony of the fact that, within just a few generations, Western societies shifted from fighting hunger to fighting obesity. There is an underlying trend towards increasing spending on food, as well as a diversification of the products that make up the diet, but the outcome is uncertain. In some aspects and contexts, this trend favours an improvement in nutritional health, and in others, it has the opposite effect (Floud et al., 2011; Montanari, 1993; Oddy et al., 2009).

These ambivalent perspectives offered by historians closely resemble Hirschman's "synthesis view", and for this reason, we find it pertinent to retain this reference for our reconstruction of the conversation that economists have had on the subject. We will also take one final idea from Hirschman: the fact that, alongside the boundaries that separate economics from other social sciences, there can also be channels that connect it to them. In a mischievous choice of words, Hirschman (1981) talks about the possibility for economists to use those channels and engage in "trespassing" and use those channels. At this point, we can turn to Schumpeter's *tour de force* to elaborate Hirschman's *petite idée*.

Throughout the book, we will pay close attention to Schumpeter's (1954, pp. 47–60) assertion that what distinguishes the professional economist from the rest of the citizens who occasionally talk about the economy is the mastery of a series of "techniques". Schumpeter specifically lists four of them: economic history, economic theory, statistics, and economic sociology. He placed history first on his list of techniques, asserting that most of the errors made by economists stemmed from their lack of historical sense. He also emphasised the importance of sociology, understood as an analysis of the reasons underlying individual behaviour, including the functioning of political institutions. Throughout the book, we will read the contributions of various economists, and the different lines of tension and feedback between them, not only in terms of what Schumpeter (1954, p. 262) calls "pure economics" but also in terms of its connection to other social sciences.

To carry out this type of reading, we will distance ourselves at several points from Schumpeter's own reading. In relation to "pure economics", we will find it more useful to adopt the view of the history of economic thought that, starting from Piero Sraffa (1951–1955), extends to the present day through Roncaglia (2005, 2019). According to this view, there is a fundamental contrast between two great paradigms: classical political economy, which understands value in objective terms and studies economic reproduction in a society based on the division of labour, and neoclassical economics, which understands value in subjective terms and studies individual decisions aimed at allocating scarce resources to satisfy unlimited wants. To this binary contrast, Roncaglia adds other paradigms that do not easily fit into it, especially the institutional-evolutionary school. In any case, the resulting picture is one of a transition from classical economics as the original orthodoxy to a new orthodoxy embodied by neoclassical economics from the late nineteenth century. Despite innumerable developments, fragmentations, and reorientations, it is this new orthodoxy that culminates in the dominant economics of today, where both classical economics and the institutional-evolutionary paradigm are part of the heterodoxy.

What kind of relationships do these different systems of "pure economics" have with neighbouring social sciences? Are they what, in a passage referring to classical political economy, Schumpeter (1954, p. 597) calls "close relations"? Or, on the contrary, are they distant relations, perhaps even eroded by the lack of frequent contact? In a fantastic exploration of what he calls "the Cambridge revival of political economy", Nuno Martins (2014) argues that the political economy tradition stemming from the classics differs from the contemporary mainstream not only due to these different anchors of economic theory but also because it shows a much greater openness to social and ethical theory. It is not that neoclassical economics entirely lacks a sociological and ethical substrate, but rather that such a substrate is thin and often implicit. For Martins, on the contrary, serious engagement with social theory and ethical theory is necessary for completing the blank spaces that would otherwise be left by an economic theory that, by its very nature, is partial. This aligns with the view recently proposed by John Stilwell (2019) of political economy as a transdisciplinary enterprise, whose challenge to economics includes a redefinition of the playing field in which the conversation should take place: a field that, according to its proponents, should be broader and more connected to history, geography, sociology, and the rest of the social sciences.

Although we sympathise with these perspectives, throughout the study, we will grant a certain degree of autonomy to both axes of analysis. One thing will be the clashes and contrasts that occur within the realm of "pure economics", and another the clashes and contrasts that occur in its engagement with the other social sciences and humanities. This way, we will be able to exploit the opportunities provided by this second axis to detect different families within the same school of economic thought, as well as to establish unexpected connections between schools. In other words, we will not initially impute certain associations with other social sciences to particular schools of economic thought, but rather we want to leave room for these associations to be constructed and deconstructed over time.

In any case, in our approach to the other social sciences, we will retain the two mentioned by Schumpeter, history and sociology, and go further by including philosophy and psychology. With philosophy, it is clear that we are taking a step Schumpeter did not deem appropriate. However, economic philosophy is key to our purposes because, as Martins (2014) elaborates, it is ethical theory that deliberates on issues such as the components of human well-being and the nature of a good life. Although often only implicitly, the economic conversation is frequently seasoned with philosophical elements that inform its framework of reference (Sedlácek, 2011). We will also pay attention to economic psychology, a field not fully developed in Schumpeter's time. It seems reasonable to think that, had it been more developed in his time, he would have probably included it among the "techniques" of the economist. Economic psychology will be of particular interest to us due to its ability to incorporate biological factors, understood in a broad sense and considered in interaction with social factors, in explaining individual behaviours and mentalities. It is likely that, in this case as well, there are many conversations economists engage in where, even if implicitly, "pure economics" is complemented or at least framed by elements of psychology.

Our reading of economic thought, therefore, will be one in terms of both "pure economics" and its integration with the other social sciences and the humanities. It will also, in the end, go beyond Schumpeter when it comes to paying attention to politics. We will not go as far as those who assert that, ultimately, economics is a political argument (Chang, 2014, p. 105). However, we will by no means see economics, or any other social science, as a purely technical intellectual exercise, disconnected from the political life that researchers share with the rest of their fellow citizens. Beyond the (variable) degree to which economic conversation may influence the political debate of the day, the latter significantly influences the former, posing questions, delineating fields of debate, and ultimately helping to shape arguments. From this perspective, even contributions supposedly situated in the strictly academic realm of "pure economics" are susceptible to political reading. This is the sense in which we will deem it pertinent to pay attention to the general political discourse in which economists' contributions are inscribed.

One final point. Just as we have retained from Schumpeter the interest in "vision" and in the possible relations (whether "close" or not) between economics and the rest of the social sciences, we will also retain his focus on what has come to be known as "structural time". Repeatedly throughout his *tour de force* on the history of economic analysis, Schumpeter privileges the identification of what he calls "classical situations", using in-depth studies of key authors and key works as a focal point around which to reconstruct long periods. For example, John Stuart Mill's *Principles of Political Economy* is taken as a "classical situation" from which to interpret the entire period between 1790 and 1870. Given the extensive nature of the project, the number of periods Schumpeter works with is consequently small. The incomplete nature of his work even leads one to speculate whether, with a little more time and perspective, the final section of the book, dedicated to the period after 1914, could have been merged with the section devoted to the 1870–1914 period without significant disruption to the narrative thread.

What Schumpeter is doing with this analysis of long periods is focusing on what, shortly after his death, Braudel (1958) would categorise as one of the three historical times: structural time, which focuses on the deep-seated inertias and trends of systems. The other two temporalities would be conjunctural time, which is suited to capturing cycles and medium-term trends, and the time of events, closely linked to specific events and short temporal scales. None of these three temporalities is superior to another; each of them simply captures certain types of historical movement better than the others. In a similar vein, the types of movements in the history of economic analysis that most interest Schumpeter are those unfolding over the long term of structural time. Throughout this book, there will be no shortage of conjunctural perspectives, and even some occasional snapshot of events, but the main focus will be on structural analysis.

Precisely for this reason, we will not opt for a balanced periodisation. In fact, we will establish four periods of significantly different lengths: the first two, from the late eighteenth century to 1870 and from that date to the Second World War, are long periods; the other two, the Cold War period and the period from 1990 to the present, are shorter periods. The reason for this imbalance is that, as we hope to show in the following chapters, these are four moments of similar significance from the perspective of their role in the making of the debate. As could be expected, this debate had a chronology heavily shaped by the very chronology of the formation and reproduction of consumer societies in the real world. Hence, our periodisation is skewed towards the period after 1945, in contrast to other histories of economic thought that, focusing on different debates or on the overall picture, justifiably aim to study the period from the late eighteenth century to the present in a more balanced way.

Conclusion: In Search of a Stepping Stone

Even those readers who have been more receptive to the options defended in the previous pages will not have failed to perceive that each and every one of them reveals the inherent limitations of the present study. Our adoption of structural time as the main temporal scale may, at best, reveal patterns of change and continuity in the long term, but it will evidently limit our ability to capture shorter-term conjunctural movements, let alone the particular events that shape the trajectory of the authors and their work. Our interest in the most purely economic question about consumer society, namely, the one relating to human well-being and social progress, may allow us to focus on a specific objective and organise our historical reconstruction accordingly, but it clearly excludes other questions that, extending across the social, the cultural, and the political, would also form part of a "total" intellectual history of consumer society.

The study will also not be without its limitations even as a work focused on economic thought and structural time. After all, the focus will be on a small number of great names and major works. Second- and third-tier researchers will play a modest role, and specialists on the great names may find reason to complain about the simplification involved in not adopting a perspective more attentive to revealing lesser works. On the other hand, while the study will certainly draw on abundant secondary literature, benefiting from numerous contributions by historians of economic thought, it will not engage extensively in dialogue with this literature. Quite the opposite, it will subject it to the discipline imposed by the central theme of the book. And although the study is aligned with the current disinterest in taking too seriously the traditional dichotomy between "rational" reconstructions and "historical" reconstructions, its limitations will be all the more evident in the second of these planes. There will be material on the social and personal context of the authors and their works, but the protagonists of the book are more the ideas themselves than their proponents or the intellectual milieu in which they operated. In particular, the intellectual history of the reception and diffusion of ideas, both in academia and beyond, will be the subject of less detailed analysis than these ideas undoubtedly deserve.

All of the above flaws collapse into one implication: the present study is far from providing its readers with a Schumpeterian *tour de force*. Such an ambitious goal would require a book of greater length and depth. That book would delve into the work of a larger number of thinkers, would examine more thoroughly the complete works of the great names, would integrate the intellectual history of economics on an equal footing with that of the other social sciences, and would offer a vibrant fresco of the human and social element involved in the rise and fall of various ideas. This book, in contrast, is more of a proposal for articulating some *petites idées* in the Hirschmanian vein. Its more modest goal is to offer a provisional framework for that sort of *tour de force*. The framework will allow us to identify the main lines of an episode in the history of economic thought. By drawing on a long-term perspective, the framework will provide an overview that places each of the analytical periods in relation to the others. Instead of immersing ourselves in detail in one of these periods and leaving the rest for a similar undertaking in the future, we will prioritise understanding each of these parts better through research into the role they play within the whole.

The final point will be less the end of a journey than an invitation to continue it. In the classic words of Alexander Gerschenkron (1962, p. 364), "For what more can be expected of any historical hypothesis than to have stimulated research to the point of becoming the stepping stone to a new hypothesis and to new research?" The path towards that stepping stone begins in the next chapter.

References

Bairoch, P. (1997). *Victoires et déboires: histoire économique et sociale du monde du XVIe siècle à nos jours*. Gallimard.
Berg, M. (2005). *Luxury and pleasure in eighteenth-century Britain*. Oxford University Press.
Blaug, M. (1968). *Economic theory in retrospect*. R. D. Irwin.
Bolt, J., Timmer, M., & van Zanden, J. L. (2014). GDP per capita since 1820. In J. L. van Zanden, J. Baten, M. Mira d'Ercole, A. Rijpma, & M. P. Timmer (Eds.), *How was life? Global well-being since 1820*. OECD.
Braudel, F. (1958). Histoire et sciences sociales: la longue durée. *Annales: Économies, Sociétés, Civilisations, 13*(4), 725–753.
Braudel, F. (1979). *Civilisation matérielle, économie et capitalisme: XVe–XVIIIe siècle*. Armand Colin.
Chang, H.-J. (2014). *Economics: The user's guide*. Penguin.
Chirat, A. (2021). *L'Économie intégral de John Kenneth Galbraith (1933-1983)*. Garnier.
Cross, G. (2000). *An all-consuming century: Why commercialism won in modern America*. Columbia University Press.

Cervantes, M. de (1605). *El ingenioso hidalgo don Quijote de la Mancha*. Empresa Pública Don Quijote de la Mancha, 2005.
de Grazia, V. (2005). *Irresistible empire: America's advance through twentieth-century Europe*. Harvard University Press.
de Grazia, V. (2016). The crisis of hyper-consumerism: Capitalism's latest forward lurch. In J. Kocka & M. van der Linden (Eds.), *Capitalism: The reemergence of a historical concept*. Bloomsbury.
de Vries, J. (2008). *The industrious revolution: Consumer behavior and the household economy*. Cambridge University Press.
Deaton, A. (1975). The structure of demand 1920-1970. In C. M. Cipolla (Ed.), *The Fontana economic history of Europe, vol. 5: The twentieth century*. Collins-Fontana.
Felice, E. (2020). *Historia económica de la felicidad: una nueva vision de la historia del mundo*. Crítica.
Floud, R., Fogel, R. W., Harris, B., & Hong, S. C. (2011). *The changing body: Health, nutrition, and human development in the Western world since 1700*. Cambridge University Press.
Francks, P. (2009). *The Japanese consumer: An alternative economic history of modern Japan*. Cambridge University Press.
Gerschenkron, A. (1962). *Economic backwardness in historical perspective: A book of essays*. Harvard University Press.
Glickman, L. B. (2009). *Buying power: A history of consumer activism in America*. University of Chicago Press.
Gordon, R. J. (2017). *The rise and fall of American growth: The U.S. standard of living since the Civil War*. Princeton University Press.
Hayek, F. A. (1954). History and politics. In F. A. Hayek (Ed.), *Capitalism and the historians*. University of Chicago Press.
Hirschman, A. O. (1977). *The passions and the interests: Political arguments for capitalism before its triumph*. Princeton University Press, 1997.
Hirschman, A. O. (1981). *Essays in trespassing: Economics to politics and beyond*. Cambridge University Press.
Hirschman, A. O. (1986). Rival views of market society. In A. O. Hirschman (Ed.), *Rival views of market society and other recent essays*. Harvard University Press. [Spanish edition: *Enfoques alternativos sobre la sociedad de mercado y otros ensayos recientes*. Fondo de Cultura Económica, 1989.]
Hirschman, A. O. (1991). *The rhetoric of reaction: Perversity, futility, jeopardy*. Harvard University Press.
Hirschman, A. O. (1994). Social conflicts as pillars of democratic market society. *Political Theory, 22*(2), 203–218.
Hobsbawm, E. (1994). *Age of extremes: The short twentieth century, 1914-1991*. Michael Joseph.

Hodgson, G. (2015). *Conceptualizing capitalism: Institutions, evolution, future.* University of Chicago Press.
Instituto Nacional de Estadística. (2025). *Encuesta de presupuestos familiares.* Instituto Nacional de Estadística.
Kocka, J. (2016). *Capitalism: A short history.* Princeton.
Kuznets, S. (1962). Quantitative aspects of the economic growth of nations: VII. The share and structures of consumption. *Economic Development and Cultural Change, 10*(2, 2), 1–92.
Kuznets, S. (1966). *Modern economic growth: Rate, structure and spread.* Yale University Press.
Leijonhufvud, A. (2006). The uses of the past. Working paper 0603, Department of Economics, University of Trento.
Levy, J. (2021). *Ages of American capitalism: A history of the United States.* Random House.
Lie, J. (1998). *Han unbound: The political economy of South Korea.* Stanford University Press.
Maluquer de Motes, J. (2005). Consumo y precios. In A. Carreras & X. Tafunell (coords.), *Estadísticas históricas de España, siglos XIX-XX.* Fundación BBVA.
Martínez Carrión, J. M. (2012). La talla de los europeos, 1700-2000: ciclos, crecimiento y desigualdad. *Investigaciones de Historia Económica, 8*(3), 176–187.
Martins, N. O. (2014). *The Cambridge revival of political economy.* Routledge.
McGilchrist, I. (2009). *The master and his emissary: the divided brain and the making of the Western world.* Yale University Press.
McGilchrist, I. (2024). Resist the machine apocalypse. *First Things*, 341.
McNeill, J. R., & Engelke, P. (2014). *The great acceleration: An environmental history of the Anthropocene since 1945.* Cambridge University Press.
Medina-Albaladejo, F. J., Martínez-Carrión, J. M., & Calatayud, S. (Eds.). (2023). *Inequality and nutritional transition in economic history: Spain in the 19th-21st centuries.* Routledge.
Milberg, W. (2019). The return of 'capitalism' and the limits of economics. *Public Seminar*, 20 September.
Mitra-Kahn, B. H. (2011). Redefining the economy: How 'the economy' was invented in 1620, and has been redefined ever since. PhD thesis, City University London.
Montanari, M. (1993). *El hambre y la abundancia: historia y cultura de la alimentación en Europa.* Crítica.
Oddy, D. J., Atkins, P. J., & Amilien, V. (Eds.). (2009). *The rise of obesity in Europe: A twentieth century food history.* Ashgate.
Offer, A. (2006). *The challenge of affluence: Self-control and well-being in the United States and Britain since 1950.* Oxford University Press.
Offer, A. (2012). Consumption and well-being. In F. Trentmann (Ed.), *The Oxford handbook of the history of consumption.* Oxford University Press.

Offer, A. (2014). Consumption and affluence. In R. Floud, J. Humphries, & P. Johnson (Eds.), *The Cambridge economic history of modern Britain*. Cambridge University Press.

Pamuk, S., & van Zanden, J.-L. (2010). Standards of living. In S. Broadberry & K. O'Rourke (Eds.), *The Cambridge economic history of modern Europe* (Vol. 1). Cambridge University Press.

Perrotta, C. (2004). *Consumption as an investment, I: The fear of goods from Hesiod to Adam Smith*. Routledge.

Perrotta, C. (2018). *Unproductive labour in political economy: The history of an idea*. Routledge.

Pinker, S. (2018). *Enlightenment now: The case for reason, science, humanism, and progress*. Penguin. [Spanish edition: *En defensa de la Ilustración: por la razón, la ciencia, el humanismo y el progreso*. Paidós, 2018.]

Polanyi, K. (1944). *The great transformation: The political and economic origins of our time*. Farrar & Rinehart.

Pomeranz, K. (2000). *The great divergence: China, Europe, and the making of the modern world economy*. Princeton University Press.

Prados de la Escosura, L. (2017). *Spanish economic growth, 1850-2015*. Cham.

Rodríguez, N. (2021). *La publicidad y el nacimiento de la sociedad de consumo: España, 1900-1936*. La Catarata.

Roncaglia, A. (2005). *The wealth of ideas: A history of economic thought*. Cambridge University Press.

Roncaglia, A. (2019). *The age of fragmentation: A history of contemporary economic thought*. Cambridge University Press.

Rostow, W. W. (1960) *The stages of economic growth: A non-communist manifesto*. Cambridge University Press. [Spanish edition: *Las etapas del crecimiento económico: un manifiesto no comunista*. Ministerio de Trabajo y Seguridad Social, 1993.]

Schumpeter, J. A. (1954). *History of economic analysis*. Oxford University Press. [Spanish edition: *Historia del análisis económico*, Barcelona, Ariel, 1994.]

Sedlácek, T. (2011): *Economics of good and evil: The quest for economic meaning from Gilgamesh to Wall Street*. Oxford University Press. [Spanish edition: *Economía del bien y del mal: la búsqueda del significado económico desde Gilgamesh hasta Wall Street*. Fondo de Cultura Económica, 2014.]

Shammas, C. (2012). Standard of living, consumption and political economy over the past 500 years. In F. Trentmann (Ed.), *The Oxford handbook of the history of consumption*. Oxford University Press.

Sraffa, P. (Ed.). (1951–1955). D. Ricardo, *Works and correspondence*. Cambridge University Press.

Stewart, E. (2021). How 9/11 convinced Americans to buy, buy, buy. *Vox*, 9 September.

Stilwell, F. (2019). From economics to political economy: Contradictions, challenge, and change. *American Journal of Economics and Sociology, 78*(1), 35–62.
Trentmann, F. (2016). *Empire of things: How we became a world of consumers, from the fifteenth century to the twenty-first*. HarperCollins.
van Zanden, J. L., Baten, J., Mira d'Ercole, M., Rijpma, A., & Timmer, M. P. (Eds.). (2014). *How was life? Global well-being since 1820*. OECD.
Vanhaute, E., Paping, R., & Ó'Gráda, C. (2007). The European subsistence crisis of 1845-1850: A comparative perspective. In C. Ó'Gráda, R. Paping, & E. Vanhaute (Eds.), *When the potato failed: Causes and effects of the last European subsistence crisis, 1845-1850*. Brepols.

CHAPTER 3

Classical Ambivalence (1770–1870)

In this chapter, we interrogate economists from the century prior to 1870 on topics that, by their very nature, could not have been on their agenda. This runs the risk of decontextualisation and presentism, but in exchange, it allows us to capture the roots of debates that, like the one we address in this book, have only more recently emerged as such. The chapter is organised into five sections. The first describes the historical context of the period, in terms of both economic thought and the real world. The second outlines how, in such a historical context, it was difficult for economists to have a vision of consumer society. Once this clarification is made, the remaining three sections embark on an exercise in backtracking (Leijonhufvud, 2006). We study three distinct moments in this period, taking Adam Smith, John Stuart Mill, and Karl Marx as our main references. The chapter's conclusions emphasise the ambivalence of the reflections that the economists of this period left us regarding the world of consumption.

The Industrial Revolution and Political Economy

The industrial revolution changed the world. Its only serious competitor for the title of principal rupture in the economic history of humanity is the Neolithic revolution that began around 12,000 years ago and transformed

F. Collantes, *Consumer Society and the Economists*, Palgrave Studies in the History of Economic Thought,
https://doi.org/10.1007/978-3-031-96645-3_3

hunter-gatherer communities into sedentary agrarian societies. The industrial revolution, which began in Great Britain in the second half of the eighteenth century, entailed a radically different path of economic change. In contrast to the organic energy base of agrarian societies, the new industrial societies came to rely on fossil fuels such as coal. In contrast to the slow evolution of techniques over the preceding millennia, technological innovation reached unprecedented speed and depth. Mechanisation and upgraded technologies in industrial sectors such as textiles and ironmaking led to an acceleration of economic growth. At a later stage, this constellation of innovations extended to the transport sector, driven by another powerful engine of growth: the railway (Cipolla, 1962; Freeman & Louçã, 2001; Landes, 2003; Wrigley, 1988).

Meanwhile, what had originally been a distinctly British event spread to the rest of Europe and the British colonies in North America. By 1870, our endpoint in this chapter, industrialisation was far from having completed what Sidney Pollard (1981) calls the "peaceful conquest" of Europe. The British advantage was clear, as was the gap between the advanced economies of the north-western part of the continent and the lagging economies of its southern and eastern periphery. However, the dynamics of industrialisation had started all across the continent. Furthermore, it must be acknowledged that the grandeur of the industrial revolution goes far beyond the changes it may have brought about during its time frame, though these were many and profound. As decisive as these changes were, the fact that the industrial revolution gave rise to a world in which that sort of change would become recurrent is equally important. From that very long-term perspective, it is not an exaggeration to assert that, through subsequent waves of technological change and economic growth, the industrial revolution continues to live on among us (Cipolla, 1973).

However, despite its undeniable historical significance, the industrial revolution did not quickly and profoundly transform the consumption patterns of households. To begin with, income levels grew rather slowly by contemporary standards, both in Great Britain and in any of its followers. While for a long time it was assumed that this historical rupture could only have led to an extraordinary acceleration of economic growth, the rates of growth actually remained at levels that, from a contemporary perspective, were modest: around 1–1.5 per cent annually, a figure that would today quickly be met with forecasts of crisis from commentators. Moreover, the income levels of most households increased by far less than this. The industrial revolution did not halt the trend of the early modern period towards increasing social inequality and, in fact, exacerbated it. The fruits of industrial growth tended to be concentrated in a few hands: business profits grew more clearly than the real wages of workers, which in fact remained virtually stagnant for a significant part of the period (Bairoch, 1997; Lindert & Williamson, 2016; Maddison, 2001; Piketty, 2014).

These circumstances seriously restricted the ability of most families to increase their spending, purchase more consumer goods, and diversify their basket. Diversification was also hindered by an additional problem: the persistence of high relative prices for food. The technological change of the industrial revolution was distinctly located in certain industrial sectors and transport, while a significant part of the economy, particularly its agricultural sector, continued to operate with organic energies and labour-intensive techniques. Even though there was some increase in agricultural productivity during the nineteenth century, the imbalance between the growth potential of the food system and that of the rest of the economy was evident. Consequently, the onset of industrialisation put pressure on food markets. At numerous points, this combined with adverse events, such as wars or unfavourable weather episodes, to produce sudden rises in food prices, with "subsistence crises" and social unrest as a result (Bairoch, 1999; Krausmann et al., 2008; Vanhaute et al., 2007).

During most of this period, in most countries, most households had consumption patterns that were not very different from the traditional ones. Their baskets became only a bit more abundant, mainly thanks to the reduction in the cost of clothing items. The composition of the basket did not experience major changes. Food continued to be, by far, the largest item in household budgets. Given that much of the population still had a poor nutritional status and given that the relative price of food remained high, families channelled much of their modest income increases towards improving their diet. This mainly involved strengthening the plant-based core of the diet, consisting of cereals, legumes, and potatoes, and only more secondarily (and less widely as one moved down the social pyramid) diversifying it through greater consumption of vegetables, fruits, or animal-based foods such as meat and milk. The fact that access to decent food at reasonable prices remained one of the main sources of social tension during this period tells us much about how little the industrial revolution revolutionised the world of consumption, at least during its early stages (Malassis, 1997; Martínez Carrión, 2012; Popkin, 1993; Pujol & Cussó, 2014).

Meanwhile, the onset of the industrial revolution coincided with what many have seen as the beginning of modern economic thought: the intellectual cycle that starts with Adam Smith continues with the rest of the economists today known as "classics", and ends with Karl Marx. This is, of course, somewhat of an exaggeration: classical political economy was, to a significant extent, an intellectual enterprise different from that pursued by most economists in most faculties around the world today. Furthermore, and just as the industrial revolution did not lack the antecedent of a certain economic dynamism during the early modern era, there are reasons to read Smith not so much as a starting point, but as the endpoint of a genealogy that would have begun several decades earlier. Nevertheless, as we argued in the previous chapter, we are dealing with an intellectual cycle capable of exerting a lasting influence, shaping the terms and instruments of economic discourse on a scale hitherto unknown. Moreover, it is a cycle that does not lack some unifying traits.

The first of these traits is the adoption of an economic perspective centred around the notions of surplus and reproduction. For the classical political economists and Marx, the economy was a network of interconnected production processes organised according to a division of labour and a social class structure. The division of labour was oriented towards the generation of value, a term understood in an objective sense: as the relative difficulty of producing a given commodity, considering the circumstances surrounding the integration of its production process with the rest of the production processes in the network. The reproduction of the network over time required that, at the end of each period, the commodities necessary to reactivate the various production processes for the next period were available. Among these, it was necessary to "reproduce" the workforce by ensuring that it had sufficient food and, in general, a basket of consumer goods that allowed it to meet its basic needs. When production exceeded the system's reproduction requirements, the resulting surplus would be reintegrated into the economic circuit. The manner in which this occurred, depending on the decisions made by the social classes entitled to appropriate the surplus, would provide the system with a direction of change (Martins, 2014; Roncaglia, 2005).

A second unifying trait lies in the way the classical economists and Marx accompanied this "pure economics" with elements of history, sociology, and philosophy. Perhaps, as in so many other aspects, it was John Stuart Mill (1865, p. 306) who best captured this *zeitgeist* when he stated that "a person is not likely to be a good political economist who is nothing else".

There was undoubtedly a move towards a more autonomous status for economic thought, and we may even speculate that the very evolution of some key figures in this cycle, such as Smith and Marx, was precisely one of moving from an economy embedded in an otherwise philosophical argument to the construction of a distinctly economic argument. In any case, even *The Wealth of Nations* or *Capital*, to cite the endpoint of both authors, were filled with historical and sociological material. In this way, the classical economists and Marx were able to formulate their arguments about the direction of economic dynamics, the social classes involved in the division of labour, and the nature of human well-being and social progress. Economic thought gained autonomy as successive authors endeavoured to identify the "principles of political economy" that served as the title for more than one of the major books of the era, but it did not break its ties with other fields (Aspromourgos, 2009; Martins, 2014). On the contrary, and as Schumpeter (1954, p. 597) reminds us, it maintained "close relations" with them.

No Vision

The classical economists and Marx could not have a vision (in Schumpeter's sense) of consumer society because, as we have pointed out in the previous section, consumer society simply did not exist in their time. Their "pre-analytic cognitive acts" led them to domains closer to the economic and social reality of the era. To begin with, their focus was on value, production, and distribution rather than on consumption. The economy of the classics and Marx was one in which various social classes participated in a division of labour that made the production of useful commodities possible, and in which institutional arrangements prevailed that regulated the distribution of that value. What each social class or the individuals that made it up later did with their income was not a major issue. It was not even commonly accepted that it belonged to the intellectual enterprise of political economy, and its significance for the field seemed almost exclusively restricted to the implications it might have for future rounds of value creation (Perrotta, 1998; Villeneuve, 2024).

It was only through this avenue that the world of consumption began to enter classical economic thought. Throughout the arc from Smith to Marx, we find a distinction between those incomes that, once distributed, were used by their recipients to reproduce and expand production circuits, and those that were not. The former were more or less equivalent to what we now call investment or capital formation, but they also included the necessary consumption for the different social classes, especially the working class, to be able to participate in the next round of production. As Marx emphasised, the reproduction of production circuits required that entrepreneurs had access to machinery, buildings, or raw materials, but also to a workforce capable of performing the required work. For the classical economists, it was obvious that those incomes allocated to ensure these starting conditions were the engine on which economic change rested, and in that sense, they could be considered "productive" expenditures. However, already in Smith (1776, pp. 424–448), we find a caution regarding "unproductive" consumption, that is, consumption oriented to ends different from the reproduction and expansion of productive circuits. Smith especially focused on the hiring of personal servants by the wealthy classes, and other authors pointed to various consumptions seen as luxurious. This set up a tension between two possible uses of the surplus: either it was used to expand, diversify, and deepen production circuits, which would lead to more value creation in the future, or it was allocated to an "unproductive" consumption of the value that had already been created. Smith strongly advocated for the first option, represented by industrious manufacturers or farmers, and condemned the second, identified with rentier aristocrats.

Only occasionally did the analytical possibility arise that the desirable scenario might not be the predominance of one or the other use of surplus, but rather a healthy balance between both. Robert Malthus (1836), in particular, suggested the possibility that consumption could lag behind investment, with the consequent retardation of future rounds of value creation. Marx (1867–1894) also entertained the possibility that the inequality inherent in capitalist society could lead to crises of underconsumption, which would contribute to the general contradictions poised to bring about the collapse of the mode of production. However, the conventional wisdom of the time was aligned with what Jean-Baptiste Say (1803) eloquently formulated: in this economy with a division of labour and intertwined production processes, the production of commodities injected purchasing power across the different social classes, ensuring that a crisis of overproduction could not occur at the economy-wide level.

In any case, the reflections on consumption by the classical economists and Marx were rooted in visions of a society in which most people seemed condemned to earn little more than a subsistence income. Let us bear in mind, to begin with, that the narratives of the classical economists and

Marx about economic dynamics were eminently asymptotic: sooner or later, growth was bound to exhaust itself (Wrigley, 1988, 2004). There would then come a stationary state, in the language of the classics, or a terminal crisis of capitalism, in Marx's language. The first generations of classical economists, in particular, did not seem to be aware that the major break that later generations would call the industrial revolution was taking place. This, of course, reflects that economic growth during the early stages of industrialisation was slow and, perhaps even more importantly, that the macroeconomic record still depended much on the large fraction of the economy that remained dependent on organic energies and labour-intensive techniques. It is true that later generations of classical economists, such as John Stuart Mill, and certainly Marx, had a more vivid perception of the significance of the technological changes taking place. But even they, for different reasons, continued to produce narratives in which, sooner or later, the sources of economic growth were bound to run out. This pushed the theoretical possibility of a permanent transformation in consumption patterns revolutionising people's material life further away.

Moreover, it was not even clear that the consumption patterns of most households were likely to change much during the phase of growth that would precede either the stationary state or the collapse of capitalism. Some narratives about the dynamics of economic change were more optimistic than others regarding the trajectory of wages, but the dominant view was that the scope for wage improvement was modest at best. Economic growth could perhaps allow for some increase in wages over time, but there were many who argued that the fruits of growth would eventually become concentrated in the hands of the elites, without workers benefiting significantly. David Ricardo (1817) argued that, since economic change was constrained by the limited growth potential of the agrarian sector, the fruits of growth would flow to landowners, while workers would remain tethered to a subsistence wage. Similarly, Marx (1867–1894) argued that, in an industrial economy, the bourgeoisie appropriated surplus value in the form of business profits, while the working class only earned a subsistence wage. Under such conditions, it was difficult for classical economists or Marx to foresee any substantial transformation in the consumption patterns of much of the population. The masses seemed to be condemned to a very rudimentary consumer basket. While it may not have been strictly a subsistence basket in the biological sense of the term, it barely included a small addition of very basic cultural standards.

The reflections of the classical economists and Marx on consumption were then shaped by considerations of social class. Rather than being reflections on the masses, they were reflections on the elites. It is true that the face of these elites changed throughout the period as the social stratification patterns of European societies evolved. At the beginning of the period, Smith reflected on how the landowning aristocracy used its wealth, whereas by the end of the period Marx focused on the luxury consumption of the industrial and financial bourgeoisie. But in either case, the masses did not seem to be susceptible to analysis regarding how they used their wealth. Their economic situation seemed to be too bad for such a problem to come to life. A partial exception is John Stuart Mill, who seemed to glimpse the possibility that a new type of middle class might emerge with a consumption pattern and lifestyle distinct from both the elites and the working classes. In general, however, neither the classical economists nor Marx, immersed in economies of slow growth and societies with highly unequal patterns of distribution, anticipated that the dynamics of capitalism might lead to the formation of mass consumer societies. Perhaps, as suggested by Diatkine (2021), Smith's work could be read as the "discovery of capitalism", but neither Smith nor his successors, nor Marx, had the chance to discover consumer society.

The political debate of the period could not do much to push the concerns of classical economists or Marx in that direction either. The central tension revolved around what some have called "centrist liberalism", which eventually became the dominant ideology and praxis, and two alternatives: conservatism, which looked back to lament the destruction of the social and political structures of the pre-market order; and socialism, which looked forward to propose a post-market order that would be more equitable. This political tension unfolded in various directions, but none of the key debates had much to do with the world of consumption. The central debates concerned institutional structures, political modes of representation, and, if we look at the socio-economic dimension, the liberalisation of economic life, international trade, and the transformation of labour, capital, and natural resources into commodities (Polanyi, 1944; Wallerstein, 2011).

Consumer society could not form part of the field of vision of the classical economists or Marx. Nevertheless, these authors offered intuitions about the world of consumption that are useful for reconstructing the origins of the debate that would take place in later periods. To this backtracking exercise we now dedicate the remainder of the chapter.

Adam Smith *In Medias Res*

Adam Smith is, for the reasons outlined in the previous chapter, our starting point. However, our reading of Smith will be *in medias res*. By the time Smith published his two major works, *The Theory of Moral Sentiments* and *The Wealth of Nations*, there were prior intellectual traditions that were impossible to ignore and with which, in fact, it was natural to engage. We will use Smith's thought as a point from which to condense these prior traditions, thus providing context for the beginning of our historical arc.

What role do material comforts play in human flourishing and the cultivation of the good life? The question had occupied thinkers since at least Ancient Greece. The Epicureans, for instance, had proposed a hedonistic ethics, based on the pursuit of pleasure and the avoidance of pain. The Stoics, by contrast, had proposed an ethics of virtue, in which tolerance and self-control were seen as playing a fundamental role. In a certain sense, we find here a sketch of what much later would become the rival views of consumer society: the progress thesis and the deviation thesis. Aristotle, who was closer to the Stoics than to the Epicureans, had given one of the first sketches of what we have called the "synthesis view". According to Aristotle, economic life should serve to allow people to satisfy their needs, but once that goal had been achieved, it made little sense to continue in a race for higher incomes and more abundant consumer baskets. Characteristically, for Aristotle the good life consisted of various dimensions, and clashes could be verified between them. Human flourishing could not be completed through the individual consumption of material goods alone; it also required, for example, the genuine development of sociability and civic life. According to some modern interpreters, the components of the Aristotelian good life and the virtues underlying them tended to follow bell-shaped curves: when any of these elements was lacking, increasing its provision contributed to flourishing; but beyond a certain threshold, it ceased to do so. Flourishing was threatened both by deficiency and by excess: it was necessary to identify the "golden mean". To do so, Aristotle relied on practical wisdom, the supreme virtue that would make us adept at the art of combining our individual virtues in a manner adapted to the context. In relation to consumer goods, as well as other components of the good life, it was this practical wisdom that had the responsibility of identifying the moment when progress would begin to turn into deviation (Bruni, 2006, pp. 18–23; Schwartz & Sharpe, 2014; Sedlácek, 2011, pp. 133–180).

Christianity had retained this type of caution against material excesses. After all, the Gospels presented several instances in which Jesus warned against the dangers of materialism and encouraged his followers to live a life of renunciation of comforts (Sedlácek, 2011, pp. 191–194). Combined with those other episodes in which we see Jesus undeniably embedded in a network of social relationships and (through this) in the consumption practices of his own time (Küng, 1976), the result probably does not differ much from Aristotle's golden mean. In the hands of the medieval scholastics, it had been this caution against materialism that had occupied the central focus of the discourse. The Protestant Reformation had done little to change this direction. In fact, at least part of its protest against Catholicism had been a critique of the distance between an austere reading of the Gospel and Rome's embrace of luxury. Outside the religious sphere, there were also numerous medieval and early modern thinkers who articulated ideas that evoked a "fear of goods" (Perrotta, 2004).

It seems reasonable to concede that, in societies so marked by scarcity, poverty, and deprivation as those before the modern era, the idea that moving towards more abundant consumer baskets could lead to a better life had been so common-sensical that it was hardly considered necessary to develop substantial intellectual efforts to defend it. Another matter, however, were the warnings about the dangers of materialism as a deviation. Some of these may have been nothing more than crude attempts to indoctrinate the masses about the necessary nature of their poverty, as well as to strengthen the social legitimisation of an unjust status quo. But others, it must also be acknowledged, had been warnings about what could happen if, in virtually stagnant economies, individuals embarked on a race to pursue unlimited material wealth: that the success of some in this race could only occur at the expense of the defeat of others. Although this theoretical vision of a zero-sum game may seem odd to the modern mindset, we would do well to appreciate the historical context in which it was framed: that of economies, as later research by historians has repeatedly shown, with truly modest growth potential (Piketty, 2014, pp. 593–594; Wrigley, 1986).

In any case, by Smith's time, a rebellion against these kinds of warnings had already taken shape. Perhaps its most forceful voice had been Bernard de Mandeville in the early eighteenth century. For Mandeville (1714), the pursuit of what he had unabashedly called "private vices" could lead to the forging of true "public virtues". There was nothing wrong with adopting a luxurious lifestyle, supported by increasing quantities of ever more refined goods and large staffs of servants. In Mandeville's view, traditional warnings about materialism not only reflected the moral authoritarianism of those who made them but also stood as obstacles to economic progress. In a certain sense, Mandeville was rescuing the Epicureans and their ethics of pleasure, adding a dose of macroeconomic consequentialism to it (Sedlácek, 2011, pp. 245–254).

It is no coincidence that, just as warnings against materialism proliferated in nearly stagnant economies, the rebellion against them had its main centres in places that were achieving some economic growth during the early modern period. Both in the Netherlands, where Mandeville was raised, and in England, where he spent his adult life, "advanced organic economies" had formed, capable of combining modest progress in agriculture, trade, and manufacturing. It was in these economies that a certain renewal of consumer culture had occurred. In fact, the demand for new consumer goods, particularly those from the expansive colonial trade, may have prompted families to intensify their work efforts. Mandeville's *Fable of the Bees* had, to no small extent, been an apologia for that "industrious revolution". This was essentially the kind of "wealth of nations" that Smith was set to investigate by the late eighteenth century (de Vries, 2008; Wrigley, 1988).

Smith's view of the world of consumption, however, was ambivalent. Like other authors of the time, for example Antonio Genovesi from Naples, Smith rather positioned himself as a mediator between the classical tradition based on virtue and the common good, on the one hand, and the new ideas about private interest and individual utility, on the other (Bruni, 2006, pp. 48–65; Pabst, 2018). On the one hand, Smith saw in the improvement of consumption patterns a potential lever for progress. It was impossible even to concede to his adversaries the use of a term such as "vice", even though Mandeville had used it with subversive intentions. What motivated consumers was simply their interest, now redefined to capture the material aspects of well-being rather than (as had traditionally been the case) the full range of human aspirations. Smith attributed to individuals a considerable ability to identify their interests and act accordingly. The purchase of goods and services allowed consumers to improve their well-being because it improved their performance in one of the various dimensions that comprised the good life. To the extent that the evolution of their income level allowed, individuals could find in consumption a means to enhance their lives. Embedded in a society in which the material life of most of the population was conditioned by serious privations, Smith resisted adopting a hard-line anti-materialistic stoicism (Bee & Paganelli, 2019; Hirschman, 1977).

This pursuit of private interest through consumption also seemed to have a broad area of convergence with the achievement of public interest. After all, consumer behaviour allowed producers to identify social needs and respond to them. In Smith's "commercial society", the market could serve as an effective mechanism of economic coordination between the two. Moreover, it could not be ruled out—indeed, perhaps quite the opposite—that the adoption of more satisfying consumption patterns could improve the situation of individuals in those other dimensions of the good life that were not directly related to material well-being. Thus, for example, the improvement of material well-being could allow for a more faithful expression of the consumer's identity and human potential. It could also facilitate their insertion into various networks of interpersonal relationships. With its dynamic effect on society as a whole, the allure of consumption could even contribute to dissolving the remnants of feudalism that still persisted in eighteenth-century Europe. If Montesquieu had spoken of a *doux commerce* capable of soothing the violent impulses of citizens and nations, Smith suggested a certain notion of *doux consommation* capable of promoting not only material well-being but also the non-material components of the good life. In this, he was advancing along a path already trodden by the aforementioned Genovesi and David Hume (Bee, 2018; Bruni, 2006, pp. 48–65; Hirschman, 1977, p.129; Sedlácek, 2011, p. 307).

However, although Smith had in mind this kind of positive feedback loop between consumption and other components of the good life, his conception of the good life was multidimensional, and this could not fail to have consequences. The hedonistic calculus along the pleasure-pain dimension was part of his ethical framework on human well-being, but by no means did it dominate it. Hirschman (1977) even speculates that the only reason why this ethical complexity in *The Theory of Moral Sentiments* was somewhat blurred in *The Wealth of Nations*, giving rise to what would later be called *das Adam Smith problem*, was precisely his confidence in positive feedback between the advancement of material wealth and the other dimensions of the good life. However, there were moments when this confidence was threatened by negative feedback loops. For instance, even in relatively prosperous societies, most of the population seemed to be trapped in a vicious circle of hard work and a lack of intellectual and social engagement, which led to their capacity for human flourishing being severely stunted (Smith, 1776, pp. 717–721). This brought Smith to the threshold of the deviation thesis, if not as a primary argument, then at least as an analytical possibility.

The key concept for uncovering this analytical possibility was unproductive consumption. Smith was moderately optimistic about the consumption patterns that the masses, or at least an emerging middle class, could eventually have within the "commercial society", but he was far less sympathetic towards the decisions made by elites on how to use their wealth. As we studied in the previous section, for Smith, the wealth of nations was better served if, for example, elites used their surplus to accumulate capital in order to promote production in the next period, rather than spending it on hiring large staffs of personal servants, which he regarded as unproductive consumption.

This line of thought has sometimes been considered a red herring, especially when interpreted as a hasty exclusion of service activities from value creation. However, even consumer goods with material content were not free from Smith's critical gaze, as he spared no derogatory terms in his evaluation of the goods that seduced the elites. For instance, men of fortune often purchased durable commodities, which was good for the "growth of public opulence" but entailed a problem:

> The latter species of expense [ ], especially when directed towards frivolous objects, the little ornaments of dress and furniture, jewels, trinkets, gew-gaws, frequently indicates, not only a trifling, but a base and selfish disposition. (Smith, 1776, p. 448)

Similar references can be found in other parts of Smith's work (Hirschman, 1977, p. 121, 1982, pp. 56–57; Trincado, 2024). Far from endorsing any consumer decisions, Smith was not a hard-line Epicurean, and his *Theory of Moral Sentiments* had already criticised the philosophical foundations of Mandeville (Smith, 1759, pp. 536–546). Smith's ethics was not one of pleasure, but of virtue.

The analytical possibility of deviation in Smith's work was linked to the spread of a particular consumer culture. Smith's consumers had a reasonable capacity to identify their interests and act accordingly, but they were also social beings whose orientations were influenced by their position within a broader network of cultural interactions with other individuals. *The Theory of Moral Sentiments* had already provided an analysis of the role of habits and fashions, suggesting that the fascination with status could lead to the moral corruption of consumers. Now, in *The Wealth of Nations*, the subsistence standard of living attributed to most of the population was not such from a strictly biological standpoint but carried a certain cultural component. Certain goods had to be consumed in order to secure some basic social integration. Smith never seemed to have much of an issue with this component of the masses' consumption baskets, which, at the time, was still frankly modest. The issue, however, lay with the very different consumer culture of the elites, particularly the aristocratic elites, who in both past and present diverted substantial resources into "sumptuous profusion". Such unproductive consumption was necessary for their social standing within their respective spheres of reference, but it neither allowed them to cultivate the good life nor was it necessarily beneficial for social progress (Smith, 1759, pp. 138–144 and 349–374, 1776, pp. 446–447, 622; Kim, 2015; Paganelli, 2009; Smith, 2013, 2016).

In sum, Smith attempted to mediate between traditional cautions against materialism and new ideas about private interest. Another author we can read in this light, Antonio Genovesi, summarised his view of the world of consumption by stating that he had as little sympathy for "rude and sordid parsimony" as for "fool and vain prodigality" (cf. Bruni, 2006, p. 58). In our view, this was also Smith's perspective. From this viewpoint, the dangers of reading Smith retrospectively as a precursor to what would eventually become the central tradition of economic thought in the twentieth century are as evident as specialists in his work have been underscoring for at least fifty years now (Arrighi, 2007; Diatkine, 2021; Rothschild, 2001; Winch, 1978).

John Stuart Mill's "Classical Situation"

Schumpeter (1954) encourages us to view John Stuart Mill, particularly his *Principles of Political Economy*, as the "classical situation" that would encapsulate the evolution of economic analysis between 1790 and 1870. We will begin from this perspective to make the leap from Smith to Mill. We will also make this jump with the liberty granted by the fact that, as argued earlier, none of the economists of the period had a vision of consumer society. We lose little by not pausing over certain intermediate vignettes, such as the role that consumption may have played in some of the waves of debate sparked by Malthus' *Essay on Population* (Collantes, 2003), or Say's (1803, pp. 217–222) digression on the "judicious kinds of consumption" and the problems of ostentation. At most, what these vignettes would make clear is the persistence of an analytical framework in which consumption was shaped by social and cultural influences, and in which the possibility of progress coexisted with that of deviation. More relevant to our exercise in backtracking is the positioning of Mill within the intellectual context that was shaping up after *The Wealth of Nations*.

Political economy was rising, and it was developing increasing synergies with utilitarian philosophy. Already in the late eighteenth century, Jeremy Bentham (1789) proposed that pleasure and pain were the two great sovereigns on the basis of which any conduct should be approved or disapproved. This, of course, was ammunition for the final assault on the political and intellectual strongholds that still preserved what we have come to call the *Ancien Régime*. It was also, and this is more important for our purposes, an update of the characteristically Epicurean position. Once the pursuit of pleasure and the avoidance of pain became normative standards, the traditional cautions against materialism were definitively neutralised (Bruni, 2006, pp. 104–105). In fact, it was no longer necessary, as in Mandeville or Smith, to try to win the battle by arguing about the potential beneficial effects of private consumption on public progress. A free and autonomous consumer made hedonistic calculations that led them to make certain decisions over others. As long as these choices did not harm others, what sense could there be in criticising them?

The adoption of utilitarianism as the default philosophy by most political economists thus had a notable impact on their work. With pleasure and pain converted into the one-dimensional metric of well-being, the type of virtue ethics that Smith had worked with was bound to recede (Rogan, 2017, pp. 83–91; Schumpeter, 1954, pp. 463–467). The space for continuing to perceive the possibility of consumption as deviation became smaller. Political economy paid little attention to the kind of ambivalent counterbalances with which Smith had viewed the world of consumption.

However, we should not exaggerate the magnitude of this movement. Intellectuals critical of nineteenth-century political economy, particularly the romantics, depicted it as an intellectual project that, in a rather gloomy manner, sought to encapsulate the richness of human experience within the dimension of private utility and material wealth. But how resistant would the one-dimensional approach, à la Bentham, have been to the fact that these political economists had been moved to reflect more systematically on the world of consumption? Take, for example, the case of a utilitarian as convinced as James Mill. Even he, after all, could end up accommodating the return of the deviation thesis through the back door. His utilitarianism seemed to be compatible with a concern about the "intemperance" of consumers as a potential obstacle on their path to happiness. Education appeared then as a *deus ex machina* meant to aid individuals in making decisions (Bianchini, 2016). At the end of the day, the signals these individuals received from the pleasure-pain axis did not seem to be good enough.

This resistance of political economists to carry utilitarianism to its logical extremes is illustrated with particular clarity by John Stuart Mill and his "classical situation". Mill the son had been raised as a Benthamite, and few would question that utilitarianism played a role in his system of thought. However, the utilitarianism of the mature Mill was not identical to that of Bentham or his father. Furthermore, it coexisted with other intellectual influences, among which (to complicate matters further) was the influence of romanticism. The result was a view of consumption that kept alive the ambivalence cultivated by Smith and projected it into the future in a more systematic way.

This story has two parts. The first consists of how Mill aligned with Smith's narrative on consumption as a potential driver of progress. By the mid-nineteenth century, while John Stuart Mill was writing the first edition of his *Principles of Political Economy*, industrialising Europe was being shaken by social and political upheavals. However, it is fair to concede that, particularly in Britain, a more benign horizon of economic and social change was beginning to take shape. Mill and his generation were becoming more aware of the economic progress that, in spite of shortcomings and imbalances, had begun to unfold since the late eighteenth century. There was also greater confidence in the ability of progress to sustain itself over time through scientific activity, technological creativity, and, after the repeal of the Corn Laws in 1846, the use of international trade as a tool to ease the bottlenecks of domestic industrialisation. By the final years of Mill's life, in the 1860s and 1870s, this more benign horizon also included some improvement in the material lives of the masses, once the most traumatic impacts of the industrial revolution in terms of social dislocation, inequality, and labour exploitation had been mitigated (Martínez Carrión, 2012; Prados de la Escosura, 2022).

Mill had no interest in denying the element of progress that this wave of economic and social change entailed. With a conciseness that partly reflected the diminishing relevance of traditional cautions against materialism, Mill (1848, p. 869) declared himself little interested in asceticism and, instead, supported all attempts by individuals to access the genuine enjoyment of the various pleasures that life might offer. Mill's consumers, like those of the other classical economists, had a considerable capacity to identify their interests and act accordingly. Their freedom of choice in the market was important because it generally led to correct choices, in the sense that these choices reflected consumers' preferences and inclinations better than any government or third party could. And freedom of choice was important also because it was part of a broader package of civic and political liberties that favoured the flourishing of genuine personalities within a diverse and vibrant society. In other words, Mill was updating the Smithian narrative: a *doux consommation* that, while allowing individuals to achieve greater material comfort, could generate positive impacts on the non-material dimensions of the good society.

This leads, however, to the second part of the story: the incorporation of deviation as an analytical possibility. Like Smith, Mill was working with an ethical theory (or, in the words he himself chose for the subtitle of the *Principles*, a "social philosophy") that conceived of well-being in multidimensional terms. This opened the door to the coexistence of the progress thesis with the deviation thesis. For Mill, Bentham's hedonistic pleasure was important, but there were "higher pleasures" and "lower pleasures". The higher pleasures were those that allowed for the development of the most genuine human potentialities, including intellectual, scientific, or artistic activity. Although these activities could only contribute to the good life insofar as they provided satisfaction to those who engaged in them, the one-dimensional scale of utilitarianism would, according to Mill, do little justice to their intrinsic superiority over the lower pleasures associated with the consumption of material goods (Dilulio, 2022; Villeneuve, 2024).

Mill had no problem admitting that, on occasion, a positive link could be observed between material progress and the non-material dimensions of the good life. After all, the accumulation of successive rounds of material progress, as could be perceived in nineteenth-century Britain, created more room for societies to orient themselves towards higher pleasures, allocating greater resources to the education of the masses or to the production and enjoyment of works of art. Here, Mill extended the theoretical framework that his predecessors had been working with, liberating the notion of unproductive consumption from the negative connotations it had previously carried. For Mill, as for other classical economists, there was indeed something that could be justifiably called unproductive consumption. It referred to resources that did not feed into the network of production processes that created economic value. This did not have to be defined in an austere way: the consumption of "a certain quantum of enjoyment which may be classed among necessaries, since anything short of it would not be consistent with the greatest efficiency of labour" (Mill, 1848, p. 52), was to be seen as productive.

However, and here comes the difference with most classical political economists, these were resources that could serve to promote higher pleasures and allow people to access a whole range of transformative experiences, from education to the enjoyment of art, which could be considered essential for their full flourishing as human beings. "It would be a great error", Mill (1848, p. 53) warned, "to regret the large proportion of annual produce, which in an opulent country goes to supply unproductive consumption". How, otherwise, could societies ever be in a position to flourish civically, spiritually, or artistically? Only a sizeable share of unproductive consumption, made possible by the accumulation of prior rounds of economic growth, could create the conditions for this. As a result, material progress could be an ally of progress in the other dimensions of the good life.

And yet, precisely because material progress made increasingly large flows of unproductive consumption possible, it was also more likely that consumption deviated from the path towards the good life. "The [thing] to be regretted", Mill (1848, p. 53) pointed out, "[...] [is] the little worth of the objects to which the greater part of it is devoted". Mill often argued that the social classes that had the possibility to go beyond merely productive consumption tended to direct their unproductive consumption towards misguided ends. Much spending was flowing towards commodities that, despite reaching considerable prices in the market, had an intrinsic value that was decidedly mediocre.

The same author who declared himself opposed to asceticism was reluctant to unconditionally embrace the progress thesis. His attitude was ambivalent: he did not retain the distinction between productive and unproductive consumption to criticise the latter as useless, but rather to assess it openly. Beneath this lay a relativistic conception of the capacity of consumers to correctly identify their interests and act accordingly. For Mill (1848, p. 953), "[T]he proposition that the consumer is a competent judge of the commodity, can be admitted only with numerous abatements and exceptions". This claim was largely valid when referring to the more basic goods of material life, but not so much when it came to "those things which are chiefly useful as tending to raise the character of human beings".

Once the multidimensional conception of well-being came to be accompanied by an open-ended view of the interaction between the different dimensions, Mill found himself in a position to execute one of his most famous shifts: the deproblematisation of the stationary state. All the classical economists, Mill included, anticipated that economic growth could not continue indefinitely because its sources, such as the division of labour and capital accumulation, tended to run out. Even though, in Mill's time, it was beginning to be perceived that the period during which growth could be sustained was perhaps longer than expected, the eventual appearance of bottlenecks was thought to be certain. However, what others had seen as an obviously gloomy scenario, Mill regarded as an opportunity that could promote, rather than hinder, the cultivation of the good life. Once the fruits of economic growth had been reaped, the advent of the stationary state could bring about a convenient shift in mentalities from the traditional pursuit of material progress to the other dimensions of the good life. The saturation of profitable investment opportunities could stimulate interest in a less materialistic lifestyle, one more aligned with genuinely human values, more focused on the pursuit of higher pleasures and on "improving the Art of Living" (Mill, 1848, p. 751). Underlying this optimistic view of the stationary state was, to a large extent, the suspicion that, once a certain level of material comfort had been reached, the continuation of economic growth could hinder, rather than promote, the cultivation of the good life. What had for a time been progress could, through a cascade of unproductive consumption of dubious value, become deviation.

According to Mill, what determined whether or not unproductive consumption took a beneficial direction? As in Smith, the answer to this question seemed to lead him to the terrain of consumer culture, or more precisely, to the different consumer cultures prevalent in different social classes. The working class participated in a consumer culture in which the purely biological components of subsistence were supplemented by moderate extras arising from custom. This basic basket allowed workers to integrate adequately into the productive and social fabric. The problem, however, lay more in the consumer culture of the elites, among whom the key values were vanity and the desire to signal social status:

> [A] great portion of the expenses of the higher and middle classes in most countries, and the greatest in this, is not incurred for the sake of the pleasure afforded by the things on which money is spent, but from regard to opinion and an idea that certain expenses are expected from them as an appendage of station. (Mill, 1848, p. 869)

Since these expenditures did not promote the good life,

> I know not why it should be matter of congratulation that persons who are already richer than any one needs to be, should have doubled their means of consuming things which give little or no pleasure except as representative of wealth. (Mill, 1848, p. 749)

Mill's hopes were placed in the gradual flourishing of an alternative culture among what we might read as a new middle class (Persky, 2016, pp. 97–98). The accumulation of successive rounds of economic growth would allow a larger proportion of individuals to enjoy a more comfortable consumption pattern, capable of satisfying their material needs and promoting a reorientation towards higher pleasures. This type of middle class might even serve as a model for the lower classes, encouraging them to redirect their energies towards higher objectives than purely material ones. In fact, it was this sociological projection that underpinned much of Mill's deproblematisation of the stationary state. The outcome, however, remained open. In other passages, Mill outlined a potential threat: once individuals were provided with sufficient material comfort, they might continue to cling to their traditional orientations and motivations. It was possible that consumer behaviour would depend on one's prior consumption experiences, such that the pursuit of higher pleasures could be obstructed by the fact that these pleasures were not important within the pre-existing consumer culture. Mill illustrated this with regard to education, but the argument could be extended to other areas. In a related vein, Mill voiced concern over the potential rise of a mass culture defined by materialism, uniformity, and mediocrity (Persky, 2016, pp. 130–131).

In sum, the prospect of a society less burdened by deprivation opened up a variety of possible paths of change. It was conceivable that new social groups would arise, who, based on significant material comfort, would seek to develop some of the most valuable human potentials. However, it was equally conceivable that such material comfort could be linked to the consolidation of consumer cultures that diverted individuals towards expenditures that were not conducive to the good life. In this way, Mill systematised the ambivalence with which Smith had initiated the cycle of classical political economy.

Das Karl Marx Problem

The rise of political economy was contested from two very different angles: romanticism and socialism. Romantics were highly critical of the long shadow cast by utilitarianism over what Thomas Carlyle famously called the "dismal science". Take, for example, the highly influential case of John Ruskin, which up to some extent can be read as the "classical situation" of romanticism in the central part of the nineteenth century. Originally an art critic, Ruskin believed that by this point in history, industrialisation had secured the necessary consumer goods for subsistence. Consequently, the emphasis should be placed on finding a virtuous allocation of resources that went beyond the purely material dimension of well-being. The monetary criterion should make way for a broader life criterion which focused on the intrinsic characteristics of consumer goods. Ultimately, in Ruskin's (1862, p. 648) world, "the manner and issue of consumption" became "the real tests of production":

> Production does not consist of things laboriously made, but in things serviceably consumable; and the question for the nation is not how much labour it employs, but how much life it produces. For as consumption is the end and aim of production, so life is the end and aim of consumption.
>
> [...] THERE IS NOT WEALTH BUT LIFE. Life, including all its power of love, of joy, and of admiration. That country is the richest which nourishes the greatest numbers of noble and happy human beings; that man is richest, who, having perfected the functions of his own life to the utmost, has also the widest helpful influence, both personal, and by means of his possessions, over the lives of others.

As in Smith, consumption was the end of all production; but, taking it one step further, life was the end of all consumption.

In the terms we have been using in this chapter, Ruskin was openly sceptical about the idea that progress in consumption patterns would be virtuous in its connection to progress in other dimensions of the good life. What, for some, was the triumphant progress of market society, for Ruskin was a deviation in which a new civilisation, obsessed with material wealth, had lost sight of the flourishing of personal and collective life (Cain, 2021; Shionoya, 2014).

One might wonder whether this argument was truly incompatible with the theoretical structure of Smith and Mill, but it cannot be denied that it was a much more vigorous formulation of the deviation thesis. What was beginning to take shape was what, much later, would become the humanist critique of consumer society. In this type of humanist critique, the romantics and the socialists were initially less separated than we might think. To appreciate this, we do not need to apply backtracking to the cooperative socialists of the early part of the period, nor to what Marx would later call the utopian socialists: Marx himself will suffice.

In 1844, four years before Mill published his *Principles*, Marx stated his own version of the deviation thesis, doing so in a way that connects directly with what would later become the conversation about consumer society. The humanist critique of capitalism that he developed in his unpublished *Economic and Philosophic Manuscripts* rested on an ideal of life whose core was the realisation of human potential within a social framework that ensured freedom from material scarcity and freedom from labour exploitation (Marx, 1844). This ideal, however, appeared painfully at odds with the reality of the working class in the mid-nineteenth century. Technological innovation had allowed for significant progress in productivity, but workers were still forced to work very long hours, so much so that they lacked the time and energy to realise their human potential. Their jobs, embedded in a rigid organisation of labour within firms, also led them to an impoverishing specialisation. By the end of the day, they lacked not only time but also the faculties to think, love, theorise, sing, or paint, to name just a few activities that Marx suggested as constitutive of humanity.

The only pursuit for which there seemed to be space in this lifestyle was the acquisition of income, a goal that sacrificed life and humanity. In fact, and this is where consumption came into play, capitalism would rely on the continuous induction of false needs by producers:

> Each individual speculates on how to create in the other a new need, compelling them to make a new sacrifice, plunging them into a new dependence, and *diverting them towards a new form of pleasure*. [...] [The] increase in production and needs becomes the ingenious and ever-calculating slave of inhuman, refined, unnatural, and imaginary whims. [...] The producer submits to the most abject whims of man, acts as a go-between between him and his need, awakens morbid appetites, and watches for every weakness in order to demand a tip for these good offices. (Marx, 1844, pp. 156–157; emphasis added)

In their pursuit of profit, manufacturers and merchants sought to create new desires among consumers, analysing their weaknesses and seducing them into the purchase of goods that did not actually help them develop their full potential as human beings. Here, Marx reproduced the ethical template known since Aristotle: the good life consisted of cultivating different dimensions, and thus there existed the possibility that an excessive emphasis on the dimension related to income, consumption, and material comfort would obstruct the flourishing of individuals in other areas. As with Aristotle (or, for that matter, Smith), the path to the good life involved an ethics of virtue that could navigate the dangerous seduction of materialism.

However, Marx's vision of capitalism left little room for the masses to actually stray down a consumerist deviation in practice. In fact, the deviation thesis did not form part of the core of his later work. In his mature writings, Marx's (1867–1894) critique of capitalism was primarily a denunciation of economic and social inequality. Capitalist society was premised upon a divide between the bourgeoisie and the proletariat, a divide that the very dynamics of capitalism only exacerbated. The working class appeared doomed to suffer a relative, if not absolute, impoverishment. While the bourgeoisie reaped the benefits of economic growth, the proletariat remained anchored at a subsistence standard of living. This was reflected in the consumption patterns of both classes. The elites had the ability to consume luxury goods, while the masses were confined to consuming basic goods.

Marx's capitalists developed new luxury needs as their wealth increased. The goods they consumed became ever more refined and varied: a "conventional dose of extravagance" that had more to do with social signalling than the intrinsic value of the goods themselves. The working class, on the other hand, consumed merely "means of life" or "means of subsistence". This was a condition for the reproduction of capital: "no more and no less than the cleaning of machines", provocatively wrote Marx (1867–1894, I, pp. 3, 370 and 500; and III, p. 191). This essentially mirrored the classical notion of productive consumption, which, in Marx's hands, became part of the social reproduction process underlying the economic reproduction of the capitalist system (Fine & Saad-Filho, 2010, pp. 79–81).

Like all the classical economists, Marx acknowledged that this basket of basic goods did not only include those strictly essential for biological survival. It also included other commodities that, in each historical period, made up a commonly accepted cultural standard (Marx, 1867–1894, I,

p. 124; II, p. 360). Ultimately, what defined goods as either subsistence or luxury goods was not any intrinsic characteristic of the goods themselves, nor the type of human need those goods were meant to satisfy, but the social class of those who consumed them: all social classes in the case of subsistence goods, only the elites in the case of luxury goods.

Marx's (1867–1894, II, p. 366) working classes could come to adopt a consumption pattern with elements of luxury only in a brief, almost accidental way. An example would be the most speculative moments of the upswing of the economic cycle. However, these changes were destined to collapse as soon as excess speculation triggered the transition to the downswing. Moreover, it is important to note that, according to Marx, this succession of cycles did not lead to long-term progress, nor did it seem to induce a softening of class barriers or the expansion of the middle classes. On the contrary, the endpoint was the collapse of the capitalist mode of production and the class structure associated with it. If anything, the role of consumption in the argument would be connected to that collapse—for example, in the sketches outlined by Marx of an unbalanced dynamic in which the sector producing investment goods expanded more rapidly than the sector producing consumer goods.

The mature Marx, consequently, left little room for the progress thesis and was no longer interested in the deviation thesis that the young Marx had proposed. The masses would never consolidate a consumption pattern that went beyond mere subsistence, but the culture that defined such a subsistence pattern was reduced to an exogenous fact. While in the *Manuscripts* Marx had suggested that capitalism could create a consumer culture that diverted individuals from the good life, in *Capital* that connection disappeared. Whether the cultural element of the subsistence consumer basket increased over time and whether this increase represented progress or deviation, as in Mill's discussion of unproductive consumption, were matters that were now outside the focus.

This transition from a humanist critique to a distributive critique was underpinned by Marx's instrumentalisation of utilitarian philosophy (Carabelli & Cedrini, 2018; Veblen, 1906–1907), even if such instrumentalisation was motivated by his desire to subvert its conventional uses. Without explicitly rejecting it, the multidimensional conception of the good life from the *Manuscripts* gradually gave way to a one-dimensional conception of well-being, in which the key factor was the level of income that each social class could obtain. This was essential for emphasising the injustice of the capitalist order, given the immense inequality it created in the distribution of collectively generated wealth. It was also essential for identifying an alternative social order based on the abolition of private property, from which would emerge a pattern of abundant consumption for the masses, not only for the elites. Note that, according to Marx's logic, this would imply the disappearance of luxury consumption, not because goods different from basic ones could not be consumed, but because the type of social segmentation of consumption that defined luxury consumption would disappear. Did this not ultimately lead to the Benthamite slogan of "the greatest happiness for the greatest number"? The mature Marx did not question that more was better; he questioned whether capitalism could guarantee "more" and "better" for the masses, which is why he called for a revolutionary transformation in the mode of production. Having set aside his youthful flirtation with the deviation thesis, Marx sought in the socialist alternative a more credible path to the progress thesis than capitalism could offer.

There is no doubt about the historical irony contained in this intellectual evolution. When the young Marx wrote the *Manuscripts* in the 1840s, the social balance sheet of the new mode of production was decidedly mediocre. Inequality in income distribution was increasing. The institutional changes associated with capitalism were causing significant social dislocation, from labour exploitation in cities to the disintegration of community self-governance in the countryside. The living standards of the masses continued to be precarious, threatened by recurrent subsistence crises and famines. By the time the mature Marx published the first volume of *Capital* in 1867, however, this historical phase was beginning to close. The income level of the masses was beginning to increase clearly, and a more solid consumption pattern was beginning to spread, including, for example, a more abundant and varied diet. Henceforth, only wars would bring back those subsistence crises and famines that, just one generation earlier, had remained common. These changes were evident in Britain by 1867, and they would become equally evident in other European countries in the remaining years until Marx's death in 1883, during which time he worked on what would become the posthumous volumes of *Capital* without showing any interest in the deviation thesis. Yet, as Mill had already perceived in 1848, partly based on the reality of his time and partly on his (more optimistic than Marx's) projections about the future, it was precisely this type of economic and social context that most encouraged loosening the straitjacket of Benthamite utilitarianism. Marx, on the other hand, took the opposite path and mobilised utilitarianism in a politically subversive sense.

It is tempting to describe this by using the formula traditionally applied to Adam Smith and speak of a Karl Marx problem. (This is something that Magness and Makovi (2023), also do, though in a different sense from the one proposed here.) Why did the young Marx's multidimensional view of the good life collapse into a single dimension—the monetary one—that the mature Marx would use to construct his influential critique of capitalism? Why did the deviation thesis come to be forgotten and replaced by an anti-capitalist version of the progress thesis? When it comes to Marx, it is impossible to avoid the suspicion that his analysis was subordinated to his broader political intentions. Retaining the deviation thesis from the *Manuscripts* in *Capital* would likely have required a less gloomy diagnosis of the evolution of income inequality, as well as a sociology of capitalism that allowed for the emergence and consolidation of middle classes. Only in that analytical context would it have been feasible for a significant, perhaps growing, proportion of the population to reach an income level that allowed them to engage in the kind of unproductive consumption that Mill saw as both an opportunity for progress and a danger of deviation.

The influence of the political context must not be dismissed either. The social balance sheet of centrist liberalism was beginning to improve, but by then, a socialist alternative was already being forged, with Marx playing a key role in the evolution of this alternative towards (allegedly) "scientific" socialism. Marx found little political value in the cultural, humanist critique offered by the utopian socialists. Instead, he preferred to subvert utilitarian philosophy, putting it to the service of a distributive critique of capitalism. The deviation thesis, with its suspicion that greater income and more consumer goods were not necessarily better for the good life, would thus disappear from a political agenda for which the central issue was combating social inequality. The subsequent dispute between orthodox Marxists and revisionist social democrats was primarily a disagreement over the most effective means to achieve this goal: anti-capitalist revolution for some, social reform for others. It is worth recalling, moreover, that while income distribution began to become more egalitarian, the distribution of wealth continued to concentrate until the outbreak of the First World War. The distributive issue remained alive, with much power to articulate interests around a socialist policy alternative to centrist liberalism. Marx's version of the deviation thesis was thus buried in the unpublished *Manuscripts* of 1844. It would only reappear in the intellectual and political culture of socialism after its publication in 1932 by the Marx-Engels-Lenin Institute of the Soviet Union.

On the other hand, and alongside these usual suspicions about the interaction between Marx's economics and politics, it is possible that there is another way of addressing our particular Karl Marx problem. This route mirrors the one that Hirschman (1977) encourages us to consider for the Adam Smith problem. For Hirschman, there is no fundamental inconsistency between Smith in *The Theory of Moral Sentiments* and Smith in *The Wealth of Nations.* It is simply that, since the former believed that economic improvement tended to stimulate improvements in other dimensions of the good life (e.g., civic virtue), it was natural for the latter to focus his subsequent efforts on analysing the conditions that made such economic improvement possible. A similar development may have occurred with Marx, albeit in the opposite direction. The Marx of the *Manuscripts* perceived a connection between class inequality and working-class poverty, on one hand, and alienation, which ultimately led people to subordinate their lives and humanity to the pursuit of money, on the other. Thus, for the Marx of *Capital*, it may have seemed natural to focus his later efforts on analysing the conditions that made the reproduction of such an economic system possible.

A great deal of ink would be spilled among later Marxist scholars attempting to resolve this tension. Some would seek ways to argue that one Marx was fully consistent with the other, while others would defend one of the two as the true and relevant one, urging their readers to subordinate their reading of the other Marx accordingly. In any case, and returning to our focus on the debate about consumer society, Marx's case completes the ambivalent picture we have been tracing of the intellectual cycle spanning from the late eighteenth century to the late nineteenth century. In an era in which economists could not be expected to have a vision of consumer society, their intuitions about the role of consumption in human flourishing pointed in diverse directions and prefigured an open space for debate.

Conclusion: Classical Ambivalence

The historical cycle of classical political economy and Marx established key references for subsequent rounds of economic debate. In the case of what would later become the conversation on consumer society, the classics and Marx left behind an ambivalent intellectual legacy. On the one hand, the classical economists carried forward the momentum of the Enlightenment and its belief in material progress made possible through the exercise of reason. In their case, this material progress entailed an increasing access of broader segments of the population to ever more abundant and diverse baskets of consumer goods. The autonomous pursuit of self-interest by mature individuals would thus make consumption a driver of the good life. Marx, of course, was highly sceptical about whether this could occur under the capitalist mode of production, but his faith on an alternative socialist order was still imbued with a variant of the progress thesis. On the other hand, both the classics and Marx simultaneously raised doubts about the capacity of consumption to promote the good life. At times, consumers made decisions that seemed inappropriate for the full development of their human potential, directing their focus towards material goods of little intrinsic value and missing the opportunity to focus on higher purposes. The incorporation of this idea into the core of political economy was embodied in the concept of unproductive consumption, and it was Mill who offered the most systematic treatment.

Regardless of the greater or lesser analytical coherence of Mill or others in integrating the theses of progress and deviation, the ambivalence of the classics and Marx suggests that the terms of economic debate were being set in a way that favoured what we have termed the "synthesis view". The deviation thesis, present in the philosophical and religious traditions prior to the Enlightenment, continued to find its space within the expansive field of political economy. This was facilitated by the fact that the classics and Marx worked within a theoretical framework centred on the twin notions of reproduction and surplus, thereby granting an important role to socio-economic processes of change over time. Their world of consumption was framed within the sphere of social reproduction, which accompanied the reproduction of an economy based on the division of labour. There was a prevailing sense that, although it would never be easy to define precisely, there existed a basic basket of consumption that could be considered sufficient for individuals to satisfy their needs and ensure the reproduction of the system. However, insofar as the economic dynamic led to the production of a surplus, the question arose of how the social classes possessing this surplus would use it. From this, it was only a small step to the emergence of unproductive consumption by analogy with unproductive labour. And it was only one step further to identifying the possibility that this unproductive consumption might feed either the progress thesis or, conversely, the deviation thesis.

It is, however, doubtful that this latter step should have been taken for reasons of economic theory alone. A second circumstance that favoured the persistence of the deviation thesis, and the consequent establishment of a discourse with the potential to evolve towards the "synthesis view", was the fact that the classics and Marx often complemented their economic theory with a philosophy that conceived well-being as a multidimensional variable. In this philosophy, the consumption of material goods could be an important dimension of well-being, but it was by no means the only one. Material goods provided comfort and enjoyment but also enabled people to develop their human potential in areas such as relationships with others, virtuous participation in civic life, or the enjoyment of "higher pleasures" related to art or nature. Yet, from the moment this Aristotelian conception of well-being retained some presence in the writings of the classics and Marx, keeping at bay what Schumpeter (1954, p. 103) refers to as "Bentham's boisterous and vulgar utilitarianism", the stage was set for reflection on the potential sign of the interaction between progress in these different dimensions of the good life. Theoretical flirtations could occur with the possibility that greater availability of consumer goods might enhance the other dimensions (as Smith sometimes suggested), or conversely, that material poverty might dull the potential for living a fully human life (as Marx, but also Smith, sometimes suggested). However, the most consistent endpoint could only be the territory that Mill reached: alongside these self-reinforcing alignments, there could be situations where the progress in one dimension of the good life crowded out progress in another. Consequently, the hypothesis of consumption as progress was forced to coexist with the hypothesis of consumption as deviation.

A final circumstance that favoured the formation of an intellectual landscape pointing towards such coexistence was the fact that the economic theory of the classics and Marx was accompanied by a sociology in which society was constituted not merely by an amalgamation of more or less autonomous individuals. In their society, there would exist stratifications and cultural structures that predated any individual considered in isolation. It was an economic theory premised on the identification of differentiated social classes: more than a representative individual of society as a whole, what we find is a variety of social classes, including the traditional aristocratic elites, the emerging industrial and commercial bourgeoisie, family farmers, the working classes, and possibly even the embryo of a new layer of middle classes. And it was within each of these social classes that a specific consumer culture seemed to prevail, directing individuals' preferences and conditioning their behaviour. This was true for both the elites, with their luxuries, and the masses, whose subsistence basket would be informed by cultural ideas about social insertion. It is true that neither the classics nor Marx paid much attention to the causes of these consumer cultures or to their potential evolution over time. Yet, this does not imply that their consumer was an individual whose behaviour did not depend on social position. This was key for the philosophical analysis discussed earlier to unfold across a broad domain, which included not only income levels or consumer prices but also a certain sociology of consumption.

On the other hand, while the classics and Marx contributed an intellectual map that favoured a certain coexistence of the theses of progress and deviation, this map also contained some blind spots that would later prove to be of great importance for the trajectory that later rounds of conversation among economists would take. The first is that, while we can find passages that propose the progress thesis and others that propose the deviation thesis, it is another matter entirely whether these different passages were articulated into an overall framework. With his dissection of unproductive consumption, Mill was the one who came closest to that. But even in this case, it is interesting to appreciate the extent to which the deviation thesis was thus framed within one of the conceptual blocks that later generations of economists would rapidly dispense with: that organised around the concept of productive labour and the notion that some economic activities could, in some sense, be more important than others. What future could such an argument have, tied as it was to what would eventually be "the most maligned concept in the history of economic doctrines"? (Blaug, 1968, p. 86).

Another blind spot, which posed a threat to the survival of the deviation thesis, was the long shadow of utilitarianism as a companion of classical political economy and Marxism. The Aristotelian vision of the good life as a multidimensional process coexisted, not always harmoniously, with the rise of a utilitarian ethics that proposed a reductionist view based solely on the axis of pleasure and pain. Smith and Marx found ways in which this reduction did not necessarily imply abandoning the Aristotelian conception, but it was likely that later generations of participants in the conversation would then proceed directly from the utilitarian dimension. It would be unjust to dissociate the economics of Smith or Mill from their philosophy, but there is no doubt about the synergies that gradually emerged between political economy, utilitarian ethics, and the political project of disembedding the economic sphere from the rest of the social spheres. In fact, there were more than a few countries where these three elements formed part of the same intellectual and political vector. This vector left far more room for the progress thesis, grounded in consumption as the rational acquisition of utility and pleasure, than for the deviation thesis.

In any event, it must not be overlooked that neither the classics nor Marx had a vision (in Schumpeter's sense) of mass consumer society. The economic and social reality of their time was too distant from this, and as a result, our reading of their works has been an exercise in backtracking. From the end of the nineteenth century, however, it began to become evident to all kinds of observers that an increasing fraction of the population was beginning to gain access to more abundant and diverse consumer baskets. Although this historical dynamic remained subject to important social and territorial limits, it was sufficiently powerful to inspire new reflections on the extent to which this embryo of a consumer society constituted progress or, conversely, deviation.

References

Arrighi, G. (2007). *Adam Smith in Beijing: Lineages of the twenty-first century*. Verso.

Aspromourgos, T. (2009). *The science of wealth: Adam Smith and the framing of political economy*. Routledge.

Bairoch, P. (1997). *Victoires et déboires: histoire économique et sociale du monde du XVIe siècle à nos jours*. Gallimard.

Bairoch, P. (1999). *L'agriculture des pays dévelopées: 1800 à nos jours*. Economica.

Bee, M. (2018). Wealth and sensibility: The historical outcome of better living conditions for all according to Adam Smith. *European Journal of the History of Economic Thought, 25*(3), 473–92.

Bee, M., & Paganelli, M. P. (2019). Adam Smith, anti-Stoic. *History of European Ideas, 45*(4), 572–584.

Bentham, J. (1789). *An introduction to the principles of morals and legislation*. T. Payne.

Bianchini, V. (2016). James Mill on intemperance and individual preferences. *Journal of the History of Economic Thought, 38*(1), 21–40.

Blaug, M. (1968). *Economic theory in retrospect*. R. D. Irwin.

Bruni, L. (2006). *Civil happiness: Economics and human flourishing in historical perspective*. Routledge.

Cain, P. (2021). Radicalism versus Ruskin: Quality and quantity in Hobson's welfare economics. In R. E. Backhouse, A. Baujard, & T. Nishizawa (Eds.), *Welfare theory, public action, and ethical values: Revisiting the history of welfare economics*. Cambridge University Press.

Carabelli, A. M., & Cedrini, M. A. (2018). Great expectations and final disillusionment: Keynes, 'My early beliefs' and the ultimate values of capitalism. *Cambridge Journal of Economics, 42*(5), 1183–1204.
Cipolla, C. (1962). *The economic history of world population.* Penguin.
Cipolla, C. (1973). The industrial revolution. In C. Cipolla (Ed.), *The Fontana economic history of Europe, 3: The industrial revolution, 1700-1914.* Collins-Fontana.
Collantes, F. (2003). Robert Malthus, un economista politico convertido en demógrafo por aclamación popular. *Revista Española de Investigaciones Sociológicas,* 101, 149–173.
de Vries, J. (2008). *The industrious revolution: Consumer behavior and the household economy.* Cambridge University Press.
Diatkine, D. (2021). *Adam Smith and the wealth of nations: The discovery of capitalism and its limits.* Palgrave Macmillan.
DiIulio, J. P. (2022). *Completely free: The moral and political vision of John Stuart Mill.* Princeton University Press.
Fine, B., & Saad-Filho, A. (2010). *Marx's "Capital".* Pluto Press. [Spanish edition: *El capital de Marx.* Fondo de Cultura Económica, 2013.]
Freeman, C., & Louçã, F. (2001). *As time goes by: From the industrial revolutions to the information revolution.* Oxford University Press.
Hrschman, A. O. (1977). *The passions and the interests: Political arguments for capitalism before its triumph.* Princeton University Press, 1997.
Hirschman, A. O. (1982). *Shifting involvements: private interest and public action.* Princeton University Press. [Spanish edition:Interés privado y acción pública. Fondo de Cultura Económica, 1986.]
Kim, K. (2015). Demand and structural change in Adam Smith's view of economic progress. *Cambridge Journal of Economics, 39*(1), 245–264.
Krausmann, F., Fischer-Kowalski, M., Schandl, H., & Eisenmenger, N. (2008). The global sociometabolic transition: Past and present metabolic profiles and their future trajectories. *Journal of Industrial Ecology, 12*(5/6), 637–656.
Küng, H. (1976). *On being a Christian.* Doubleday.
Landes, D. S. (2003). *The unbound Prometheus: Technological change and industrial development in Western Europe from 1750 to the present.* Cambridge University Press.
Leijonhufvud, A. (2006). The uses of the past. Working paper 0603, Department of Economics, University of Trento.
Lindert, P. H., & Williamson, J. G. (2016). *Unequal gains: American growth and inequality since 1700.* Princeton University Press.
Maddison, A. (2001). *The world economy: A millennial perspective.* OECD.
Magness, P. W., & Makovi, M. (2023). The mainstreaming of Marx: Measuring the effect of the Russian revolution on Karl Marx's influence. *Journal of Political Economy, 131*(2), 656–672.

Malassis, L. (1997). *Les trois âges de l'alimentaire: essai sur une historie sociale de l'alimentation et de l'agriculture*. Cujas.

Malthus, T. R. (1836). *Principles of political economy considered with a view to their applications*. Pickering.

Mandeville, B. (1714). *The fable of the bees, or private vices, public benefits*. J. Roberts.

Martínez Carrión, J. M. (2012). La talla de los europeos, 1700–2000: ciclos, crecimiento y desigualdad. *Investigaciones de Historia Económica, 8*(3), 176–187.

Martins, N. O. (2014). *The Cambridge revival of political economy*. Routledge.

Marx, K. (1844). *Manuscritos: economía y filosofía*. Alianza, 1980.

Marx, K. (1867–1894). *Capital: A critique of political economy*. O. Meisner. [Spanish edition: *El capital: crítica de la economía política*. Fondo de Cultura Económica, 2000.]

Mill, J. S. (1848). *Principles of political economy, with some of their applications to social philosophy*. Longman, Greens and Co., 1923.

Mill, J. S. (1865). *Auguste Comte and positivism*. Trübner. Reprinted in vol. 10 of *Collected works of John Stuart Mill*. Routledge and Kegan Paul, 1979.

Pabst, A. (2018). Political economy of virtue: Civil economy, happiness and public trust in the thought of Antonio Genovesi. *European Journal of the History of Economic Thought, 25*(4), 582–604.

Paganelli, M. P. (2009). Approbation and the desire to better one's condition in Adam Smith: When the desire to better one's condition does not better one's condition and society's condition…. *Journal of the History of Economic Thought, 31*(1), 79–92.

Perrotta, C. (1998). Consumption. In H. D. Kurz & N. Salvadori (Eds.), *The Elgar companion to classical economics*. Edward Elgar.

Perrotta, C. (2004). *Consumption as an investment, I: The fear of goods from Hesiod to Adam Smith*. Routledge.

Persky, J. (2016). *The political economy of progress: John Stuart Mill and modern radicalism*. Oxford University Press.

Piketty, T. (2014). *Capital in the twenty-first century*. Harvard University Press.

Polanyi, K. (1944). *The great transformation: The political and economic origins of our time*. Farrar & Rinehart.

Pollard, S. (1981). *Peaceful conquest: The industrialization of Europe 1760–1970*. Oxford University Press.

Popkin, B. M. (1993). Nutritional patterns and transitions. *Population and Development Review, 19*(1), 138–157.

Prados de la Escosura, L. (2022). *Human development and the path to freedom: 1870 to the present*. Cambridge University Press.

Pujol, J., & Cussó, X. (2014). La transición nutricional en Europa occidental, 1865-2000: una nueva aproximación. *Historia Social, 80*, 133–155.

Ricardo, D. (1817). *On the principles of political economy and taxation*. John Murray.

Rogan, T. (2017). *The moral economists: R. H. Tawney, Karl Polanyi, and E. P. Thompson*. Princeton, Princeton University Press.
Roncaglia, A. (2005). *The wealth of ideas: A history of economic thought*. Cambridge University Press.
Rothschild, E. (2001). *Economic sentiments: Adam Smith, Condorcet, and the Enlightenment*. Harvard University Press.
Ruskin, J. (1862). *Unto this last: Four essays on the first principles of political economy*. [Selected texts: "John Ruskin on population and the quality of life", *Population and Development Review, 20*(3), 1994.]
Say, J. B. (1803). *Traité d'économie politique*. Deterville. [English edition: *A treatise on political economy*. Batoche Books, 2001.]
Schumpeter, J. A. (1954). *History of economic analysis*. Oxford University Press. [Spanish edition: *Historia del análisis económico*. Ariel, 1994.]
Schwartz, B., & Sharpe, K. (2014). *Practical wisdom: The right way to do the right thing*. Riverhead.
Sedlácek, T. (2011). *Economics of good and evil: The quest for economic meaning from Gilgamesh to Wall Street*. Oxford University Press. [Spanish edition: *Economía del bien y del mal: la búsqueda del significado económico desde Gilgamesh hasta Wall Street*. Fondo de Cultura Económica, 2014.]
Shionoya, Y. (2014). Ruskin's romantic triangle: Neither wealth nor beauty but life. *History of Economic Ideas, 22*(1), 15–50.
Smith, A. (1759). *The theory of moral sentiments*. Kincaid and Bell. [Spanish edition: *La teoría de los sentimientos morales*. Alianza, 1997.]
Smith, A. (1776). *An inquiry into the nature and causes of the wealth of nations*. W. Strahan and T. Cadell. [Spanish edition: *La riqueza de las naciones*. Alianza, 2001.]
Smith, C. (2013). Adam Smith's 'collateral' inquiry: Fashion and morality in *The theory of moral sentiments* and *The wealth of nations*. *History of Political Economy, 45*(3), 505–522.
Smith, C. (2016). All in the best possible taste: Adam Smith and the leaders of fashion. *European Journal of the History of Economic Thought, 26*(4), 597–610.
Trincado, E. (2024). Adam Smith's criticism of David Hume. Lecture given at Adam Smith's Panmure House.
Vanhaute, E., Paping, R., & Ó'Gráda, C. (2007). The European subsistence crisis of 1845-1850: A comparative perspective. In C. Ó'Gráda, R. Paping, & E. Vanhaute (Eds.), *When the potato failed: Causes and effects of the last European subsistence crisis, 1845-1850*. Brepols.
Veblen, T. (1906–1907). The socialist economics of Karl Marx and his followers. *Quarterly Journal of Economics, 20*(4) and *21*(2), 578–595 and 299–322.
Villeneuve, L. (2024). John Stuart Mill and the art of consumption. *European Journal of the History of Economic Thought, 31*(1), 1–19.

Wallerstein, I. (2011). *The modern world system, IV: Centrist liberalism triumphant, 1789-1914*. University of California Press.
Winch, D. (1978). *Adam Smith's politics: An essay in historiographic revision*. Cambridge University Press.
Wrigley, E. A. (1986). Elegance and experience: Malthus at the bar of history. In D. Coleman & R. Schofield (Eds.), *The state of population theory: Forward from Malthus*. Basil Blackwell.
Wrigley, E. A. (1988). *Continuity, chance, and change: The character of the industrial revolution in England*. Cambridge University Press.
Wrigley, E. A. (2004). *Poverty, progress, and population*. Cambridge University Press.

CHAPTER 4

A Battlefield in the Making (1870–1945)

The economic debate on consumer society began to take shape during the period 1870–1945. These were years of wide-ranging socio-economic transformations, during which the emergence of mass consumer societies started to become evident. The period also witnessed substantial changes in economic thought, as the process of institutionalising economics as a social science progressed decisively. The present chapter begins with a section dedicated to presenting this context. We then delve into the so called marginalist revolution and the way in which it promoted a certain bias towards the progress thesis. Next, we consider the approaches that championed the deviation thesis, particularly that of Thorstein Veblen. A subsequent section explores the attempts to produce a "synthesis view" by Alfred Marshall and John Maynard Keynes. Finally, we witness the birth of the sovereign consumer and the role this played in the efforts of authors such as Ludwig von Mises to establish the progress thesis on economic and political grounds. The chapter's conclusions highlight the existence of a plurality of views on the changing world of consumption at the time, but also the outlines of what would later become a frontal clash between them. This is the sense in which, as the chapter title suggests, we are witnessing a battlefield in the making.

F. Collantes, *Consumer Society and the Economists*, Palgrave Studies in the History of Economic Thought,
https://doi.org/10.1007/978-3-031-96645-3_4

Towards Consumer Society, Towards Economics

Between 1870 and the Second World War, the history of capitalism entered a new phase. A trajectory of technological change based on fossil fuels and industrial machinery continued, but now under the form of a "second industrial revolution". Within a renewed energy base, incorporating electricity and petroleum, the technological frontier shifted to sectors such as steel, chemicals, cars, and the food system, to name just a few. This was a technological revolution more connected to the advancement and application of cutting-edge scientific knowledge. The success of large American and German firms in these fields contributed to the rise of "managerial capitalism", replacing the personal capitalism characteristic of British leadership in the previous period. Significant political changes also took place. In contrast to the liberal capitalism of much of the nineteenth century, a variant of capitalism emerged in which the state played a more active role. Partly as a self-protection mechanism for society against the threats of dislocation posed by liberal capitalism, the state became more prominent in various areas of socio-economic life, from the provision of public services to greater regulation of markets and industries (Chandler, 1990; DeLong, 2022; Freeman & Louçã, 2001; Landes, 2003; Lindert, 2004; Polanyi, 1944).

During this new phase in the history of capitalism, an embryo of mass consumer society began to take shape in North America and Western Europe. For most of the period, these economies grew at a faster pace than during the initial phase of industrialisation. Moreover, industrialisation spread to an increasing number of countries. As a result, household expenditure tended to rise more clearly than in the previous period. Additionally, the dispersion of households relative to this average tended to narrow, as income distribution became more equitable. The relative position of the working class improved, and there was a widening of the middle class (Bairoch, 1997; Maddison, 2001; Piketty, 2014).

This made it possible to diffuse substantial changes in the consumer baskets of most households. What later generations of researchers would call a "nutritional transition" began to unfold. Caloric intake increased and became less subject to seasonal fluctuations. Basic plant-based foods such as cereals and potatoes continued to be a significant part of the diet, but now they were more frequently accompanied by animal-based foods like meat and milk. This changing diet remained the main expenditure in household budgets, but its share began to decline in favour of new types of spending, some directed towards meeting other basic needs such as clothing and housing, while others aimed at incorporating new consumer goods like household appliances. A less austere consumer culture took shape, and this culture ultimately permeated the new notions of citizenship and democracy that restructured political life during these decades (de Grazia, 2005; Deaton, 1975; Floud et al., 2011; Gordon, 2017; Malassis, 1997; Popkin, 1993; Trentmann, 2016).

The limits of these transformations were certainly evident, and thus we can view them more as an embryo than as a fully realised version of consumer society. A significant portion of households remained relatively untouched by these changes in consumption patterns, or at least incorporated them in a delayed, decidedly incomplete manner. The embryo of a consumer society was much more visible in the United States, which, over these decades, came to occupy a leadership position in the world economy, than in most of Europe, where the consolidation of middle-class households with plentiful consumer baskets advanced more slowly. This was still a distant horizon for most of the global population, in an era when much of the Global South saw its economic gap with the North widen. Furthermore, even in the North, it was clear that the long-term trend came to be drastically interrupted by the impact of the two world wars and the post-1929 Great Depression. Nonetheless, despite these social and temporal limits, few would question that the period from 1870 to the Second World War witnessed a transformation in material life that clearly anticipated what, after the war, would become the full development of mass consumer societies.

The transformation that was taking place in economics as a social science also anticipated the landscape that would consolidate after the war. The discipline became increasingly institutionalised. Its practitioners adopted the label "economics" to designate a field of study more clearly differentiated from other social sciences. This economics, in turn, came to be characterised by a significant break from the previous tradition of political economy: the abandonment of theories centred on reproduction and surplus, in favour of those focused on equilibrium and scarcity. Along the way, the focus of analysis shifted from society and its various classes to individuals, and the common language began to be substituted with mathematical language. In all these aspects, the so-called marginalist revolution (a term as misleading with regard to the chronology of the process as it is accurate with regard to its nature) and its subsequent evolution into a school of thought known as neoclassical economics laid the foundations for what would become the mainstream of economic thought after the Second World War (Martins, 2014; Roncaglia, 2005; Tribe, 2022).

However, we should not fail to recognise that this vector of change advanced slowly and that the overall picture of economic thought during this period was characterised by pluralism. The neoclassical school gained influence in Britain, but for much of the period, its proponents faced considerable difficulty in dominating the conversation in the United States and Germany, where the institutionalist and historical schools (respectively) were stronger. The neoclassical school also coexisted with the Austrian school, which had a distinct identity, and towards the end of the period, it even gave rise, in the figure of John Maynard Keynes, to an analytical line that would later be seen as a school in its own right. To this, we must add the consolidation of a Marxist variant of economic analysis. Pluralism already existed in the less specialised intellectual world before the late nineteenth century, but now it was more explicit and significant. Therefore, we would do well not to project onto this period later images of a hegemonic school surrounded by small heterodox groups (Hodgson, 2001, 2004; Morgan & Rutherford, 1998).

The pluralism of the period between 1870 and 1945 is reflected in the variety of views that economists began to develop about the world of consumption.

The Marginalist Consumer and the Purchase of Pleasure

The beginning of the 1870s is commonly regarded as the key turning point in the paradigm shift from classical political economy to marginalist economics. Independently from one another, William Stanley Jevons (1871), Carl Menger (1871), and Léon Walras (1874) laid the foundations of a new conception of economic analysis. In this framework, the labour theory of value, which had informed the work of classical economists in one way or another, was abandoned, and a subjective theory was embraced. The value of goods, according to the marginalists, was not an intrinsic characteristic of the goods themselves or a measure of the objective circumstances involved in their production. Instead, value was attributed subjectively by each individual, depending on the degree to which they expected the good in question to satisfy their needs or desires. Obviously, there were as many attributions of value as there were consumers. Not all consumers would necessarily value goods in the same way, and in fact, significant differences could be expected between the value attributions made by different consumers, depending on their circumstances and tastes.

Each consumer had their own utility scale for each good, and this scale was expected to decrease with the level of consumption: the utility provided by the first loaf of bread to a hungry consumer was greater than that of a hypothetical second loaf, and so on, until reaching a point where a fully satisfied consumer would no longer derive any utility from an additional loaf. Each consumer would also have some orientation when comparing the expected satisfactions derived from the consumption of different quantities of various goods, allowing them to determine whether consuming the second loaf of bread (to retain the example) would provide greater or lesser expected utility than consuming the first glass of wine. The key to these orientations lay in the margins, especially at those points at which the additional unit of a good no longer provided utility or no longer provided utility comparable to that of an additional unit of a different good (Méndez Ibisate, 2004).

The result was an optimising consumer. Taking into account their preferences and the prevailing market prices, the consumer would choose to purchase the quantity of each good that maximised their utility. From this core, it was possible to develop various extensions aimed at expanding the scope of analysis to consider several goods simultaneously. The so-called indifference curves, proposed by Francis Edgeworth and systematised by Vilfredo Pareto, allowed for the identification of those baskets whose combinations of goods provided the consumer with comparable levels of total utility. These curves, in turn, could intersect with others representing the budget constraint faced by consumers, depending on their available income level and the prevailing price structure in the market at any given time. The optimising consumer would select that basket which, by absorbing all their income, offered the highest possible level of expected utility. In the words of Jevons (1871, p. 81), economic behaviour was about "maximising happiness by purchasing pleasure, as it were, at the lowest cost of pain".

This narrative fit well with the historical context of the decades leading up to the First World War, when it was becoming clear that an embryo of consumer society was taking shape. The image of an optimising consumer, altering their decisions based on how changes in their budget constraint interacted with their map of expected utilities, was more compatible with this reality than the traditional image of a consumer bound to a mere subsistence basket. The image also aligned with the consolidation of liberalism as a political project and, in general, with the prevailing confidence of the period that humanity—or at least those regarded as its "civilised" peoples in this "age of empire"—was capable of progress through the application of reason to the resolution of practical problems (Gallego, 2022; Hobsbawm, 1987).

There was a significant degree of continuity, both analytically and politically, between this marginalist narrative of an optimising consumer and the progress thesis, as it had been prefigured by classical economists. The market order described by the marginalists led to a social optimum, in which consumers were positioned as well as possible within the constraints imposed by their budget, and producers strived to satisfy the desires of these consumers in order to maximise their profit. The maximisation of utility pursued by the consumer thus linked with the classical idea that there was a broad space for convergence between the pursuit of private interests, identified by each individual and expressed in the economic behaviour they freely chose to follow, and the achievement of social progress. The marginalists retained this dimension of classical political economy, illuminated it with a powerful beam of light, and introduced a mathematical language that would, over time, facilitate its formalisation, systematisation, and expansion. However, other dimensions were obscured. As a result, the characteristic ambivalence of the classics began to fade away.

By abandoning the classical focus on surplus and replacing it with a focus on scarcity, the marginalists eliminated the analytical space that, up to that point, had been occupied by the classical dichotomy between productive and unproductive consumption. Along the way, the notion of sufficiency that had permeated this dichotomy and underpinned the evaluation of unproductive consumption in terms of progress or deviation also lost its relevance. The desires of the marginalist consumer were potentially insatiable and that was all. The marginal utility associated to the consumption of any individual good was decreasing, but the focus could always shift to some other good after all. In fact, by moving away from a focus on reproduction over time to one centred on equilibrium at a particular point in time, the marginalists reduced the space in which the deviation thesis could continue to develop. This thesis, by its very nature, was a statement on history: it was the assessment of a temporal sequence. But if the focus shifted to market equilibria achieved as a result of rational decisions made by autonomous consumers, the narrative would become one of successive equilibria in each of which consumers had maximised their utility. While the reproduction of the classics could go on a good or a bad path, the equilibria of the marginalists depicted the best possible path given the preferences and constraints to which consumers were subjected.

The marginalist break was not just a matter of economic theory and its historical associations; it also had to do with its connections to sociology and philosophy (Martins, 2014). The rise of marginalism weakened these connections. When it comes to the social, it is true that the classics and Marx had not developed dense analyses of the social contexts that shaped consumer preferences. But they had sketched out some ideas, particularly the role of social class as the domain in which the reproduction of consumer cultures took place. Such emergent properties were, however, absent from marginalist analysis (Hodgson, 2004; Lawson, 1997). Society was reduced to the aggregation of the different individuals composing it. Each of them was equipped with a map of preferences and expected utilities, the origin of which remained unexplained. This closed off the route through which Mill and other classical economists had suggested images of deviation in consumption patterns: identifying the consumer culture that led a given social class to spend in ways that did not promote the good life.

If economic sociology was eliminated, economic philosophy disappeared from the explicit debate and was reduced by default to utilitarianism. Every consumer was supposed to maximise their expected utility and position themselves at that point on the pleasure-pain axis that, given the circumstances, was the best possible according to their preferences. Each step forward on the pleasure-pain axis could be considered a step towards the good life. In this way, human well-being began to be defined in a one-dimensional manner. Utilitarianism had not been unfamiliar to classical economists or (as we saw) Marx, but it had rarely reigned supreme. Even when it seemed to do so, it had been based on the premise that other dimensions of the good life could be expected to positively feed into the material dimension. The underlying philosophy of marginalism, however, tended to exclude those other dimensions. Consequently, it closed off the route through which economists of previous generations, especially Mill, had discovered the possibility of consumption as deviation.

This sociological and philosophical thinning of the economic mind must be linked, at least in part, to the efforts of a new generation to push for the institutionalisation of economics as an autonomous field of study.

The marginalists' silence on the social origin of consumer preferences and the non-material dimensions of the good life contributed to positioning their work as strictly economic in nature. At times, the narrowing of economic thought has also been connected to the way the spectre of Marxism, understood both as an intellectual programme and (even more so) as a political programme, gradually gained ground in the public debate of European societies in the decades leading up to the First World War. If Eric Wolf (1982, p. 20) is correct in stating that the social sciences constitute a long dialogue with the ghost of Marx, it is likely that this phrase also applies to the type of economic science that emerged under the influence of the marginalist revolution. The representation of society as an aggregation of autonomous individuals, rather than a fabric composed of social classes, denied the very premise on which Marxism was based, supporting a narrative more in line with the triumphant liberalism of the period.

However, as has often been pointed out, the political ideas of the early marginalists were varied, as were the ways in which they refined their core arguments. There was nothing inherent in the theory of the marginalist consumer that prevented the integration of those sociological and philosophical perspectives that had initially been excluded from the analysis. Specialists in Walras, for example, remind us that his influential "pure economics" cannot be read in isolation from his lesser-known "social economics", in which individual behaviour was significantly shaped by social influences (Arena, 2021). There was also considerable space for incorporating elements of economic psychology. Menger (1871, pp. 108, 112, and 133), for instance, had sensed that the marginalist consumer could make mistakes. Their value attributions could be mere fantasies, especially in the case of "foolish people, driven by their ignorance". They might fall into the danger of "giving more importance to those satisfactions of needs that promote their well-being in a more intense, though fleeting, manner, rather than to those that depend on less intense but more permanent satisfaction". They could even end up making consumption choices that, rather than bringing pleasure, could be harmful or even threatening to their health. Menger thus uncovered a path that, if followed diligently, could only lead to the deviation thesis.

The use of marginalist tools could be compatible with a variety of alternative directions for the evolution of economic discourse. Someone like Vilfredo Pareto intuited that the future lay in a "pure economics" that would not make value judgements or explored the kind of non-instrumental behaviour that was better left to sociology (Bee and Desmarais-Tremblay,

2023; Bruni, 2006, pp. 109–113). Others, like Alfred Marshall (whose case we will explore later in this chapter), were less inclined to make such a radical break. During the interwar period, a range of different visions of the world of consumption would emerge among neoclassical economists. What would later come to be known as "the" theory of demand in mainstream economics did not actually stabilise until the end of our period—partly due to disagreements within pure economics and partly due to disputes concerning the non-strictly economic elements surrounding the analysis of the marginalist consumer (Mirowski & Hands, 2006).

However, by then, a variety of economic schools of thought were flourishing in directions well apart from marginalism, including institutional economics in the United States, historical economics and social economics in Germany and Central Europe, and Marxism. All of these proposed views of the world of consumption that were different from that of the marginalists. By venturing down the paths blocked by the marginalist project—particularly the influence of emergent properties on consumer behaviour (on the one hand) and the multidimensional nature of the good life (on the other)—these economists would rediscover the deviation thesis and, in fact, would state it with greater vigour than had been the case until then. The pioneer and most influential of them was, without a doubt, Thorstein Veblen.

Thorstein Veblen and the Rediscovery of Deviation

The economy and society of the United States were undergoing rapid transformation in the decades before the First World War. More and more households were gaining access to more abundant and diversified baskets of consumer goods. The country was leading a "second industrial revolution" that ultimately pushed its GDP per capita well above that of Europe. For an American observer, however, there was something more. The country's self-image as a republic of equal citizens was increasingly difficult to reconcile with the growing accumulation of wealth and power in the hands of business elites. By 1910, the proportion of national wealth held by the top 10 per cent of wealthiest families had reached a historical peak of 43 per cent. While this figure was still lower than in most European societies, its sociological impact was destined to be much more significant. Europeans, after all, had a long tradition of estate-based societies, where political life was based on the premise of inequality between social classes. It was only more recently that these *Ancien Régime* societies had disappeared, and when they had, they had left numerous legacies to the new liberal societies. In contrast, in the absence of a feudal past, American political life had been much more centred around the vision of free and equal citizens. How, then, could this premise fit in an era in which, unlike the time of the Founding Fathers in the late eighteenth century, economic growth was very rapid, and its fruits were distributed with an increasing level of inequality (Levy, 2021; Mayer, 1981; Piketty, 2014)?

This was the context in which Thorstein Veblen published *The Theory of the Leisure Class*, which remains to this day one of the most vigorous formulations of the thesis of consumption as deviation (Veblen, 1899). Once the more elementary stages of economic evolution were surpassed, Veblen argued, consumption had little to do with the maximisation of individual utility through the purchase of goods. The Veblenian consumer was not an isolated and autonomous individual, but one whose behaviour was largely influenced by their social position. Yet, this social position was not neatly defined by a scheme of a few rigidly defined social classes. The social structure consisted of a multitude of strata based on small differences and was equipped with ladders that allowed for upward or downward mobility. The role of consumption in social reproduction, then, was precisely to help build the social image of each stratum. What the Veblenian consumer sought in the goods they purchased was not the satisfaction of a need or the cultivation of the good life, but the signalling of the social status they had achieved.

In fact, consumer behaviour was largely shaped by what Veblen identified as an instinct of emulation. Each social stratum took as a reference the consumption patterns of the stratum just above them and directed all their efforts to try to emulate them. And this same dynamic, which drove emulation bottom-up, led to ostentation top-down. From this, Veblen derived the key concept of his analysis: conspicuous consumption. Consumers of higher social status had a basket of goods that, while perhaps irrelevant in terms of human needs, were extremely effective at signalling status: they provided a public demonstration of the magnitude of discretionary income that the consumer could now direct as they saw fit. At the top of the social pyramid, the leisure class—whose income came from rents (whether from overwhelming business success or simply inheritance)—could indulge in a hedonistic lifestyle in which not only the goods they consumed but also their long leisure time signalled, unambiguously, the social status they had reached. This was the social milieu that the novelist F. Scott Fitzgerald, with a critical spirit probably influenced by his reading of Veblen, would immortalise a quarter of a century later in *The Great Gatsby* (Canterbery, 1999). However, Veblen's narrative was not structured around a dichotomy between an opulent elite and impoverished masses. On the contrary, there were numerous strata positioned just below the leisure class, each also hierarchically organised according to the greater or lesser ability of their consumer baskets to signal status. In a society where the majority of the population had left behind the baskets of mere subsistence, Veblen described a positional race among the broad range of social strata that the rapid economic growth of the period was generating.

Veblen's narrative of ostentation and emulation strongly suggested that America's embryonic consumer society was deviating from the ideal of the good life:

> [In order for] consumption to effectively enhance the consumer's reputation, it must be of superfluous items. To cultivate a good reputation, such consumption must be wasteful. [...] This expenditure is referred to here as "waste" because it does not serve human life or the collective well-being, not because it represents a waste or deviation in effort or expenditure, when viewed from the perspective of the individual consumer who makes the choice. (Veblen, 1899, pp. 103–104)

Instead of dedicating their energies to the cultivation of the good life, individuals were engaged in a vain race for status. Moreover, the companies supplying these consumer goods had no hesitation in allocating substantial resources to advertising campaigns which, in the view Veblen (1904) would later provide in subsequent works, did not contribute to social progress. The overall picture was of a society that, instead of dedicating its resources to solving relevant problems, was wasting them.

Veblen managed to convey these sentiments without explicitly stating any ethical theory. His ethics were rather implicit in the sharp, detached character of his prose. His choice of words with negative connotations to coin key concepts stood out. But the analytical gap through which a Veblenian consumer took shape, in opposition to the marginalist consumer, had more to do with the reintroduction of a sociology of consumption. When individual preferences were derived from their interaction with other individuals and their belonging to a shared culture, the possibility arose that the rationality of the consumer within that culture could be compatible with the absurdity of that culture itself:

> [The] problem is not whether, under the given circumstances of individual habit and social custom, a particular expenditure leads to the satisfaction or spiritual peace of a specific consumer, but whether—setting aside acquired tastes and conventional decorum and custom—its result represents a net gain in terms of the community or the fullness of life. (Veblen, 1899, p. 106)

This was connected to one of the key ideas that would permeate Veblen's thought repeatedly over the years: his aversion to teleological perspectives and his attachment to the idea of a "blind drift" in economic evolution. "Instrumental" institutions promoted progress, but they were in constant tension with "ceremonial" institutions, including various forms of mentalities and customs. The outcome remained open-ended (Hodgson, 2004).

In the years prior to the First World War and during the interwar period, this sociological gap became the entry point of other versions of the deviation thesis. Some were more or less direct followers of Veblen, such as the institutionalist Wesley Mitchell (1912) and his views on the "backward art of spending money". Others came from different research programmes that were flourishing with vitality in Germany and Central Europe: the new generation of the German Historical School, economic sociology, and social economics. Like Veblen and the American institutionalists, none of these interconnected programmes accepted the marginalist starting point of an isolated consumer with preferences whose origin was left unspoken. Instead, authors like Karl Polanyi, Werner Sombart, and Max Weber proposed a consumer whose behaviour depended on their incorporation into a network of social relations that shaped their orientations, interests, and propensities (Arrighi, 2001).

The result was, as in Veblen's work, a vision in which the way in which changing consumer cultures would condition individual behaviour—and, by extension, the direction of consumer society—remained open-ended. Nothing guaranteed any kind of teleological sequence towards progress and the good life: deviation was perfectly possible. In fact, at numerous points, these authors produced narratives about the overall evolution of the economic system that reflected this tenor. Polanyi's *The Great Transformation* (1944) was probably the most representative of these: a story about how the liberal civilisation constructed during the nineteenth century was built on deceptively progressive premises and contained within it the seeds of a deviation that would ultimately become evident when fascism emerged as an alternative during the interwar period.

This family of arguments variably mobilised the other dimensions left behind by the marginalist revolution. On the one hand, they incorporated historical time in order to identify dynamics and sequences of change. On the other hand, and although there were important differences between authors, they could sometimes draw upon ethical elements. The case where both points were most deeply combined was probably that of R. H. Tawney. In particular, in *The Acquisitive Society*, Tawney (1920) criticised how, in his view, capitalism exacerbated individuals' orientation towards the acquisition of income and the purchase of consumer goods, thus creating a moral climate that hindered progress towards a better society.

Tawney's figure is also distinctive because he more clearly than Veblen pointed to the incorporation of consumption into the political debate of the time. In early twentieth-century Britain, Tawney attained considerable stature as a representative of a gradualist form of socialism. His version was one inspired by his Christian faith and, as a result, placed significant emphasis on the moral problems attributed to utilitarianism and market society. It was also one of the several streams of political discourse converging towards what would eventually become the policy paradigm of social democracy (Offer & Söderberg, 2016). Despite their differences, these variants shared a rejection of the revolutionary path of orthodox Marxism and advocated for the integration of private entrepreneurship and private property rights within an inclusive political economy where the state would offer solutions to citizens affected by issues of economic insecurity. It is interesting to note that, although Tawney did not fully elaborate the implications of his argument for the realm of consumption, he nonetheless offered a clear entry point for its inclusion within the social democratic agenda. For Tawney (1920), social democracy was not to focus solely on the fight against inequality; it also had to remind industrial society of the purposes that made the pursuit of wealth worthwhile. Enhancing the purchasing power and material conditions of the masses could not be the sole objective (Rogan, 2017).

Meanwhile, the deviation thesis resurfaced within academic Marxism, especially during the interwar period. The Bolshevik revolution had created an alternative economic system in Russia and, from the perspective of Western public debate, the world of consumption seemed to be one of its weaknesses. Central planning had a bias for public investment and heavy industries and a bias against private consumption and consumer goods. The system also placed strong restrictions on consumer choice. This was the context in which Marxist economists like Maurice Dobb questioned whether the emerging consumer society developing in the West was as progressive as this line of critique implied. For Dobb, capitalism was a system that allocated increasingly larger amounts of resources to the manipulation of consumers through corporate advertising. Furthermore, the preferences of the masses were heavily influenced by the conventions and standards set by high-class consumers. Not everyone, even in socialist circles, agreed: Abba Lerner, for instance, criticised what he saw as an argument tainted by paternalism. Nonetheless, in Dobb we find a new path through which a sociological look, and the consequent rejection of the marginalist conception of the individual consumer with exogenous preferences, favoured the reappearance of the deviation thesis (Chirat, 2021, pp. 421–459; Olsen, 2019, pp. 170–171). This was undoubtedly a path consistent with Marx's critiques of the "Robinsonades" of economists, but also with the type of socialised consumer sketched by the classical economists.

In the 1930s, Marxism began to pay more attention to the deviation thesis for a second reason. The *Economic and Philosophic Manuscripts* Marx had written in 1844 were published for the first time in 1932. As we studied in the previous chapter, these drafts contained an explicit presentation of the deviation thesis centred around alienation and the effects of capitalism on the masses' ability to cultivate a full human life. The publication of the *Manuscripts* posed an important question to Marxist scholars: How consistent was the declared anti-utilitarianism of the young Marx with the premises of the academic and political movement that had grown out of the work of the mature Marx? Regardless of each scholar's response to this question, the Marxist conversation could not help but begin to reserve more space to reflect on the multidimensional conception of the good life and its implications. From this space, a distinctively Marxist formulation of the deviation thesis would eventually emerge in the decades following the Second World War.

With all their nuanced differences, these new formulations of the deviation thesis during the period from 1870 to 1945 shared a feature that also connected them to the intuitions produced by the classical economists and Marx before 1870. These were formulations framed within a conception of the economist's task that led them to position the strictly economic elements of analysis within a broader context, in which history, sociology, and philosophy played an important role. The deviation thesis could emerge more forcefully if economists took an interest in open-ended processes of change over time, rather than focusing on transitional sequences between allegedly optimal equilibrium points. The same occurred if economists placed consumer behaviour within a social and cultural matrix, instead of assuming that it was governed by exogenous preferences. Finally, the deviation thesis emerged more effectively if economic analysis was accompanied by a multidimensional conception of the good life, rather than the one-dimensional view of utilitarianism. The schools of thought that formulated the deviation thesis during this period highlighted these contrasts, especially the one related to cultural conditioning. Nevertheless, we would do well to see that the foundations upon which the deviation thesis was growing were quite similar to those of the previous period: less dispersed and more systematic, but similar, nonetheless.

The new versions of the deviation thesis were, of course, more powerful than the glimpses and scattered intuitions found in the works of the classical economists and Marx. To begin with, they were based on something much closer to a vision (in Schumpeter's sense) of consumer society. Moreover, and most importantly, they were much more successful in the stage of conceptualisation that comes after vision. Concepts were coined, such as that of conspicuous consumption, that were destined to leave a profound mark. Although the classical economists had anticipated the Veblenian idea on multiple occasions (see, for instance, Wisman, 2019), and although Mill had coherently formulated it within his (broader) notion of unproductive consumption, it was Veblen who gave it a name and made it a central element in his arguments. Along the way, Veblen and the other proponents of the deviation thesis facilitated an argumentative leap of enormous importance for the later evolution of the debate: what, in the hands of the classical economists, had been a critique of the consumer culture of the elites, gradually became a critique of consumer cultures in other social strata, in particular the middle classes.

However, it was another matter entirely to frame the powerful concept of conspicuous consumption within a general theoretical framework. In the past, the deviation thesis had been well inserted in the respective theoretical perspectives of the classical economists and Marx. It was not a very long journey from the labour theory of value to a subset of unproductive consumption that was not conducive to the good life. It is less evident, however, how conspicuous consumption connected with Veblen's overall perspective. In retrospect, we can read conspicuous consumption as one of the many "ceremonial institutions" that Veblen thought to be entangled in a tension with the instrumental institutions upon which economic dynamism depended. But it is no less true that in the absence of a general treatise akin to Mill's *Principles* or (for that matter) Marx's *Capital*, the exercise of situating conspicuous consumption within a comprehensive analysis of the economic life remained pending.

The Possibilities of Cambridge

As consumer society began to enter the economists' field of vision, some voices attempted to articulate some form of combination between the theses of progress and deviation. The classical economists and Marx had identified both theses and allowed them to coexist in an ambivalent atmosphere, but neither had explored these theses in depth nor had they proposed any explicit combination of them. As new conversations among economists between 1870 and 1945 led to more vigorous narratives in terms of progress or deviation, the likelihood increased that some economist would turn the ambivalent intuitions into an explicit articulation of both theses. This amounted to working towards what we call the "synthesis view", and in our case, it was the perspective adopted by the two most prominent economists of Cambridge during the period: Alfred Marshall and John Maynard Keynes.

Considering Marshall and Keynes together may go against some of the usual conventions in the history of economic thought. After all, Marshall was the leading figure of the neoclassical school into which the marginalist revolution of the 1870s evolved, whereas his disciple Keynes broke so thoroughly with this research programme that the Keynesian school is often (and rightly) regarded as a distinct school of thought. Marshall was a great synthesiser of the emerging economics of the period, while Keynes believed he had identified a gap of such magnitude in that economics that he considered himself in a position to propose a "general theory" that subsumed it as a particular case and, along the way, transformed the political coordinates of the conversation. However, these rightful appreciations, built largely with the benefit of hindsight and in the framework of academic battles that would erupt at a later date, should not blind us to the fact that there were elements of continuity between Marshall and Keynes, and that the men themselves seemed to be openly aware of them. Furthermore, as we will see in this section, Marshall and Keynes accompanied their economic theories with similar elements of sociology and philosophy. With these accompaniments, Marshall's neoclassical economics led to a different playing field from that with which the neoclassical project would later be associated, particularly in the decades following the Second World War. Marshall and Keynes, who were involved in the movement towards institutionalising a separate discipline, preferred the label economics over political economy, but their economics was often joined by considerations of what John Stuart Mill had called "social philosophy". This is the substrate from which the synthesis views of Marshall and Keynes would grow.

Like many other economists of his generation, Marshall had little doubt that the development of industrial capitalism had ended up producing an embryo of consumer society that, leaving behind the grim social conditions of early industrialisation, was allowing the material life of most of the population to be more comfortable. The successive equilibrium points at which supply and demand curves met in each market were allowing more and more consumers to access a wider and more diverse basket of goods. This, in turn, enabled them to reach a higher level of utility. At the beginning of the twentieth century, Marshall (1907, pp. 204–205) estimated that "more than half, and perhaps even three-quarters, of the total income of the nation is devoted to purposes that lead to happiness and the elevation of life".

Furthermore, like Smith and Mill before him, Marshall thought that material progress could lead to parallel advancements in other components of the good life: better education, broader interests, enriching personal relationships, etc. The problem of the working-class man, to a large extent, was that "if his toil has been fierce, and so his brain is dulled, he is apt to seek there only the coarser pleasures —drink, ignoble jests, and noise" (Marshall, 1873, p. 187). But precisely because of this, it could be expected that, as the material situation of the working class improved, they would gain a greater capacity for personal flourishing. This is the sense in which Marshall even predicted the eventual disappearance of the working class: it would persist economically, as large masses of people would still rely on a wage for their livelihood, but it would no longer exist sociologically, as fewer and fewer individuals would have their cultural flourishing hindered by the material deprivations of daily life (Marshall, 1873, p. 184).

However, at the same time as he reformulated this kind of expanded version of the progress thesis, Marshall warned of the possibility that consumer society might also lead to a deviation. Already in his *Principles of Economics*, he acknowledged feeling compelled to examine whether growing wealth was really contributing to greater happiness and well-being. A major concern in this regard was that economic progress might lead less to an increase in the "standard of living" than to a mere rise in the "standard of comfort", resulting from the increasing satisfaction of "artificial wants" (Marshall, 1890, p. 109; cf. Bruni, 2006, pp. 94–95). Furthermore, in his article "The Economic Possibilities of Economic Chivalry", Marshall (1907, p. 8) asserted that a significant fraction, at least a quarter, of the expenditures made by British consumers in the early twentieth century were socially useless:

> It is a common saying that we have more reason to be proud of our ways of making wealth than of our ways of using it. Even the working classes buy many things that do them little good and some things that do them harm. And the well-to-do classes expend vast sums on things that add little to their happiness and very little to their higher well-being, but which they regard as necessary for their social position.

For Marshall, consumer expenditure should logically cover the basic needs and comforts that constituted workers' "necessaries for efficiency". This was quite similar to the productive consumption described by the classical economists. Moreover, like Mill, Marshall was not at all inclined to view the rest of consumption expenditure under a negative light simply because it exceeded a basic standard. He, too, regarded those "things that yield solid, unostentatious pleasure of a wholesome kind" as being oriented towards cultivating the good life. However, and again like Mill, there was a portion of this expenditure that could not be considered oriented in that direction. Consumers, especially those from higher classes, were engaged in "a vast expenditure which contributes very little towards social progress, and which does not confer any large and solid benefits on the spenders" (Marshall, 1907, p. 9).

The prospect of a more materially prosperous society thus outlined a cultural crossroads of the utmost importance. There existed the danger that the seduction of materialism would spread values that downplayed education, and with it, the non-material dimensions of well-being. That path would lead society into "social waste", driven by the "combative" (rather than "constructive") advertising efforts through which companies sought to seduce consumers. It was urgent, therefore, to take a different path: the generalisation of "a spirit of chivalry" that would guide individuals in orienting their pattern of wealth utilisation towards the public good and the good life. What was required was an ethical and moral transformation that, once material life had improved, would allow people to lead truly better lives. It should not be dismissed that the state might need to play a role in this dilemma. For instance, it could extract resources from ostentatious consumption and inject them into bringing "the beauties of nature and art within the reach of the ordinary citizen" (Marshall, 1873, pp. 194 and 197, 1907, p. 27, 1920, p. 305). In sum, according to Marshall, the future of what would later be called consumer society was open-ended: it could be progress, but it could also be deviation (Caldari & Nishizawa, 2020; Nishizawa, 2021).

Just four years after Marshall's death, his former student John Maynard Keynes adopted most of his approach and arguments to formulate his own synthesis view. He did so in an essay that was actually very reminiscent of Marshall's 1907 article: it was also speculative in nature, and its title was "Economic Possibilities for Our Grandchildren" (Keynes, 1930). In his "Possibilities", Keynes also constructed an argument about the direction that, in his opinion, societies should take once a certain degree of material wealth had been achieved. Over time, affluence would allow humans to resolve their "economic problem" and focus their efforts on more noble objectives. The capacity of capitalism to generate economic growth was beyond doubt, and it would make it possible for advanced societies, within the span of just a couple of generations, to reach income levels sufficient for all their citizens to live in comfort and abundance. Here, Keynes echoed the tradition of the classical economists, Marx, and Marshall regarding the improvement of consumer baskets as an important component of the good life. Although he did not refer directly to the emerging consumer society, his argument was, up to this point, aligned with the progress thesis.

But Keynes advanced the argument in a way that eventually created room for the deviation thesis. Indeed, once the economic problem was resolved, it would be feasible to transform the productivity gains into reductions in working hours, rather than higher income levels. People could work only three hours a day, and this would be mainly to satisfy the "Adam within us all". The time thus freed could be devoted to cultivating human relationships, engaging with art and nature, and, in general, pursuing beauty and happiness. Keynes was moderately optimistic about the plausibility of this sequence. In fact, among those who listened to the lectures in which he presented the essay before its publication, there were some who saw it as a provocatively carefree attitude, especially those who attended them after the 1929 crash and the onset of the Great Depression (Clar, 2024).

Nevertheless, throughout the text, this identification of a post-materialist path towards the good life coexisted with the identification of a troubling alternative. What if people, instead of considering their economic problem resolved and reorienting their life priorities, continued to cling to a materialistic mindset? After all, Keynes' consumers were not only seeking to satisfy what he called absolute needs, more or less dependent on biological imperatives, but also relative needs arising from comparison with others, which were therefore virtually limitless. The upper classes of his time offered reasons for concern about what could happen to the masses a few generations later. They seemed incapable of breaking free from their cycles of getting and spending:

> [There] is no country and no people, I think, who can look forward to the age of leisure and abundance without a dread. For we have been trained too long to strive and not to enjoy [...] To judge from the behaviour and the achievements of the wealthy classes to-day in any quarter of the world, the outlook is very depressing! For these are, so to speak, our advance guard—those who are spying out the promised land for the rest of us and pitching their camp there. For they have most of them failed disastrously, so it seems to me—those who have an independent income but no associations or duties or ties to solve the problem which has been set them. (Keynes, 1930, p. 330)

Keynes then confronted his readers with the abyss: the possibility that consumer society, a vehicle of progress during one historical period, might turn into deviation in the next. The grandchildren of Keynes' generation would find themselves with great economic possibilities, but would they be able to use them to lead a truly better life? Would they manage to "keep alive and cultivate into a fuller perfection the art of life itself"? Or, conversely, would they become "people with intense, unsatisfied purposiveness who will blindly pursue wealth", and in doing so, will "sell themselves for the means of life" (Keynes, 1930, pp. 330–331)? The strength of the essay lay in its effectiveness in posing this question, rather than in defending one or another of the possible answers.

As in the case of Marshall, this approach was embedded within a system of thought that Keynes developed in his youth and maintained throughout the rest of his life with notable consistency. The multidimensional conception of well-being that underpinned the essay, and from which its core question-message derived, had been present in Keynes' work since his early writings on ethics. Indeed, some links have been found between this conception and his contributions to the theory of probability, based on the incommensurability of events and dimensions (Carabelli, 2021; Carabelli & Cedrini, 2011).

However, the fact that Marshall's and Keynes' contributions were fully consistent with the overall framework of their thought, and the fact that they themselves felt this was so, does not imply that these contributions occupied a central position within that framework. Marshall never succeeded in producing his longed-for synthesis between the neoclassical edifice of his *Principles* and his research on economic dynamics and industrial change over time. Some of this research was at least published in the form of independent works, but his book on progress was never published. Keynes, for his part, was far more influential through his contributions regarding what needed to be done during those two generations in which the "economic problem" would still need to be addressed. And in these contributions, he advocated for a type of consumer quite different from the post-materialist individual of "Economic possibilities". With his calls to restore effective demand through the promotion of spending by lower-income social groups with a higher propensity to consume, Keynes (1936) did much to prefigure the type of mass consumer society that would emerge after the Second World War. In the short term, more continued to be better (Skidelsky, 1996).

In any case, the contributions of Marshall and Keynes inform us that the chances of moving towards a "synthesis view" did not have to be dramatically affected by the transition from political economy to economics. Even though a theory based on surplus was abandoned, thereby blurring the typologies of consumption based on the latter's contribution to the good life, economic thought could still be accompanied by a history that created room for a variety of possible paths of evolution over time, a sociology that spoke about the collective foundations of individual preferences, and a philosophy grounded in a multidimensional conception of human well-being.

From this perspective, Marshall and Keynes essentially continued to cultivate the broad field defined by the classical political economists. Their sociology of consumption may certainly remind us of Veblen, with his emphasis on how an individual's position in the social stratification pyramid shaped a characteristic consumer culture. But neither Marshall nor Keynes cited Veblen. Their sociological insights seemed instead to stem from a kind of conventional wisdom characteristic of Old World societies.

After all, these societies had undergone a long period of stratification, which had clearly conditioned their transition to liberalism. In fact, there are voices among historians who encourage us to appreciate the political and sociological influence that the *Ancien Régime* still had on early twentieth-century Europe (Mayer, 1981). By portraying the upper classes engaged in ostentatious spending and absorbed in "relative" needs, Marshall and Keynes were quietly subscribing to the type of sociology that Mill had already employed in his analysis of unproductive consumption. Marshall added to this an idea that would eventually become fundamental to the debate on consumer society: consumer desires, far from being an autonomous variable, were in no small part a derivative of the activities of producers (Nishizawa, 2021).

Similarly, Marshall and Keynes were attempting to maintain the link between what Schumpeter calls "pure economics" and what Mill had referred to as "social philosophy". For Marshall (1907, p. 201), there were "ideals and ... ultimate ends of economic activities", and these consisted of appropriately combining the different dimensions involved in the good life and social progress (Nishizawa, 2021). In what was an ethics of virtue rather than a utilitarian ethics, the "end of life" was "the growth of a man's (*sic*) mind" and "his spiritual cultivation", and "material wealth, houses and horses, carpets and French cookery" were "merely means" (Marshall, 1873, p. 197). For Keynes, the economist contributed to clarifying issues related to "practical ethics", understood as the identification of the means by which it would be possible to ensure the material conditions that allowed individuals to flourish in the higher dimensions addressed by "speculative ethics". Transferred to the world of consumption, this was an economic philosophy that resisted accepting the utilitarian proposal of collapsing human well-being into a single dimension of a subjective nature. Keynes, in particular, lamented how Benthamism had led to an overvaluation of the importance of economic motivations, as well as to an ethical project that, in its underlying assumptions, sought to isolate the valuation of the mental states achieved by individuals from the valuation of the objective contexts associated with those mental states (Carabelli & Cedrini, 2018).

In sum, although Marshall's neoclassical economics had willingly abandoned the political economy label, it retained sociological and philosophical elements that had permeated the work of the classical economists and had led to some kind of coexistence between the theses of progress and deviation. The same can be said for what, over time, became Keynes' idiosyncratic economics. But Marshall's was just one of the possible interpretations of the nature of neoclassical economics. A small but growing group of economists was developing a more disruptive reading of the nature of the new paradigm of economic thinking. The core of this reading was based in Austria, but during the interwar period, it successfully branched out to Britain, even to what had once been Marshall's Cambridge. A decisive implication for our purposes is that, as we will see in the next section, adopting this reading meant banishing the deviation thesis from analyses of the world of consumption.

The Sovereign Consumer and the Reconstruction of Liberalism

The crisis of liberalism was one of the central themes in the political life of the interwar period. The outbreak of the First World War had been a serious corrective to nineteenth-century optimism regarding social and moral progress. The onset of a conflict of unprecedented scale made it increasingly difficult to maintain belief in the thesis of *doux commerce*, according to which commercial liberalism was not only beneficial from the perspective of national wealth but also for geopolitical stability and peace. The First World War also was the beginning of a time of increasing state intervention in economic life. This was not just, nor predominantly, about interventions tied to the military performance of the belligerents. It was also a more permanent transition from nineteenth-century liberal capitalism to a more coordinated variety of capitalism, particularly following the social crisis triggered by the Great Depression from 1929 onwards. Whether in the democratic form of the US New Deal or the authoritarian form of Nazi Germany (to name two characteristic examples), more and more measures were introduced to regulate a wide range of microeconomic areas and to experiment with macroeconomic management. This also needs to be considered in light of the impact that the Bolshevik Revolution of 1917 and the subsequent consolidation of an anti-capitalist system in the Soviet Union had on Western social and political life. Regardless of where one stood in the fragmented political spectrum of the period, it was difficult to escape the sense that would be immortalised for future generations in the memoirs of Austrian writer Stefan Zweig. As he titled his autobiography, completed from Brazilian exile during the Second World War, the world before 1914 had become, indeed, the "world of yesterday" (Bairoch, 1997; Frieden, 2006; Hobsbawm, 1994; Tooze, 2014; Zweig, 1942).

This was the turbulent context in which various authors sought to rebuild the liberal project and adapt it to the new times. Out of the efforts of some of them, particularly economists belonging to the so-called Austrian school, emerged a proposal for reorienting economic thought. Their influence would reach members of the neoclassical school and, in this way, have a significant impact on the education of future generations of economists. In the specific case of our analysis, the world of consumption was set to play a central role in this proposal for reorientation. If there was a central economic concept within it, it was that of consumer sovereignty. According to this perspective, market society was governed by a multitude of decisions made daily in a decentralised manner by countless consumers (Olsen, 2019).

It is unclear who coined the term "consumer sovereignty" or when it was first used. We will follow the work of Austrian economist Ludwig von Mises as a guiding thread, but not without first making two important clarifications. The first relates to the chronological framing of his work, which straddles both our period and the post-Second World War period. We place Mises in this period because, even if some of his ideas only gained a global audience following their publication in English after the war, it was during this period when he presented them for the first time. The second clarification is that we do not intend to attribute to Mises the same prominence that, for example, one might justifiably give to Veblen when discussing conspicuous consumption. For example, the way in which another Austrian economist, Friedrich Hayek (1935), invoked the image of the sovereign consumer in his critique of what he called "collectivist economic planning" in 1935, was highly influential (Boettke, 2018). A year later, British economist William Hutt (1936) published a book that might contain the first mature formulation of consumer sovereignty (Desmarais-Tremblay, 2020; Persky, 1993). But Hutt (1940) himself, who claimed to have arrived at this point in an unpublished work written in 1931, was not entirely sure that he was the first to use the term. And even if he had been, Hutt admitted, expressions that prefigured it, such as the phrase "the customer is always right", had long been in widespread use. There have been voices encouraging us to look much further back in time for the origins of the term. After all, the idea of a market society governed by the desires of consumers had been latent throughout the cycle of classical political economy. Had not Adam Smith (1776), to take an illustrious example (and one that could still hardly be considered seminal), written that in a market society the butcher did not put meat on the market out of benevolence but to make money by satisfying consumer needs?

Even though he was not a radical innovator on this point, Mises brought together elements that appear more dispersed or incomplete in other authors. To begin with, there is a strictly historical element: Mises was one of the first authors who, drawing from one of the branches of the marginalist revolution, set about constructing a system of economic thought around it in which consumer sovereignty would be central. Mises began developing this intellectual framework in his early German-language publications, and throughout the rest of his career, he consistently worked to perfect this design and provide it with further developments, content, and extensions. From this perspective, his 1949 book *Human Action*, whose core ideas were first published in German in 1940, constitutes an indispensable reference. Moreover, it is a contribution that, beyond its substance, explicitly sets out the methodological foundations upon which the family of arguments that it formed part of was based. Finally, it should be noted that throughout his career, Mises had a significant influence on younger economists who would later play a pivotal role in defining the Austrian research programme, such as the aforementioned Hayek, or (which will be more important for our purposes) the neoclassical research programme, such as Lionel Robbins (Olsen, 2019).

Mises' (1949) vision of consumer society, closely aligned with what we have called the progress thesis, stemmed from his radical adherence to one of the ruptures proposed by Menger one generation earlier: the subjective conception of value. Once value was seen as a mental attribution made by each individual consumer, rather than as an objective characteristic of the commodity or its production process, the way was cleared for consumer behaviour to be understood as a set of signals directing producers to put some goods on the market rather than others. The result was the arrival at equilibrium points in which markets cleared, and no economic resource could be used more profitably for another purpose: producers maximised their profit, and consumers maximised their utility. The trajectory of consumer society, embedded in the sequence of equilibrium points produced by the spontaneous functioning of markets, was progressive. Under capitalism, entrepreneurs could only thrive if they provided consumers with those goods which they had grounds to consider valuable. Consequently, for Mises it was evident what Hayek (1954) would later seek to stress in *Capitalism and the Historians*: the development of capitalism from the nineteenth century onwards had led to a notable and widespread improvement in the living standards of common people. Capitalism would have "poured a horn of plenty upon the masses of wage earners", making it possible for the masses to enjoy more goods and more leisure time (Mises, 1949, pp. 730–736 and 893).

A theoretical issue that Mises and other members of the Austrian school found decisive concerned the role of markets as organisers of information. Since economic value was based on subjective attributions by consumers, no ruler or researcher could hope to obtain the necessary information to interfere in the actions each consumer took in search of their own well-being. This perspective became particularly significant in the new academic and political discourse ignited by the Bolshevik Revolution and the consolidation of the Soviet state. The Mises who returned from the battlefields of the First World War felt that the core of the economic debate had become the tension between statism and liberalism (North, 2016). It was in this context that the figure of the sovereign consumer began to play a central role in his political discourse. The marginalist consumer could not only be expected to effectively pursue their well-being but also be expected to stand as a bastion of individual freedom against the totalitarian winds that were gaining momentum during the 1920s and 1930s. Consumer society brought about a higher standard of living among the masses, but also an affirmation of democracy.

Mises and other new liberals then chose to present consumer society as a sort of economic democracy. Like political democracy, consumer society incorporated the masses into the decision-making process, ensuring that this process aligned with the general interest. Just as democracy required every citizen to express their political opinion at the ballot box, consumer society relied on the preferences expressed by consumers through their purchasing actions. Similarly, just as electoral outcomes moved rulers and political parties to make decisions that best reflected public opinion, consumer society compelled firms to produce and market those goods that were truly desired by the public:

> The direction of all economic affairs is in the market society a task of the entrepreneurs. Theirs is the control of production. They are at the helm and steer the ship. A superficial observer would believe that they are supreme. But they are not. They are bound to obey unconditionally the captain's orders. The captain is the consumer. Neither the entrepreneurs nor the farmers nor the capitalists determine what has to be produced. The

> consumers do that [...] They determine precisely what should be produced, in what quality, and in what quantities. They are merciless egoistic bosses, full of whims and fancies, changeable and unpredictable. (Mises, 1949, pp. 328–329)

Mises even went one step further in this analogy, arguing that consumer society was actually more inclusive and legitimate than political democracy itself. After all, the latter was an all-or-nothing affair: the voice of the minorities was forgotten once their electoral defeat had been confirmed. In contrast, in consumer society, although the majority was well represented in dominant trends, the economic "votes" (so to speak) of minorities also received a proportionate share of representation (Mises, 1949, p. 330). In terms we would use today to describe this contrast, in democracies there were only regimes, whereas in consumer societies there were regimes and there were also niches. This view of consumer society can be seen as belonging to a larger family of arguments related to what today Chirat (2022) calls "demand-side democracy".

The intellectual edifice that Mises built was completed with an explicit reflection on methodological foundations. Economics had to be what Schumpeter would later call "pure economics", in his case a set of theoretical propositions designed to explain the market behaviour of individuals. What role, then, were the other "techniques" that Schumpeter considered crucial to the economist's work supposed to play? None of any significance. History and statistics were secondary, and Mises did not hesitate to express his scepticism about research programmes based on collecting large quantitative data sets. His influence in this regard was so small that it is not worth dwelling on. It is enough to note that, for our topic, there seemed to be an insurmountable barrier from the Austrian perspective: it was not possible to obtain data on what was truly crucial, namely the mental processes through which individuals attributed value to goods.

Much more influential was the way Mises resolutely broke ties with sociology and philosophy. For Mises, the economist had to take the preferences and orientations of consumers as given. He should not attempt to explain that data as such an intellectual enterprise would be unproductive in an analytical framework focused on the consequences of said preferences and orientations. The origin of that data was something relevant only to those "moralists" and "sermonisers" who sought to blame entrepreneurs for consumer tastes, but not to an economist. Economists should be scientists who never attempted to indicate people the goals they should strive for, but they simply discovered the most suitable means to achieve those goals (Mises, 1949, pp. 11 and 363).

Mises reacted vehemently to the possibility that the economist might cross the line and begin to make value judgements about the ultimate ends of economic activity. In Mises' intellectual world, this was nothing short of authoritarian: the economist-philosopher as a superior being who considered themselves legitimised to impose a particular philosophy of life on his fellow citizens (Mises, 1949, pp. 295–296). Like Hayek (1944), any step in that direction could only start a painful journey down the "road to serfdom":

> If one abolishes man's freedom to determine his own consumption, one takes all freedoms away. The naive advocates of government interference with consumption delude themselves when they neglect what they disdainfully call the philosophical aspect of the problem. They unwittingly support the case of censorship, inquisition, religious intolerance, and the persecution of dissenters. (Mises, 1949, p. 865)

This applied even in cases where consumer behaviour might raise certain concerns for an external observer. Menger had acknowledged that his optimising consumer could indeed make mistakes, and during the interwar period, an emerging "nutritional science" exerted considerable influence on policymakers by offering recommendations for healthier diets (Biltekoff, 2012). But for Mises (1949, p. 295), "Those who issue such opinions and recommend that governments act on such criteria intend to treat men as cattle". And what analytical importance could conspicuous consumption really have? Even if an economist believed a consumer was being driven by pointless vanity, how could one deny that such behaviour increased consumer satisfaction (Mises, 1949, p. 295)?

Mises' true originality lay not so much in the economic theory he employed—essentially a derivation of Menger's branch of marginalism—but rather in the way he embedded that theory in a broader political discourse aimed at reconstructing liberalism, and in his effort to insulate economic theory from sociological and philosophical complements. Sociology disappeared from the picture, while philosophy was reduced to the bare minimum: the good life was simply whatever each person believed it to be. Once the terms of the conversation were fixed that way, the deviation thesis could not survive.

This set of ideas was destined to have a profound impact on how subsequent generations of economists would view consumer society. This was due to the selective infiltration of these ideas into the research programme of the neoclassical school. A key figure in this regard was Lionel Robbins. In his youth, Robbins had been a socialist-leaning economist, but his participation in Mises' seminar in Vienna profoundly reshaped his intellectual life and reoriented him towards the reconstruction of the liberal project (Olsen, 2019). This reorientation was accompanied by a reading of the marginalist revolution and the neoclassical programme that was markedly different from that of Marshall.

Away from Cambridge, at the London School of Economics Robbins (1932) drew two red lines regarding what an economist should and should not be. The first was that the economist should avoid lines of inquiry that, by their very nature, belonged to the realm of sociology. The economist had to begin with an individual endowed with certain resources and preferences, without delving into the origins of those preferences. On that basis, economics would be a science of choice under conditions of scarcity: individuals had to allocate limited resources to alternative ends in order to satisfy potentially unlimited needs or desires. The second red line was that the economist had nothing to gain from adopting ethical criteria. As with Mises, each individual knew better than anyone else what they should do to pursue their own interests, and it was presumptuous for an external researcher to claim the authority to define what desires or ends the individual should seek.

In Robbins' vision, the subject of economics was the "economising" of individuals, and thus retaining ties to sociology and philosophy would be of little help. An economist could cultivate such "outside interests", but without allowing them to contaminate the "neutral area of science". One had to be careful, because the "borderlands of Economics" with other social sciences were, in fact, "the happy hunting-ground of the charlatan and the quack" (Robbins, 1932, pp. 83 and 134–135). Along the way, the history of consumer society could hardly be seen as anything other than a sequence of equilibrium points, each representing the best of all possible worlds at each particular moment. From there to the progress thesis was but a short step—almost more intuitive than analytical.

By then, Cambridge was no longer the Cambridge of Marshall, anyway. Marshall had appointed Arthur Pigou as his successor, and Pigou's welfare economics can be interpreted in two quite different ways concerning the debate on consumer society. On the one hand, there is no doubt that

Pigou (1920) used marginalist tools to formalise at least part of the argument Marshall had sketched in his "Possibilities" article. In Pigou's world, there were instances where the level of consumption of a particular good in society might not align with what could be considered socially optimal. Consequently, once an external criterion for evaluation was introduced, the door was opened for public policies to influence individual decisions in order to better align them with social utility. Since certain goods—such as those related to access to culture in Marshall's view—might be under-consumed relative to what was desirable, while others, particularly those associated with conspicuous consumption, were over-consumed, there was an economic argument for the state to extract fiscal resources from private consumption of the latter and redirect them to promote the former. There was also an argument in favour of initiatives aimed at fostering "educated preferences" among consumers, helping to guide them towards needs that had been neglected under their initial "raw preferences" (Yamazaki, 2021, pp. 112–115).

However, there was one important point where Pigou deviated from Marshall, much to the latter's dismay. Marshall had retained a multidimensional conception of human well-being, which enabled him to articulate a discourse in which the utilitarian dimension coexisted with others and did not necessarily have to be aligned with them. In contrast, Pigou's welfare economics unfolded along a single dimension, representing a kind of amended version of the utilitarian tradition. Social welfare could be expressed on a single utility scale, and the amendment consisted in the economist retaining the right to identify a social utility that did not necessarily correspond to the aggregation of individual utilities. Yet, as Pigou himself made clear at the outset of his major work, the analysis was confined to phenomena that could be studied through a monetary metric.

This was not at all inconsistent with the many passages in which Marshall had adopted what Schumpeter (1954, p. 1162) calls a form of "revived Benthamism" to lay the groundwork for the future of welfare economics. However, it did bury Marshall's deeper agenda of progress, which was concerned not only with material wealth but also with moral improvement (Nishizawa, 2021). In fact, Pigou was inclined to dispense with Marshall's suspicion that these two types of improvement might not necessarily go hand in hand. The political agenda still left ample room for the state to intervene in economic life to correct "market failures" caused by discrepancies between social and private utility curves. Even so, there remained a blind spot in which the economist's philosophical positions continued to filter through implicitly: namely, in the identification of such discrepancies. From this perspective, there was still a significant gap between Pigou's welfare economics and the ethically neutral welfare economics of Pareto (Yamazaki, 2021).

That said, although current specialists in Pigou are right to remind us of these and other aspects of his work that align him more closely with reformism than with Mises' project of reconstructing liberalism (Kumekawa, 2017), abandoning the multidimensional conception of the good life had decisive implications. From then on, the deviation thesis could only arise among neoclassical economists if they could claim that some form of negative externality or market failure was involved. However, once Robbins cast doubt on the idea that a good economist could rely on ethical considerations, such a claim had to be grounded in utilitarian terms. This destroyed much of the field where previous authors, including Marshall, had cultivated the deviation thesis.

In any case, it would be an exaggeration to claim that the Austrian winds channelled by Robbins radically altered the conversation among economists in the interwar period. Robbins' definition of economics would only become dominant in the decades following the Second World War (Backhouse & Medema, 2009). Only then would the intrinsic limitations of the type of welfare economics envisaged by Pigou be extensively developed. Meanwhile, during the 1930s, some neoclassical economists maintained at least an ambivalent attitude towards consumer society. Consider the case of economists from the University of Chicago, one of the strongholds of neoclassicism in a country still heavily influenced by institutionalism. It cannot be said that authors like Frank Knight or Henry Simons were staunch adherents of the progress thesis; rather, they questioned the social value of advertising and highlighted the fragile nature of consumer autonomy (Backhouse, 2021, pp. 187–189; Olsen, 2019, pp. 171–172).

In fact, not even all economists within the Austrian orbit were aligned with Mises. Schumpeter abandoned the notion of a sovereign consumer. For him, the *primum mobile* in economic life came from producers:

> Needs, whatever they may be, are never more than conditioning factors, and in many cases merely the products of entrepreneurial activity; it is not they that set the capitalist machine in motion. (Schumpeter, 1939, p. 442)

It was the entrepreneurs who, through their innovation strategies, took the risk of launching new products onto the market for which it was not clear that any demand existed. It was up to them to engage in persuasive efforts to prompt potential consumers—often somewhat apathetic—to take an interest in these products:

> The great majority of changes in commodities consumed has been forced by producers on consumers who, more often than not, have resisted the change and have had to be educated up by elaborate psychotechnics of advertising. (Schumpeter, 1939, p. 50)

Perhaps some goods targeted essential biological needs that could be taken as given, but many others targeted "manufactured needs" that the economist should treat as a variable. In other words, using the terminology employed by Schumpeter himself when listing the "techniques" that distinguished the economist, it was necessary to venture into a certain sociology of consumption to explain preferences and, in doing so, offer a realistic view of the role of consumption within the "capitalist process". This is likely what Schumpeter (1954, p. 585) had in mind when he noted that "a theory of consumption worthy of the name" had yet to be developed and that, when it emerged, it would incorporate the "social, moral, and cultural conditions" of household economies. Ultimately, Schumpeter (1942) transferred his view to the realm of political democracy, which in his conceptualisation could no longer be seen as a system truly governed by sovereign voters, but rather as a form of monopolistic competition between political elites. This amounted to a radical reworking of the standard analogy between the market order and democracy (Chirat, 2022).

In summary, Mises and Robbins drew red lines that would prove highly influential in shaping future debates among economists about consumer society. However, it would be a mistake to assume that these red lines immediately and universally acquired such status. This occurred as part of a historical process—gradual, not without counterforces, still notably incomplete by the time the Second World War ended.

Conclusion: A Battlefield in the Making

Between 1870 and 1945, an embryo of mass consumer society began to emerge. Although its material, social, and territorial limitations were evident, it was also clear that the masses were no longer condemned to gravitate around a rudimentary pattern of subsistence consumption. The introduction of new and sophisticated consumer goods, the diversification of consumer baskets, and the increase in spending by broad segments of the population led the economists of the period to envision the nascent consumer society with greater clarity than had been possible for the classical economists.

Since the economists of this period formed a diverse group, their views on consumer society were equally varied. These economists, though united by their participation in the institutionalisation of the discipline, worked within different paradigms. Even among those working within the same paradigm, there were significant differences in their conceptions of "pure economics" and, even more so, in the role that history, sociology, and philosophy could play as complements. This pluralism created broad spaces for the cultivation of both the progress and the deviation thesis. The former aligned well with the marginalist conception of an optimising consumer whose autonomous behaviour allowed him to achieve the highest possible level of utility. The deviation thesis, by contrast, flourished among economists who, like the institutionalists, were interested in the sociological dimensions of consumption and framed their analysis within philosophical frameworks different from utilitarianism.

In this intellectually plural landscape, some proposals emerged to articulate both theses and move towards something resembling a "synthesis view". Both Marshall and Keynes sketched an approach in which consumer society could serve as a vehicle for progress for a time but then risked veering into deviation. Progress lay in the capacity of consumer society to guarantee the material preconditions necessary for people to live a good life. The danger of deviation, however, arose once this objective was achieved. Consumerism could continue to absorb resources that would be more fruitfully devoted to the non-material components of the good life—such as the cultivation of culture, interpersonal relationships, and activities that generated existential meaning.

By no means do we intend to convey to the reader that this "synthesis view" was a fully satisfactory endpoint. It was a synthesis only in the weak sense of the term: more diachronic than synchronic. Consequently, it left important unresolved questions. For instance, what exactly was the pattern of consumption that could be considered sufficient to solve the "economic problem"? Did it differ from the basic ("productive") consumption pattern identified by John Stuart Mill in his nineteenth-century synthesis view? There is no doubt that these and other related questions could have inspired a new generation of "synthesis views" framed within a pluralistic conversation.

However, this kind of conversation was threatened during the interwar period, particularly in the 1930s, when some economists began to advocate for a conception of economic research that left little room for the development of the deviation thesis. This shift was partly due to the internal inertia of the neoclassical paradigm. As Marshall's case had shown, it was one thing to identify elements of both progress and deviation and quite another to integrate that dynamic vision into a theoretical framework—such as the neoclassical one—that gravitated towards static equilibrium positions. Although the replacement of the classical paradigm with the neoclassical paradigm did not necessarily imply a rigid adherence to the progress thesis, it did complicate the task of fitting the deviation thesis into a broader narrative about how the economy worked. It was more natural, so to speak, for equilibrium-based thinking to evolve into a teleological narrative in which every equilibrium point represented the best possible of the worlds at every given moment. In terms of neoclassical "pure economics", this outcome could only be avoided if, like Pigou, the researcher retained the right to draw maps of social utility that were, by their very nature, even less empirically observable than the individual utility maps that supported the standard neoclassical framework.

While these internal tensions were unfolding, the neoclassical project was also decisively influenced by contributions from the Austrian school. It was Austrians such as Mises who completed the journey from Menger's marginalist consumer to the vision of market society as an economic democracy governed by sovereign consumers. Although Austrian "pure economics" was not particularly innovative in this area, the political discourse framing their work gave their messages notable resonance in an era marked by the rise of totalitarian regimes. The Austrian school also exerted a direct and indirect influence on the neoclassical project by promoting a reading in which "pure economics" did not need to be accompanied by history, sociology, or philosophy. This shaped a playing field in which the deviation thesis could hardly flourish.

Pluralism remained prevalent during the interwar period, but from the 1930s onwards we begin to perceive the contours of the battlefield on which a great clash would take place after the war. In this battlefield, one side—represented by an increasingly dominant neoclassical orthodoxy—would firmly adhere to the progress thesis. This adherence was based not only on their substantive examination of consumer society but also on their definition of the professional economist as a specialised practitioner of "pure economics". Other schools of thought—particularly the institutionalists and some of the Marxists—would continue to identify elements of deviation in the dynamics of consumer society. Yet, embedded as they were in an intellectual environment that now left little room for history, sociology, or philosophy, their arguments were increasingly perceived as heterodox and of questionable scientific validity. Thus, as we will explore in the next chapter, ideas that had long been part of the economic conversation were relegated precisely when mass consumer societies were coming into full bloom in the real world.

References

Arena, R. (2021). To which kind of welfare did Léon Walras refer? The theorems and the state. In R. E. Backhouse, A. Baujard, & T. Nishizawa (Eds.), *Welfare theory, public action, and ethical values: Revisiting the history of welfare economics*. Cambridge University Press.

Arrighi, G. (2001). Braudel, capitalism, and the new economic sociology. *Review, 24*(1), 107–123.

Backhouse, R. E. (2021). Individualism and ethics: Samuelson's welfare economics. In R. E. Backhouse, A. Baujard, & T. Nishizawa (Eds.), *Welfare theory, public action, and ethical values: Revisiting the history of welfare economics*. Cambridge University Press.

Backhouse, R. E., & Medema, S. G. (2009). Defining economics: The long road to acceptance of the Robbins definition. *Economica, 76*(s1), 805–820.

Bairoch, P. (1997). *Victoires et déboires: histoire économique et sociale du monde du XVIe siècle à nos jours*. Gallimard.

Bee, M., & Desmarais-Tremblay, M. (2023). The birth of *homo œconomicus*: The methodological debate on the economic agent from J. S. Mill to V. Pareto. *Journal of the History of Economic Thought, 45*(1), 1–26.

Biltekoff, C. (2012). Critical nutrition studies. In J. M. Pilcher (Ed.), *The Oxford handbook of food history*. Oxford University Press.

Boettke, P. J. (2018). *F. A. Hayek: Economics, political economy and social philosophy*. Palgrave Macmillan.

Bruni, L. (2006). *Civil happiness: Economics and human flourishing in historical perspective*. Routledge.

Caldari, K., & Nishizawa, T. (2020). *Alfred Marshall's last challenge: His book on economic progress*. Cambridge Scholars Publishing.

Canterbery, E. R. (1999). Thorstein Veblen and *The Great Gatsby*. *Journal of Economic Issues, 33*(2), 297–304.

Carabelli, A. M. (2021). *Keynes on uncertainty and tragic happiness.* Palgrave Macmillan.

Carabelli, A. M., & Cedrini, M. (2011). The economic problem of happiness. Keynes on happiness and economics. *Forum for Social Economics, 40*(3), 335–359.

Carabelli, A. M., & Cedrini, M. A. (2018). Great expectations and final disillusionment: Keynes, 'My early beliefs' and the ultimate values of capitalism. *Cambridge Journal of Economics, 42*(5), 1183–1204.

Chandler, A. D. (1990). *Scale and scope: The dynamics of industrial capitalism.* Harvard University Press.

Chirat, A. (2021). *L'Économie intégral de John Kenneth Galbraith (1933-1983).* Garnier.

Chirat, A. (2022). Démocratie de la demande *versus* démocratie de l'offre: Reconstruction et interpretation des analogies démocratie-marché. *OEconomia: History, Methodology, Philosophy, 12*(1), 55–91.

Clar, E. (2024). El pensamiento económico de Ortega. unpublished manuscript, University of Zaragoza.

de Grazia, V. (2005). *Irresistible empire: America's advance through twentieth-century Europe.* Harvard University Press.

Deaton, A. (1975). The structure of demand 1920-1970. In C. M. Cipolla (Ed.), *The Fontana economic history of Europe, vol. 5: The twentieth century.* Collins-Fontana.

DeLong, J. B. (2022). *Slouching towards utopia: An economic history of the twentieth century.* Basic Books.

Desmarais-Tremblay, M. (2020). W. H. Hutt and the conceptualization of consumers' sovereignty. *Oxford Economic Papers, 72*(4), 1050–1071.

Floud, R., Fogel, R. W., Harris, B., & Hong, S. C. (2011). *The changing body: Health, nutrition, and human development in the Western world since 1700.* Cambridge University Press.

Freeman, C., & Louçã, F. (2001). *As time goes by: From the industrial revolutions to the information revolution.* Oxford University Press.

Frieden, J. A. (2006). *Global capitalism: Its fall and rise in the twentieth century.* W. W Norton. [Spanish edition: *Capitalismo global: el trasfondo económico de la historia del siglo XX.* Crítica, 2007.]

Gallego, D. (2022). *Los caminos del progreso: una historia del desarrollo económico.* Comares.

Gordon, R. J. (2017). *The rise and fall of American growth: The U.S. standard of living since the Civil War.* Princeton, Princeton University Press.

Hayek, F. A. (1935). The present state of the debate. In F. A. Hayek (Ed.), *Collectivist economic planning: Critical studies on the possibilities of socialism.* Routledge.

Hayek, F. A. (1944). *The road to serfdom*. University of Chicago Press. [Spanish edition: *Camino de servidumbre*. Unión Editorial, 2007.]
Hayek, F. A. (1954). History and politics. In F. A. Hayek (Ed.), *Capitalism and the historians*. University of Chicago Press.
Hobsbawm, E. (1987). *The age of empire, 1875-1914*. Weidenfeld and Nicolson.
Hobsbawm, E. (1994). *Age of extremes: The short twentieth century, 1914–1991*. Michael Joseph.
Hodgson, G. (2001). *How economics forgot history: The problem of historical specificity in social science*. Routledge.
Hodgson, G. (2004). *The evolution of institutional economics: Agency, structure, and Darwinism in American institutionalism*. Routledge.
Hutt, W. (1936). *Economists and the public: A study of competition and opinion*. Jonathan Cape.
Hutt, W. (1940). The concept of consumers' sovereignty. *Economic Journal, 50*(197), 66–77.
Jevons, W. S. (1871). *The theory of political economy*. Macmillan. [Spanish edition: *La teoría de la economía política*. Pirámide, 1998.]
Keynes, J. M. (1930). Economic possibilities for our grandchildren. In L. Pecchi & G. Piga (Eds.), *Revisiting Keynes: Economic possibilities for our grandchildren*. MIT Press, 2008. [Spanish edition: "Las posibilidades económicas de nuestros nietos", en *Ensayos de persuasion*. Folio, 1997.]
Keynes, J. M. (1936). *The general theory of employment, interest and money*. Macmillan.
Kumekawa, I. (2017). *The first serious optimist: A*. Princeton University Press.
Landes, D. S. (2003). *The unbound Prometheus: Technological change and industrial development in Western Europe from 1750 to the present*. Cambridge University Press.
Lawson, T. (1997). *Reorienting economics*. Routledge.
Levy, J. (2021). *Ages of American capitalism: A history of the United States*. Random House.
Lindert, P. H. (2004). *Growing public: Social spending and economic growth since the eighteenth century*. Cambridge University Press.
Maddison, A. (2001). *The world economy: A millennial perspective*. OECD.
Malassis, L. (1997). *Les trois âges de l'alimentaire: essai sur une historie sociale de l'alimentation et de l'agriculture*. Cujas.
Marshall, A. (1873). The future of the working classes. In A. C. Pigou (Ed.), *Memorials of Alfred Marshall*. Macmillan. [Spanish edition: "El porvenir de las clases obreras", en A. Marshall, *Obras escogidas*. Fondo de Cultura Económica, 1949.]
Marshall, A. (1890). *Principles of economics*. Macmillan. [Spanish edition: *Principios de economía*. Instituto de Crédito Oficial, 2005.]

Marshall, A. (1907). The social possibilities of economic chivalry. *Economic Journal, 17*(65), 7–29.
Marshall, A. (1920). *Industry and trade*. Macmillan.
Martins, N. O. (2014). *The Cambridge revival of political economy*. Routledge.
Mayer, A. J. (1981). *The persistence of the Old Regime: Europe to the Great War*. Pantheon.
Méndez Ibisate, F. (2004). *Marginalistas y neoclásicos*. Síntesis.
Menger, C. (1871). *Grundsätze der Volkswirtschaftslehre*. Wilhelm Braumüller. [Spanish edition: *Principios de economía política*. Orbis, 1985.]
Mirowski, P., & Hands, D. W. (2006). Introduction to 'Agreement on demand: Consumer theory in the twentieth century. *History of Political Economy, 38*(supplement), 1–6.
Mises, L. v. (1949). *Human action: A treatise in economics*. Yale University Press. [Spanish edition: *La acción humana: tratado de economía*. Unión, 2007.]
Mitchell, W. C. (1912). The backward art of spending money. *American Economic Review, 2*(2), 269–281.
Morgan, M. S., & Rutherford, M. (1998). American economics: The character of the transformation. *History of Political Economy, 30*(supplement), 1–26.
Nishizawa, T. (2021). Alfred Marshall on progress and human wellbeing. In R. E. Backhouse, A. Baujard, & T. Nishizawa (Eds.), *Welfare theory, public action, and ethical values: Revisiting the history of welfare economics*. Cambridge University Press.
North, G. (2016). Ludwig von Mises. Lecture given at the Mises Institute (Auburn). Retrieved 15 May 2024, from www.youtube.com
Offer, A., & Söderberg, G. (2016). *The Nobel factor: The prize in economics, social democracy, and the market turn*. Princeton University Press.
Olsen, N. (2019). *The sovereign consumer: A new intellectual history of neoliberalism*. Palgrave Macmillan.
Persky, J. (1993). Retrospectives: Consumer sovereignty. *Journal of Economic Perspectives, 7*(1), 183–191.
Pigou, A. C. (1920). *The economics of welfare*. Macmillan.
Piketty, T. (2014). *Capital in the twenty-first century*. Harvard University Press.
Polanyi, K. (1944). *The great transformation: The political and economic origins of our time*. Farrar & Rinehart.
Popkin, B. M. (1993). Nutritional patterns and transitions. *Population and Development Review, 19*(1), 138–157.
Robbins, L. (1932). *An essay on the nature and significance of economic science*. Macmillan.
Rogan, T. (2017). *The moral economists: R. H. Tawney, Karl Polanyi, and E. P. Thompson*. Princeton University Press.
Roncaglia, A. (2005). *The wealth of ideas: A history of economic thought*. Cambridge University Press.

Schumpeter, J. A. (1939). *Business cycles: A theoretical, historical, and statistical analysis of the capitalist process.* McGraw-Hill. [Spanish edition: *Ciclos económicos: análisis teórico, histórico y estadístico del proceso capitalista.* Prensas Universitarias de Zaragoza, 2002.]

Schumpeter, J. A. (1942). *Capitalism, socialism, and democracy.* Harper and Bros. [Spanish edition: *Capitalismo, socialismo y democracia.* Orbis, 1988.]

Schumpeter, J. A. (1954). *History of economic analysis.* Oxford University Press. [Spanish edition: *Historia del análisis económico.* Ariel, 1994.]

Skidelsky, R. (1996). *Keynes.* Oxford University Press. [Spanish edition: *Keynes.* Alianza, 1998.]

Smith, A. (1776). *An inquiry into the nature and causes of the wealth of nations.* W. Strahan and T. Cadell. [Spanish edition: *La riqueza de las naciones.* Alianza, 2001.]

Tawney, R. H. (1920). *The acquisitive society.* Collins.

Tooze, A. (2014). *The deluge: The Great War, America, and the remaking of the global order, 1916-1931.* Allen Lane.

Trentmann, F. (2016). *Empire of things: How we became a world of consumers, from the fifteenth century to the twenty-first.* HarperCollins.

Tribe, K. (2022). *Constructing economic science: The invention of a discipline 1850-1950.* Oxford University Press.

Veblen, T. (1899). *The theory of the leisure class: An economic study in the evolution of institutions.* Macmillan. [Spanish edition: *Teoría de la clase ociosa.* Fondo de Cultura Económica, 1974.]

Veblen, T. (1904). *The theory of the business enterprise.* C. Scribner's Sons W. Strahan and T. Cadell.

Walras, L. (1874). *Éléments d'économie politique pure.* Corbaz. [Spanish edition: *Elementos de economía política pura (o teoría de la riqueza social).* Alianza, 1987.]

Wisman, J. D. (2019). Adam Smith and Thorstein Veblen on the pursuit of status through consumption versus work. *Cambridge Journal of Economics, 43*(1), 17–36.

Wolf, E. R. (1982). *Europe and the people without history.* University of California Press, 1997.

Yamazaki, S. (2021). Pigou's welfare economics revisited: A non-welfarist and non-utilitarian interpretation. In R. E. Backhouse, A. Baujard, & T. Nishizawa (Eds.), *Welfare theory, public action, and ethical values: Revisiting the history of welfare economics.* Cambridge University Press.

Zweig, S. (1942). *Die Welt von Gestern: Erinnerungen eines Europäers.* Fischer Verlag.

CHAPTER 5

The Great Clash (1945–1990)

In the decades following the Second World War, the battlefield that had begun to take shape during the period 1870–1945 hosted a direct confrontation between rival views of consumer society. This confrontation is, in a sense, the climax of our historical reconstruction. It not only incorporated much of the material that had emerged during the previous two periods, but it also had a decisive impact on the period that would come afterwards.

This chapter is organised in five sections. The first presents the historical context of the period 1945–1990, characterised by the emergence of mass consumer society and the hegemony of neoclassical economics. The second section is dedicated to the key economist of the period when it comes to the topic of this book: the institutionalist John Kenneth Galbraith, who sparked a heated debate on what he called the affluent society. The third section examines other authors who, from heterodox or dissenting perspectives, developed similar arguments, insisting that there were elements of deviation in the consumer society of their time. The fourth section reconstructs the response of mainstream economists and how, as a result, the progress thesis became firmly entrenched within the profession. The fifth section analyses how by the end of the period, consumer society had become something of an intellectual mirage, increasingly absent from the economists' field of vision. The conclusions reflect

F. Collantes, *Consumer Society and the Economists*, Palgrave Studies in the History of Economic Thought,
https://doi.org/10.1007/978-3-031-96645-3_5

on the factors that led to a change in direction, disrupting the kind of "synthesis view" that, at least in part, had begun to take shape during the preceding period.

Irresistible Empires

Mass consumer societies flourished in the decades following the Second World War, first in the United States and then in Western Europe and Japan. In country after country, average incomes began to grow more rapidly than ever before. With industries such as steel, car production, and chemicals as the most visible leaders in innovation, the growth potential of economies skyrocketed. This potential was particularly high in those countries most affected by the destructions of the war, as well as in those that still had large supplies of agricultural population susceptible to be transferred to other sectors. That this growth potential was realised, leading to what some have referred to as a "golden age" (Maddison, 2001), had much to do with the political history of the period. In the United States, the New Deal order was consolidated, and in Western Europe a form of "coordinated capitalism" emerged. At least until the 1970s, this kind of active economic management by the state promoted growth. Furthermore, Western economies and Japan benefitted from the construction of a new international economic order and the subsequent revitalisation of trade and investment. This played a crucial role, for example, in the transfer of technology from the American leader to its followers and partners (Eichengreen, 2007; Freeman & Louçã, 2001; Frieden, 2006).

While economic growth accelerated, social inequality continued to decline. Governments implemented measures aimed at strengthening social cohesion, including social public expenditure programmes, progressive taxation, and labour market reforms. Inequality also decreased because the massive transfer of populations from rural areas to cities led to a reduction in income dispersion. As a result, during the post-war growth surge, a truly broad mass of consumers with growing purchasing power emerged for the first time (Lindert, 2004; Piketty, 2014; Prados de la Escosura, 2008).

The growth of this purchasing power was, in fact, greater than what income or equity data alone might suggest because consumers were able to benefit from declines in the relative price of some of the goods that played a central role in their baskets. Food, in particular, became significantly cheaper as its production chain underwent transformations such as the "green revolution" in agriculture, the industrialisation of food production, and the rise of large supermarket chains (Brassley, 2009; Malassis, 1997; Oddy & Drouard, 2013). Additionally, many durable consumer goods, which had started out at high prices at the beginning of the period, became substantially cheaper and, as a result, more affordable for population segments that had previously been unable to afford them. The automobile may be the most characteristic example.

While these drivers of consumer society were taking shape, there were no less important transformations in consumer culture. Companies made unprecedented investments in advertising to attract the attention of the consuming masses created by the "golden age". Over time, this advertising reduced its strictly informative component and incorporated ever more elements that appealed to the emotions of the consumer. In Western Europe and Japan, where many elements of the aristocratic and stratified culture that had enveloped the world of consumption since the *Ancien Régime* and the Tokugawa era had persisted, the American-style conception of mass consumer culture spread (de Grazia, 2005; Francks, 2009).

The result was the full blossoming of mass consumer societies. The vast majority of households experienced a material revolution that was all the more striking the greater the hardships that the war had imposed on their daily lives. Families mobilised unprecedented volumes of expenditure to purchase a much more abundant and diversified basket of consumer goods. The first thing they did was ensure a diet that embodied the endpoint of what we have referred to as the "nutritional transition". Not only were their caloric intakes more than sufficient for biological survival, but larger quantities of animal-based foods, such as meat, milk, fish, and eggs, as well as fruits, vegetables, and various types of processed foods, were incorporated into their diet. Households also mobilised increasing amounts of resources to purchase larger and better-equipped homes. None of this prevented most households from venturing into increasing expenditure on goods and services that satisfied needs that were less essential. A range of durable consumer goods, including cars and household appliances (from refrigerators and washing machines to television sets), spread rapidly. Even experiences traditionally reserved for the upper classes, such as tourism, began to filter down the social ladder. The result was a transformation of surprising magnitude in lifestyles and mentalities, completed within a generation or two. Although none of these trends were without precedent in the period 1870–1945 (or even earlier), after the Second World War they reached a territorial scale and social depth that were incomparably greater (Alonso & Conde, 1994; Cross, 2000; Francks, 2009; Gordon, 2017; Levy, 2021; Malassis, 1997; Popkin, 1993).

A similar observation can be made regarding the evolution of economic thought. Economics became a fully institutionalised academic discipline and, as such, participated intensively in the wave of expansion in higher education that unfolded after 1945. In this expanding profession, neoclassical economists gained a dominant position. Along the way, the other schools that had populated the pluralist scene of the interwar period, such as the historical school in Germany and institutionalism in the United States, became openly heterodox groups (Hodgson, 2001, 2004; Lee, 2009; Wallerstein, 1996).

The neoclassical programme expanded in various directions and began to identify itself with "economic theory". In fact, a striking parenthesis was opened in the history of economic thought, as economic theory gained intellectual primacy over applied economics. The profession then coalesced strongly around the production and discussion of mathematically formalised theoretical models. The very notion of what it meant to be an economist, and how the mind of a truly deserving economist should work, was deeply influenced as a result. The version of the neoclassical project that Lionel Robbins defended in the 1930s gradually became dominant during the post-war decades: a science concerned with the allocation of scarce resources in a world of unlimited needs, which were to be taken as exogenous data. This science also seemed to have a remarkable capacity to integrate ideas and intuitions that had originally arisen from other schools of economic thought. The most prominent example was the development of the so-called neoclassical synthesis to try to absorb the macroeconomic message of Keynes. It was only from the 1960s onwards that greater importance began to be placed on econometric tools, which, in the positivist language favoured by mainstream economists, were meant to provide empirical tests of theoretical hypotheses. However, beneath the internal tensions that began to close the parenthesis of high theory, there is no doubt that the very diffusion of econometrics played a significant role in continuing to differentiate mainstream economists from other economists and social scientists (Backhouse & Cherrier, 2017; Roncaglia, 2005, 2019).

Although the generalisation may be somewhat simplistic, the heterodox schools struggled to develop a narrative and set of cohesive practices of comparable strength. Furthermore, the institutionalisation of economics as an academic discipline began to threaten the pluralism that had prevailed during the interwar period. Personnel selection and the funding of research projects became more systematic, and along the way, the criteria involved reflected the theoretical and methodological premises of mainstream economics. This made it difficult for heterodox schools to reproduce themselves, at least in the cores of the academic map. On top of this, the political landscape of the Cold War had an influence. In the West, there were of course far more Marxist academics than "bourgeois" social scientists could ever be in the Soviet Union, but their personal and professional positions could become complicated. In the specific case of economics, the growing identification of the economist with the neoclassical economist entailed not just a political rejection of Marxism, but also an academic rejection of the intellectual playing field in which Marx's economic analysis had emerged.

It is also important to recognise the significance of a historical accident. The full formation of a mass consumer society in the West coincided with the Cold War. Within each country, mass consumption was inscribed within the reformulated post-war social contract. More and more explicitly, the possibility of accessing a plentiful and diverse consumer basket was incorporated into the notion of citizenship that served as the premise for Western democratic regimes. Even in those enclaves of the US side of the Cold War, where, as in Spain, dictatorial regimes persisted, these regimes also sought to mobilise the world of consumption to shore up their political legitimacy (Alonso & Conde, 1994). In a way, American-style mass consumer society ended up functioning as a kind of "irresistible empire" to which Cold War Western Europe adhered (de Grazia, 2005). This connection must be kept in mind when studying the evolution of economic thought during the period.

John Kenneth Galbraith's Affluent Society

If post-war America was the time and place for some economist to conduct the first in-depth analysis of consumer society, John Kenneth Galbraith brought with him a life trajectory that made him the ideal candidate. Galbraith had been born in 1908 in rural Canada, where he spent a childhood shaped by farm life, hard work demands and limited material rewards. Galbraith (1999) knew first-hand what it was like to live in the economy of scarcity that he would later discuss in his works. Like many of his generation, Galbraith's transition to adulthood was marked by the traumatic experience of the Great Depression and the material deprivations it caused for large sections of the population. In his case, moreover, his work as an economist for the US government allowed him to gain first-hand insight into the reconstruction problems of war-torn 1940s Europe. Looking back from his office at Harvard University at the age of fifty, how could one not appreciate the enormous distance that separated the American society of the late 1950s from rural Ontario at the turn of the century, or from the United States during the Great Depression, or from war-shaken Europe (Chirat, 2021, pp. 349–389)?

Galbraith (1958) made this distance the starting point for *The Affluent Society*. There had been a time when economists lived in societies marked by scarcity. It was not surprising, therefore, that the main body of economic theory had been built around that notion. It was also not surprising that the practical recommendations of economists had focused on policies they believed could be most useful in promoting economic growth. What seemed abnormal, Galbraith continued, was that economic discourse continued to be anchored in these notions and concerns in the very different context of post-war affluence.

In Galbraith's affluent society, consumers were no longer concerned with whether they would be able to make it through the day having eaten enough or satisfied their other basic needs. Most of the population lived relatively comfortable lives. This was good news for them as consumers but bad news for the business community and perhaps even for them as workers: how could business activity continue to expand now? The prospect of stagnation would negatively impact on profit expectations and, by extension, on the labour market. As the business community frequently reminded, it was crucial that production continued to grow. And, to achieve this, it was necessary for companies to induce new needs and desires among consumers. Consumers had to be diverted from the feeling of satiety: if their traditional needs were already well met, there would always be new needs that had not yet been properly addressed. In the affluent society, companies thus made multimillion-dollar investments in advertising campaigns to induce the formation of new preferences and desires among consumers. The production processes of companies were no longer limited to meeting the needs perceived in the consumer public: now, they included the immaterial production of new needs through images, slogans, and jingles.

When this induction of needs was successfully achieved, the result was a restoration of an economy driven by scarcity. And, with it, the social arrangements and ideas that pointed to economic growth as the societal priority were reaffirmed. Investors restored their profit expectations, while the general population smoothly integrated into the labour market and accessed a consumer basket that (now) had reasons to consider superior to the previous one. The wheel could continue to turn indefinitely as long as the threatening bottleneck of consumer satiation was removed. Even other socio-economic concerns, such as inequality and security, seemed to be well addressed by the ripple effect of each new cycle of growth.

But how good was the direction in which the affluent society was heading? For Galbraith, it was by no means the best possible direction: rather, it was a great opportunity wasted. Affluence should have served to diminish the importance of economic objectives in people's lives and, by extension, in the social and political life of the community. However, the affluent society clung an economy driven by scarcity, so that once certain consumer objectives were achieved, it shifted to pursue new ones. Now, how valuable were these new objectives? Galbraith (1958, pp. 382–383) questioned whether each new wave of consumer society was necessarily progress:

> To furnish a barren room is one thing. To continue to crowd in furniture until the foundation buckles is quite another. To have failed to solve the problem of producing goods would have been to continue man (*sic*) in his oldest and most grievous misfortune. But to fail to see that we have solved it and fail to proceed hence to the next task would be fully as tragic.

In other words, nothing guaranteed that the new demands induced by the business community would align well with the new challenges facing the affluent society. Before affluence, it was more plausible that the functioning of the economic system, oriented towards meeting fundamental needs, would contribute to solving important social problems. Now, however, each new turn of the wheel could lead entrepreneurs, workers, and consumers to coordinate around secondary, irrelevant, or even pernicious objectives.

But what then would be the "next task"? The conclusion of Galbraith's argument was that the affluent society needed active public policies to provide those public goods and services that, by their very nature, would not be supplied by the business community in the market (or at least not in sufficient quantities). If powerful business structures were to promote all sorts of new and more refined needs among consumers, the state should not lag behind: it should (for example) make substantial investments in areas such as education, healthcare, and environmental protection. Otherwise, the vested interests in the sphere of production, combined with the dominant ideas about the centrality of economic growth as a social and political objective, could dismantle the necessary balance between the private and public sectors. The state needed to capture fiscal resources from those activities of "furniture crowding-in" and inject them into the provision of public goods that addressed the "next task" on the path towards a better society.

The line of argument in *The Affluent Society* was clearly integrated into the core of Galbraith's thought. Some of his ideas had begun to be explored long before. This was the case with his interest in making consumer preferences endogenous, a topic he had addressed in the 1930s, or his mistrust of the market's ability to allocate resources to the most important social goals, which he had elaborated while participating in price administration during the Second World War. Nine years after *The Affluent Society*, with *The New Industrial State*, Galbraith (1967) would attempt (in his own words) to complete the house that *The Affluent Society* had constituted a window to, emphasising the importance of business planning within American capitalism and the links between business power and political power. Regarding the world of consumption, *The New Industrial State* gave him the opportunity to elaborate more thoroughly on the social formation of preferences, stressing (among other aspects) that the materialistic values of business elites could filter down the social ladder to promote mass consumption patterns. Later, Galbraith (1983) ventured into what he considered a general theory of power, in which, along with more explicit forms of it, he assigned a significant role to "conditional power", or the power of persuasion, which in his work had been illustrated by the influence of business advertising on consumer orientations. In other words, it was not just that Galbraith produced with *The Affluent Society* the first in-depth economic examination of consumer society, but that the subject never strayed far from the centre of his expansive intellectual project (Chirat, 2021, pp. 257–348).

Often, and not without reason, Galbraith is presented as a successor to Veblen. After all, Galbraith, with his interest in the organisation of firms and the social influences on individual economic behaviour, was continuing the institutionalist tradition that had dominated American economics during the first decades of the twentieth century. Also, he had extensively developed Veblen's intuition that the evolution of consumer society was "blind" and could lead to unfortunate pathologies. And his use of common language was as devilishly cunning as that which had been characteristic of his predecessor. Galbraith himself did not hesitate to highlight the distance between him and the central tradition of economic thought, which in his view originated from the classics.

None of this, however, is incompatible with viewing Galbraith as a successor to Mill, Marshall, and Keynes in the search for a "synthesis view". More clearly than Veblen, Galbraith began by making room for the progress thesis and only then introduced the deviation thesis. The structure of his argument, particularly well synthesised in the earlier quoted passage about furnishing the room, aligned with Hirschman's idea that each thesis could have a province, in this case temporal, where it could be correct. As in Mill, Marshall, or Keynes, Galbraith proposed a first phase of progress, in which more and better consumption allowed for the overcoming of scarcity, and a second phase of deviation, in which continuing along that path diverted individuals and society from more urgent goals.

The differences between Galbraith's institutionalist school and the schools represented by each of the other three authors (classical political economy, neoclassical economics, and Keynesianism) were evident, but they did not obstruct the pathway to a synthesis view. The key was not so much in economic theory, but in the perception that "pure economics" should be complemented by elements of sociology and philosophy. Like Mill, Marshall, or Keynes, Galbraith mobilised an economic sociology in which individual consumer behaviour was rooted in social positions and interactions. He also mobilised an economic philosophy that understood human well-being as a multidimensional variable, in which there could be both synergies and blockages between the various dimensions. In other words, Galbraith recreated the substratum from which the synthesis view had been emerging in previous periods, bringing it to a superior level of systematisation and centrality.

Other Routes to Deviation

Galbraith was part of a chorus of voices that warned the American public that consumer society was maybe leading them away from genuine progress (Horowitz, 2004). Sociologist David Riesman (1950, 1964) portrayed with concern a "lonely crowd" and asked: "Abundance, for what?" Journalist Vance Packard (1957) denounced that American economic and social life was manipulated by "hidden persuaders", working in marketing and advertising departments, making consumers buy things they did not really need. And, above all, there were the philosophers of the so-called Frankfurt School. Erich Fromm (1955, 1976) proposed a synthesis of Marx's philosophy and Sigmund Freud's psychology to argue that materialism and consumerism were undermining people's capacity to practise "the art of loving" and to unleash their human potential, moving away from the ideal of a "sane society". Herbert Marcuse (1964), for his part, argued that advanced industrial society created false needs among the working class in order to consolidate their submission and alienation within contemporary capitalism. In a way, Marcuse turned around the confidence that Adam Smith and the young Marshall had placed in the idea that material progress would bring additional advantages for personal ethics and civic life. Rather, Marcuse saw consumer society not only as a dubious path towards personal well-being but, more broadly, as an obstacle to the awakening of revolutionary consciousness and the collective search for a better world.

All these authors, like Galbraith, were born around the turn of the century, and during the post-war decades they became mass-market editorial phenomena with their critiques of consumerism. This chorus of critical voices had a significant influence on the intellectual life of the West, and some of them, particularly Marcuse, ended up being influential on the so-called countercultural movement of the 1960s. If, at the beginning of the decade, novelist Richard Yates had condemned the conformism of the 1950s and the end of what once had been America's *Revolutionary Road*, by the end of the decade anyone watching Dennis Hopper and his bikers in *Easy Rider* could hardly avoid the feeling that, at least for some, the revolutionary road remained open. The counterculture was, among other things, a protest against the replacement of the individual by a "mass-man" who dedicated his existence to working in a monotonous job devoid of deep meaning, to secure a consumer basket full of superfluous goods. Galbraith, Marcuse, and the other critics of consumerism contributed to this cultural transformation and, as it began to gain ground, they undoubtedly benefited from it, having the opportunity to reach a broader and more receptive audience for their books than would have been the case under other circumstances.

Galbraith was not the only economist who felt compelled by these changes associated with the triumph of consumer society. The most distinguished Marxist economists of the time, Paul Baran and Paul Sweezy, had significant differences with Galbraith in their analysis of American capitalism and their political discourse, but their *Monopoly Capitalism* seemed to incorporate important elements of Galbraith's thought without major tensions. The influence also went the other way, as Galbraith acknowledged the influence of Sweezy in the development of some of his ideas. The starting point for Baran and Sweezy was that the historical stage of competitive capitalism, based on small price-taking firms, had been left behind. Advanced economies had entered an era of monopolistic capitalism dominated by large firms capable of exerting power in the market and outside of it. Within this framework, Baran and Sweezy did not hesitate to label the enormous spending on advertising associated with consumer society as a vast waste of resources. Instead of allocating these resources to improving people's material lives, consumer society squandered them by feeding a gigantic machinery of consumer persuasion and manipulation (Baran & Sweezy, 1966, pp. 93–115).

If, as Baran had emphasised for some time, the key to economic dynamics was how societies made use of their surplus, it was hard not to see here a dimension in which consumer society was entailing a deviation rather than progress:

> [Our] society is very much richer now than at any previous time. Productivity and per capita output and income are much higher than ever before; and the gap between what is and what *could* be has never been so glaring as it is now [...] [Monopolistic] capitalism, for all the productivity and wealth which it has generated, has utterly failed to provide the foundations of a society capable of promoting the healthy and happy development of its members. (Baran & Sweezy, 1966, pp. 226–227)

Similar to Veblen's consumers, Baran and Sweezy's consumers placed their hopes of social recognition in the possession of material goods. However, in the absence of moral codes adapted to the conditions of abundance characteristic of monopoly capitalism, this led them into a spiral of dissatisfaction and inner emptiness (Baran & Sweezy, 1966, pp. 273–279).

The questioning of consumer society was seamlessly integrated into the thinking of various groups of heterodox economists that began to emerge in the United States during the 1960s and 1970s. The deviation thesis floated in the intellectual atmosphere of a new generation of institutional economists organised in the newly established Association for Evolutionary Economics, as well as in the neo-Marxist economists grouped in the Union for Radical Political Economics and the reformist economists of the post-Keynesian school. Through their respective leaders, each of these groups maintained cordial relationships with Galbraith and contributed to reinforcing the argument that American consumer society had ceased to be progressive (Chirat, 2021). This was an argument also present in the popular writings of heterodox "maverick" economists like E. F. Schumacher (1973).

However, and as had occurred during the early part of the twentieth century, it was not necessary to be a heterodox economist to find value in the deviation thesis and mobilise it within some kind of "synthesis view". The deviation thesis also emerged among some economists who, rather than being heterodox, were dissidents. By this we mean that they were internal, rather than external, to the mainstream. Some, like E. J. Mishan (1967), followed in Pigou's footsteps and argued that economic growth entailed serious social costs. For Mishan, the premise of growth was discontent: the identification by consumers of unmet needs. Hence, very similarly to Galbraith's world, there was a structural tendency towards the generation of discontent by means of corporate advertising. The end point was not any utopia, but a "waste land of Subtopia" in which the cycle of discontent-production-consumption was repeated over and over again. Along the way, Mishan continued, worrying environmental impacts were generated.

In a somewhat different way, Fred Hirsch's work also conveyed the sense of a deviated consumer society. For Hirsch (1976), many of the goods that consumers coveted were actually "positional goods": desired less for their intrinsic characteristics than (as in Veblen) for their ability to signal status. Consequently, when consumer society degenerated into a race for the acquisition of positional goods, it deviated from its promise of improving people's lives. Only a few would ultimately manage to access the coveted positional goods, while the rest would remain dissatisfied, no matter how larger their basket of non-positional goods had become. An additional problem of consumer society, according to Hirsch, was that the increasing commodification of economic life led to a deterioration in the quality of certain goods and services, especially those traditionally consumed for free through participation in family and cultural groups.

The deviation thesis also emerged among other economists whose dissidence consisted of getting closer to psychologists. As we saw, the neoclassical version of the progress thesis had largely hinged on a subjective notion of utility that did not seem to be subject to empirical verification. Psychology, however, could be concerned with measuring the mental states of individuals, and by the post-war decades this approach had reached a significant level of maturity (Hands, 2010). Thus, psychology offered a way to study phenomena such as consumer satisfaction and dissatisfaction. If there was something akin to the pleasure-pain axis of utilitarianism, psychology could claim it as one of its objects of study. In a sense, psychology could be seen as another one of those "techniques" whose mastery, according to Schumpeter, distinguished the professional economist from other commentators of economic life. For the debate on consumer society, the interest of some economists in incorporating elements of psychology into their analysis led to the same outcome than had previously been the case with sociology or philosophy: it fertilised the ground for the emergence of the deviation thesis.

The economist who contributed the most to this was Tibor Scitovsky. In the mid-1940s, Scitovsky had participated alongside Galbraith in the US government's inquiry about the effects of strategic bombing on the German economy. It is likely that, just as in Galbraith's case, this first-hand contact with societies marked by scarcity helped shape his later perception that there were fundamental qualitative differences between such societies and mass consumer societies. In fact, Scitovsky viewed Galbraith's works positively and concluded from them that, for consumer sovereignty to be operational, state intervention was necessary (Chirat, 2021, pp. 349–389). However, Scitovsky was not particularly interested in the way Galbraith had constructed his argument. Rather than relying on "techniques" (in Schumpeter's sense) like sociology and philosophy, Scitovsky (1976) relied on psychology. Beyond the influence that someone like Erich Fromm had on his thought (Di Giovinazzo, 2019), what Scitovsky found most interesting about psychology was the promise of a path to go beyond the assumptions incorporated into the notion of the sovereign consumer and study how real-world consumers actually behaved.

For Scitovsky, consumer psychology was governed not by a unidimensional axis of pleasure and pain, but rather by a tension between two distinct axes: comfort and stimulation. It was not necessary for large companies to induce needs through advertising for individuals to yearn for a continuous renewal of their consumption patterns. Economic progress led to greater comfort, which was good because it meant freedom from basic deprivations, but over time this comfort led to boredom and a search for new stimuli. Hence, the reproduction of consumer society was closely tied to consumer dissatisfaction, which for Scitovsky had more psychological than sociological roots. Dissatisfaction was the premise of each new round of demand for consumer goods. The result was an increasing demand for short-term stimulation, which, in Scitovsky's view, displaced the demand for other pleasures and consumptions with greater potential to sustain well-being over time. One of his examples was the enjoyment of classical music, which required the uninitiated to overcome a threshold of discomfort in order to gradually acquire the necessary skills. Consumer society, on the other hand, led to a loop in which most individuals lacked the capabilities to enjoy this type of consumption, so they ended up seeking short-term gratification.

This quickly led back to boredom, dissatisfaction, and, since better consumption skills were not developed, a bias for short-term gratification. "It is strange", concluded Scitovsky (1976, pp. 227–228), "that in our society, where people work so hard and do so for income and not for fun, we are so negligent in spending that income". While the bulk of the book cultivated the deviation thesis from the perspective of this negligence, Scitovsky (1976, p. 297) concluded by suggesting a complementary perspective: consumer society had a substantial environmental impact and the outlook of its international spread was in that sense a reason for concern. This would become a central theme in the versions of the deviation thesis produced by future generations.

Scitovsky's argument was grounded in sophisticated psychological research, but the interest of some dissenting economists in empirical measurements of satisfaction could take place through simpler conceptual routes. The most influential of these was, without a doubt, the one opened by Richard Easterlin in 1974. In a modest chapter within a multi-author book, Easterlin (1974) questioned whether economic growth led to higher levels of happiness. In the United States, higher-income social groups did tend to describe themselves as happier than those with lower income, which was certainly in line with the progress thesis. As in the neoclassical and Austrian discourse of the interwar period, consumers knew what they were doing and used their income to purchase goods that made their lives better. However, and here lay the surprise, Americans' happiness had remained stable over time. This was intriguing: how could the postwar economic boom and the formation of a mass consumer society have had such an insignificant impact on the reported well-being of individuals? This posed what would eventually come to be called the Easterlin paradox.

Like Scitovsky, Easterlin was not relying on the kind of economic sociology or philosophy that Robbins and Mises had considered inappropriate for a true economist. In particular, he was by no means relying on any ethical argument about the multidimensional nature of the good life. His was an empirical argument about exactly the same kind of subjective well-being on which the entire neoclassical edifice of utility, consumption, and demand was based. But this edifice had been built upon a notion of utility that was not empirically observable: it was, rather, an a priori deduction. For a long time, this deduction had seemed common-sensical, but now it was possible to try to approach utility empirically by asking people about their level of life satisfaction or happiness. Consequently, there was no longer any reason to favour the progress thesis. For reasons that were unclear at the time of Easterlin's seminal work, the equilibrium points towards which consumers were heading had surprisingly difficult-to-anticipate consequences: they could increase their happiness, but they might also not do so.

In summary, although Galbraith was the earliest and most prominent voice among economists who suspected that there were elements of deviation in post-war consumer society, he was far from being the only one. In various forms, the deviation thesis also emerged among other heterodox economists, especially Marxists, and dissidents. However, the deviation thesis would encounter far more trouble at gaining acceptance among mainstream economists.

Milton Friedman's Pencil Rules

Although Galbraith achieved significant success among the non-academic public with his institutionalist approach to consumer society, most economists interested in consumption were affiliated with the neoclassical school. As such, they focused their efforts on developing the marginalist theory of utility and demand, the core of which had become remarkably stable (Mirowski & Hands, 1998, 2006). The key task was to produce extensions: to make the theory applicable to a wider range of situations as well as to a greater number of empirical fields. As an advanced textbook from the final period of this era admirably clarified, the neoclassical theory had been based on assumptions that, while simple, useful, and reasonable, did not necessarily hold in all circumstances (Deaton & Muellbauer, 1980). For example, why assume that the budget constraint under which consumers maximised their utility was linear? Why assume that the indifference curves representing the consumer's subjective utility map should have a concave shape? The challenge lay in modelling less conventional assumptions and deducing the new equilibrium points that would emerge from them. Mathematical formalisation was almost intrinsic to these attempts to extend the neoclassical theory of utility and demand. In the same spirit, it was also possible to extend the theory to new empirical domains. Beyond the consumption of goods as such, the logic of utility maximisation could be applied to the study of marriage, justice, or electoral behaviour, to name just a few examples.

Nothing prevented some of these extensions from recycling institutionalist intuitions in neoclassical language. James Duesenberry (1949), for instance, designed a model in which the demand curve for certain goods could have a positive slope: the higher the price, the higher the demand for these goods. This assumption directly contradicted the usual neoclassical scenario, where the demand for a good decreased as its price increased. But what if consumers used certain goods to signal status? In that case, an increase in the price of these goods could make them more reliable status markers and, consequently, stimulate (rather than reduce) demand for them. Duesenberry aptly termed these goods "Veblen goods".

Along the way, Duesenberry was also anticipating what would become the main conceptual direction of neoclassical consumption theory during the post-war decades: the treatment of consumption as an activity of utility production by consumers (Becker, 1965). As Kelvin Lancaster (1971) would systematise, the end towards which consumers directed their efforts was not the goods themselves, but the utility derived from their various characteristics. There was no single translation of consumption into subjective utility; in fact, each good promised to contribute to that utility from different angles. A Veblen good could be useful in itself, but also as a marker of status. Consequently, the optimisation programme attributed to the neoclassical consumer was more complex than had previously been thought. Just as an entrepreneur had to choose from a range of possible technical combinations of production factors, the consumer chose between a range of possible consumer baskets. And, just as inputs ended up being transformed into outputs, consumer goods were transformed into utility. The neoclassical consumer thus came to be equated with the producer of a peculiar but notable commodity: utility.

None of this, in itself, was particularly damaging to the prospects of accepting the debate that Galbraith was proposing about the affluent society. Even in the most influential textbook of the post-war decades, that of Paul Samuelson, there was room for the marginalist consumer, with their stable preferences and full rationality, to coexist with a more unpredictable consumer, somewhat vulnerable to the seduction of advertising (Olsen, 2019, pp. 144–153). In fact, on this basis welfare economics was ready to identify all sorts of "negative externalities" in consumption patterns. By extension, there would be those who made this kind of Pigouvian reading of Galbraith, not to mention internal dissidents like Mishan, Hirsch, or Scitovsky. In other words, while the marginalist framework had brought neoclassical thought closer to the progress thesis, the neoclassical subfield of welfare economics created more room to consider the possibility of deviation.

The necessary leap for this to occur, of course, involved crossing one of the red lines drawn by Robbins and the Austrian tradition: incorporating elements of philosophy, particularly ethical theory, into economic analysis. Yet, this became an increasingly contentious matter as the proportion of economists willing to accept the initial Pigouvian framework decreased. It is interesting to note that, as late as 1946, some of the leading mainstream economists in the United States (including, once again, Samuelson) had called for wartime price controls to be extended into the post-war period, based on a distinction between "important" and "unimportant" commodities that aligned much more with the spirit of a Marshall than with that of a Mises (Weber, 2021, p. 57). But as the sense of wartime exceptionalism receded, suspicions arose that the social utilities that were being used to define externalities were even less observable than private utilities. Therefore, they were dangerously sensitive to the ethical preferences of the researcher. Even those, like Samuelson, who acknowledged that ethics was destined to play a role in welfare economics, tended to feel more comfortable with ethical propositions that could be considered so universally accepted that they might almost be regarded as ethically neutral (Backhouse, 2021).

It was also unclear whether this was a sound basis for correcting alleged externalities. Kenneth Arrow (1951) presented an influential mathematical model aimed at demonstrating the serious operational difficulties inherent in the type of social choice that had hovered over analysis since Pigou. Later, Ronald Coase (1960) revolutionised the economic analysis of externalities by proposing that market mechanisms, when properly redesigned, could generate a spontaneous order capable of aligning selfish individual behaviour with the general interest. In retrospect, historians have seen this as the beginning of the end for the type of welfare economics championed by Pigou, which, in fact, had never managed to establish a truly solid tradition (Medema, 2020). Neoclassical economists continued to be interested in "market failures", but they felt that their measurement and correction had to rely on technical instruments rather than on subjective ethical appraisals.

If the space for economic philosophy was contracting, what about economic sociology? Adhering faithfully to the separation established by Robbins (1932, p. 118) between economic science and the "sociological penumbra", an increasing number of economists understood that their work was not to explore the origin of consumer preferences. The influence of social and cultural structures on individual consumer behaviour was definitively removed from focus. For sociologists, preferences might be a variable, but for economists they were a datum. This relegated a significant part of the terrain where the deviation thesis had emerged, both among institutionalists such as Veblen and Galbraith and among classical economists like Mill, early neoclassicals like Marshall, and Keynes. Once preferences were downgraded to the status of an exogenous datum, the way was clear to view consumer society as a progressive succession of equilibrium points in which consumers maximised their utility.

There was a major exception to these theoretical trends. Yet, it developed within the same epistemological framework and in no way was mobilised to support the deviation thesis. This was the proposal by George Stigler and Gary Becker that preferences be considered endogenous variables rather than exogenous data. For Stigler and Becker (1977), it was not necessary to resort to sociology to explain preferences: it could be done within what Schumpeter would have called "pure economics". The key was to recognise that the consumption of any good depended on the extent to which the consumer had access to resources that enhanced the expected utility of that good. Many habits, for example, could be modelled simply in terms of a function where the present consumption of a good was a direct function of its past consumption. This was an ingenious way for economists to begin to unpack the "black box" of preferences without betraying the division established by Robbins; that is, without turning into practitioners of a discipline, like sociology, that neoclassical economists tended to see as much less rigorous from a scientific perspective.

In the process, the implications for the increasingly intense association of neoclassical economics with the progress thesis were potentially devastating. Not for nothing had Stigler and Becker begun with examples like that of drug addicts, offering formal models portraying addiction as rational behaviour on the part of individuals whose expected utility maps were vastly different from those of people who had not had stimulating experiences with drug consumption. If preferences became endogenous, even without recourse to a sociology of consumption and without explicit support from a multidimensional philosophy of well-being, the deviation thesis could re-emerge within neoclassical soil. The initial influence of the new approach proposed by Stigler and Becker, however, was modest. If anything, their neoclassical readers tended to view it as just another extension of the many that had blossomed in the theory of utility and demand during the post-war decades: a new dose of ingenuity that was injected into the protective belt of the paradigm and did not have any major consequences on its hard core.

It was precisely by gravitating around that hard core, which was ultimately allowing its access to a position of hegemony within academia, that neoclassical economists rejected the deviation thesis. This became evident in the hostility with which they received Galbraith's work. Mainstream economists could ignore someone like Marcuse, who, after all, was a philosopher engaged in a different conversation. But Galbraith was different because he presented himself as an economist and not just any economist. He was a professor of economics at one of the most prestigious universities in the world and, by 1972, had even served as elected president of the American Economic Association. His public profile was very high due to his regular collaboration with the Democratic Party, both in technical roles and in more overtly political ones (for instance, his service as ambassador to India during John F. Kennedy's presidency). And, to top it off, he was extremely popular among the non-academic public, who had turned books like *The Affluent Society* or *The New Industrial State* into genuine bestsellers. It was impossible to ignore Galbraith: most economists could not help but feel challenged by the notable distance between Galbraith's world, with his extraordinary popular success, and the neoclassical conversation that the profession was involved in. In a way, Galbraith had short-circuited the conventional channels of economic conversation, favouring books on broad topics written for the general public over specialised articles in journals dedicated exclusively to other academics (Chirat, 2021). From the neoclassical perspective, it was time to fix the short circuit.

Few texts encapsulate the virulence of the neoclassical response as well as the review that Robert Solow (1967) wrote about *The New Industrial State*. First and foremost, the short circuit was presented as proof that, at its core, Galbraith's work lacked scientific rigour. Galbraith's book was deemed "for the dinner table, not for the desk". Economists, according to

Solow (1967, p. 101), were "determined little thinkers" concerned with practical, concrete problems, not with grand exercises in "Whither We Are Trending". From this perspective, Galbraith was portrayed more as a successful populariser than as a rigorous scientist. The problem, of course, was that to neoclassical economists, the science Galbraith popularised had little to do with the actual science practised in academia: neither in its theoretical framework, its methodological approach, nor in its conclusions (Chirat, 2021, pp. 719–776).

Like other mainstream economists of the time, Solow questioned the empirical support for Galbraith's theses. When it came to the world of consumption, did large corporations really have as much power to shape consumer preferences as Galbraith suggested? Solow was sceptical. He thought that Galbraith had provided no proof that advertising effectively altered consumer behaviour and, so to speak, greased the wheels of consumer society. It would soon become a standard part of the neoclassical response to cite examples of business ideas that failed because they could not seduce consumers. The most famous of these became the ill-fated Edsel car launched by Ford in the late 1950s (e.g. Tobin, 1974, p. 1297). The market economy continued to be governed by sovereign, autonomous, and unpredictable consumers, far more so than Galbraith claimed. The empirical conclusion was that Galbraith had mistaken the part for the whole, offering a distorted image of the dynamics of capitalism and consumer society.

Consumer sovereignty was defended not only as an explanation of the market order but also as a political doctrine. By criticising the notion of a sovereign consumer, Galbraith had crossed a red line that most economists were unwilling to cross. Solow (1967, pp. 100 and 107) portrayed him as a member of the upper class who criticised the pleasures of ordinary people from his chalet in Gstaad. "His attitude toward ordinary consumption", Solow (1967, p. 108) continued, "reminds one of the Duchess who, upon acquiring a full appreciation of sex, asked the Duke if it were not perhaps too good for the common people". It was essential to respect the preferences and tastes of consumers, avoiding value judgements about them. In a geopolitical era marked by the Cold War, the ideas of Mises and Hayek, who argued that it was better to live in a system governed by a multitude of free consumers rather than under the authoritarian principles of a minority (whether political or intellectual), had firmly taken root among neoclassical economists (Olsen, 2019, pp. 158–161).

Hayek himself did not hesitate to deny Galbraith the status of economist, calling him a "moral entrepreneur" (Chirat, 2021, p. 563). However, if there was one economist who brought together these various dimensions and ultimately achieved a prominent status as a public intellectual opposed to Galbraith, it was Milton Friedman. Friedman was only four years younger than Galbraith, and on the surface, their life trajectories had several points in common. Friedman had also witnessed the outbreak of the Great Depression in the midst of his transition to adulthood. He had also started his career as an economist working for the Roosevelt administration. However, his economic and political ideas were diametrically opposed to Galbraith's. Friedman was an enthusiastic supporter of free markets, as well as a sharp critic of state intervention in economic life. The range of topics in which Friedman deployed this vision was formidable, covering everything from monetary policy and consumption theory to the management of education and national infrastructure. Unlike Galbraith, Friedman was not on the Democratic side of the US bipartisan system, but rather in the Republican Party. And within this, he aligned with a libertarian wing that was uncomfortable with many of the public interventions that the party did tend to support. In this sense, he was a consistent follower of the tradition represented by Mises and Hayek: a vigorous defence of economic liberalism as a key component of political liberalism (Friedman, 1962). In fact, he would share membership with both as a prominent member of the Mont Pelerin Society that Hayek had founded in 1947 to promote the values of free markets and open societies. From this perspective, Friedman clashed not only with Galbraith, but also with a substantial fraction of the neoclassical establishment that was receptive to Keynes' message (Burns, 2023; Wapshott, 2021).

The gap between Friedman and Galbraith was not just political: it was also professional. In a very influential way, Friedman (1953) had argued that value judgements were a dangerous companion for a good economist. He added that the key issue was not building models based on realistic assumptions but creating models capable of predicting the future reliably. This was, obviously, a conception of economics as a discipline very different from Galbraith's. For Friedman it made little sense to see Galbraith "as a scientist seeking explanations". He was rather "a missionary seeking converts" (Friedman, 1977, p. 30).

Building on these foundations, Friedman (1977) became the antithesis of Galbraith. His theory of consumption not only challenged the Keynesian notion of the propensity to consume, as is often noted: it also represented a substantial departure from those theories—such as those advanced by authors like Duesenberry—that had pointed towards some sort of neoclassical synthesis incorporating institutionalist insights into the social significance of consumption (Trezzini, 2012). The key lay in emphasising the importance of so-called permanent income: since household income fluctuated throughout different stages of people's life cycles, consumers tended to adopt behaviour that smoothed the impact of those fluctuations (Friedman, 1957). Consumer preferences could remain in a "black box". After all, what truly improved the predictive power of economic models was taking into account variables like permanent income and the life cycle. Understanding why consumers wanted what they wanted was a task burdened by the worst possible affliction in Friedman's world of methodological instrumentalism: it was useless.

Even worse, and inappropriate, was to judge consumer behaviour from paternalistic premises. "Denigrating the tastes of ordinary people" had been *The Affluent Society*'s main theme to Friedman's (1977, p. 14) eyes. But economists and politicians had to respect the freedom of consumer choice. The so-called crisis of consumer society, where profit-driven entrepreneurs allegedly stimulated false values in consumers, was just another of the many "collectivist fallacies" that legitimised ever-increasing state intervention in economic life (Friedman, 1994, p. 354). The only legitimate state intervention in the realm of consumption consisted in providing consumers with the best available information so that they could then make their sovereign decisions (Friedman & Friedman, 1979, pp. 313–315).

Friedman immortalised the mainstream view for the general public when in 1980 he recorded his television series *Free to Choose* (Friedman, 1980). It may be worth mentioning that the series seemed to have originated in part from the desire of some factions within the conservative spectrum to offer viewers a response to the arguments put forth by Galbraith, who had recorded his own series a few years prior (Chirat, 2021, pp. 851–853). In one of the most famous moments of the series, Friedman picked up a pencil and used it to show viewers that the market economy could be seen as an effective mechanism for cooperation between economic agents. In response to consumers' desire to own a pencil, a whole production chain was activated, comprising various links located in different parts of the world. The people occupying these spaces in the production chain rarely needed to relate to each other; in fact, they did not even have to know each other personally or live in the same country. The end result was that sovereign consumers were sending signals that prompted producers to manufacture what they wanted. The economy operated from the bottom up: from consumers to the various production activities that were organised to meet their demands.

In Friedman's pencil story, based on "I, Pencil" by Leonard Read, there was no trace of the economy functioning from the top down, in the manner Galbraith had described—that is, from companies trying to induce new needs in consumers and then preparing to meet those needs. Preferences remained in the black box, and value judgements were unnecessary. In the text on the subject that Friedman prepared for his book *Free to Choose*, the reader's attention is swiftly diverted from the issue: "Suppose that, *for whatever reason*, there is an increased demand for lead pencils" (Friedman & Friedman, 1979, p. 32; emphasis added). This uncertain point of departure, barely illustrated with the assumption of a baby boom increasing school enrolment, is never revisited thereafter. In fact, by using a simple good whose consumption was strongly associated with instrumental motivations, Friedman avoided any commodities that might be most associated with Veblen's conspicuous consumption. In one stroke, the pencil allowed Friedman to sidestep the question of why consumers wanted what they wanted and whether the result could be considered a vector of social progress. Consumers must have wanted the pencil to write something important to them, and it was clearly positive that they could finally do so.

After years of academic criticism of Galbraith's theses, mainstream economics had established an effective platform to counterattack in the territory traditionally dominated by him: communication with the general public (Burgin, 2012, 2013). By then, however, the context had changed substantially from that of the post-war decades, both in the real world and in academia. And this was going to have a significant impact on the conversation economists seemed to have started about consumer society.

Eclipse of a Vision

The bestsellers of Galbraith, Marcuse, and other researchers who mobilised some version of the deviation thesis were all published during the post-war "golden age". Never had Western economic growth been so rapid, and never again would it be. In the late 1960s, the international monetary order established at the Bretton Woods Conference started to break down, as the dollar became weaker and its convertibility into gold was cancelled. Later, in 1973 and 1979, geopolitical tensions in the Middle

East led to two unexpected surges in oil prices, sparking an inflationary spiral that quickly combined with rising unemployment rates to create an unprecedented dynamic of "stagflation". Beneath these short-term turbulences, a longer-term structural adjustment was taking place: the exhaustion of the Fordist path of technological and corporate change that had characterised economic growth after the Second World War (Freeman & Louçã, 2001; Frieden, 2006).

Contemporaries were not fully aware of how exceptional the post-war boom had been and mistakenly took it as a new normal. The work of economic historians like Paul Bairoch (1993) would later debunk the myth that the Industrial Revolution of the eighteenth and nineteenth centuries had been a period of accelerated economic growth comparable to that of the post-war decades. Viewed in this light, the growth slowdown that began to manifest in 1973 was not at all a disaster. Although Western economies would never again reach the growth rates of the "golden age", they would continue to experience rates generally higher than those typical of the nineteenth century or the first part of the twentieth. But political debates and public opinion perceived the crisis as a terrible pathology that had brought an end to the (alleged) macroeconomic normality of the post-war decades. It should also be noted that the macroeconomic turbulences were triggering an unexpected social crisis. Through the labour market channel, the impact of the slowdown in growth was concentrated in the middle and lower classes, particularly among unskilled manual workers in the now-declining industrial sector (Brenner, 2006; Hobsbawm, 1994).

The economic conversation was drastically changed. The expansive post-war decades, especially the 1960s, had provided a fertile context for some voices to suggest that perhaps there was a misguided cult of economic growth. International institutions like the OECD responded to this intellectual climate by developing a new set of social indicators to better capture the quality of life of individuals than could a macroeconomic aggregate like GDP per capita. The conversation was so lively that by 1972, two respected economists, William Nordhaus and James Tobin, felt compelled to ask, "Is Growth Obsolete?" Nordhaus and Tobin (1972) did not believe it was, and they understood that much of the scepticism surrounding macroeconomic progress was unfounded. However, the title and structure of their paper clearly signalled how vibrant the conversation on the topic had become in the years leading up to the oil shock. The 1970s shocks, the macroeconomic slowdown, and the social crisis firmly re-established what Mathias Schmelzer (2016) calls the "hegemony of growth". Reviving growth became the primary objective of economic policy. It was understood that this was a prerequisite for reducing unemployment and overcoming the social cohesion problems that were emerging. The concerns of the "golden age" about affluence were quickly sidelined, if not condemned as the pretentious luxury of a few intellectuals from a bygone time. The OECD, to revisit its case, did not entirely abandon its interest in social indicators but decisively shifted towards an agenda centred on promoting growth through the liberalisation and internationalisation of economies.

This, of course, aligned with a fundamental shift in the political economy of the period: the transition to a neoliberal policy paradigm, which, with great electoral success during the 1980s, placed its hopes for reactivating growth in deregulation and free markets (Gerstle, 2022). It is symbolic that Ronald Reagan, poised to become one of the leaders of this turn, was already by the late 1970s among the voices criticising Galbraith's economic thought as elitist and simplistic (Chirat, 2021, p. 854).

The fall of the Berlin Wall also helped to create an intellectual atmosphere in the West much less anxious about the potential problems of consumer society. It was a fact that, even at its best, Soviet economic growth had relied on the systematic sacrifice of household consumption. By the 1980s, with this growth model deep in structural crisis, the mediocrity of the Soviet world of consumption contributed to the weakening of the regime's social legitimacy and, eventually, to its collapse. To Western eyes, the images of Soviet consumers waiting in long, arduous lines for a modest basket of low-quality, limited goods could only underscore the superiority of capitalism and consumer society. In fact, by the time the Berlin Wall fell, it was already evident that Western capitalism had shown a remarkable ability to absorb the type of countercultural criticism that had erupted in 1968. What had been a critique of massification, Fordism, and homogeneity had been mobilised by new business ventures focused on diversification, flexible specialisation, and the fragmentation of consumption styles (Boltanski & Chiapello, 1999; de Grazia, 2005; Piore & Sabel, 1984).

Meanwhile, consumer sovereignty was making significant advances outside its original realm. In part due to autonomous dynamics, and in part because of the way the crisis was eroding the legitimacy of state intervention in economic life, consumer sovereignty became a guiding principle in various plans to reform public administration. Even in Scandinavia, where social democracy had been dominant until then, the notion of the consumer began to occupy spaces that had been traditionally reserved for the notion of the citizen. Emphasis was placed on the idea that the functioning of the *res publica* should revolve around the satisfaction of the consumer, understood as both the user of public services and the voter participating in elections. This was a project originally linked to neoliberalism, but, like many elements of it, it was eventually absorbed by a social democracy undergoing electoral reconstruction (Olsen, 2019, pp. 227–258).

These real-world developments, from the drastic reversal of the macroeconomic and social environment to the political naturalisation of the sovereign consumer, did much to blur the vision (in Schumpeter's sense) of consumer society that underpinned both the progress thesis and (even more) the deviation thesis. This shift was reinforced among economists by additional developments in academia. The hegemony of the neoclassical school was nothing new. As we studied at the beginning of this chapter, it had already become evident in the post-war decades that neither institutionalism nor historicism was as influential as before. It was also clear that genuine Keynesianism had ended up as just another alternative school, regardless of the fact that some of its elements had been recycled into the "neoclassical synthesis". The type of economics advocated by Robbins in 1932 became dominant in the post-war decades. As these decades progressed, the centrality of the neoclassical school was amplified by its success in dominating the academic labour market. Neoclassical standards on what constituted a quality economist began to be imposed much more severely than would have been possible in the pluralist interwar landscape or even in the 1950s. The space for the reproduction of heterodox schools, where (as we have seen) the deviation thesis was more likely to emerge, began to contract rapidly.

The case of Galbraith and Harvard, in fact, offers an eloquent illustration. In the era of *The Affluent Society*, at the end of the 1950s, mainstream economists were engaged in fluid dialogue with Galbraith, as published reviews and private correspondence show. Still at the beginning of the 1960s, someone like Paul Samuelson could address the attendees at his presidential lecture for the American Economic Association to assure them that *The Affluent Society* was part of the economic canon (Chirat, 2021, pp. 19–20). A decade later, during the period of *The New Industrial State*, these bridges had begun to break down. Although a significant proportion of American Economic Association members expressed some level of agreement with Galbraith's ideas, his election as president of the association in 1972 was widely contested. The neoclassical mainstream was also hostile to the alternative associations that had been emerging, such as the evolutionary and "radical" schools. In a telling twist, the same James Duesenberry who had modelled "Veblen goods" in 1949 became, a quarter-century later, the department head warning Harvard PhD students that radical economics was not a legitimate field of study. Meanwhile, the department closed its doors to the professional reproduction of heterodoxy by blocking, against the opinion of (among others) Galbraith, the promotion of one of the most visible leaders of the radical movement, Samuel Bowles. Galbraith himself increasingly became what one empathetic observer could not help but describe as a "dinosaur". He refrained from forming disciples, and the question remains as to what might have happened to them had Galbraith aimed to create a group of followers. By the 1970s, it was becoming evident that future generations would not have the opportunity to take the path that had made him the most popular economist of his time and president of the American Economic Association (Chirat, 2021, pp. 817–860 and 949–957).

New generations of economists, in fact, were being trained within a conception of the profession that allowed them to ignore Galbraith and his agenda in a manner that would have seemed excessive even to the most outspoken critics of a previous generation (Lerner, 1972). This ultimately removed consumer society from the economic conversation. In 1980, two brilliant young economists from the neoclassical tradition, Angus Deaton and John Muellbauer (1980), published a book aptly titled *Economics and Consumer Behavior*. Aimed primarily at an audience of graduate students of economics, the book provided an updated state of the art on neoclassical theories of utility, demand, and consumption. There, on the one hand, was the theoretical core forged during the first half of the twentieth century: a rational consumer with exogenous preferences seeked to maximise the utility derived from their consumer basket within the constraints imposed by their available income and the prices of goods. On the other hand, there was an extensive presentation of the many extensions that neoclassical economists had produced after the Second World War by modelling "non-conventional situations". Moreover, and in line with the increasing formalisation and mathematisation of neoclassical economics in the preceding decades, Deaton and Muellbauer provided thorough explorations of the pros and cons of alternative methods for empirically testing theoretical models.

Consumer society, however, did not appear in Deaton and Muellbauer's field of vision. Where an institutionalist idea could be translated into neoclassical language, such as the modelling Duesenberry had done of the Veblenian emulation effect, the corresponding extension of the basic model was offered without issue. At times, Deaton and Muellbauer even toyed with the idea that some of their models contained so many assumptions breaking with traditional neoclassical premises that they perhaps deserved a different label. However, the debate on consumer society seemed to be non-existent, not even to the extent of re-defining it as a "non-debate". Galbraith's intellectual agenda was absent from the scene, not even to be subjected to the type of criticisms that earlier generations of neoclassical economists had devoted to it in the years prior.

Beneath their numerous theoretical extensions and carefully considered empirical reflections, the work of Deaton and Muellbauer reflects the extent to which Lionel Robbins' ideas on economics and economists had triumphed among the new generations educated after the Second World War. A worthy economist seemed to have little to gain from engaging with history, sociology, or philosophy. The focus was on the behaviour of an abstract individual consumer and their reaching stable equilibrium points, rather than on the dynamics of social change and the identification of distinct structural periods. On the other hand, the society of Deaton and Muellbauer was merely an aggregation of individuals, with no social bonds uniting them. Well-being was defined as a one-dimensional variable along the subjective axis of utility. All of this illustrated how much the respect for consumer sovereignty as a political foundation of market economies—following the footsteps of Mises, Hayek, and later Friedman—had become a standard among mainstream economists.

It is interesting to note that even internal dissidents were having little impact on the mainstream at this stage. Once consumer society had disappeared from the field of vision, Mishan's social costs and Hirsch's positional goods were reduced to theoretical extensions with little presence in the central conversation. When Scitovsky began circulating among colleagues the ideas that would form part of *The Joyless Economy*, the reaction was so "unanimously hostile" that, when the time came to write the book's preface, the author felt the need to assure readers that he had not become an old fool (Scitovsky, 1976, p. 16; see also Di Giovinazzo, 2025). The Easterlin paradox, buried in a low-status publication after having been quickly rejected by the *American Economic Review*, received little attention, and Easterlin himself would later reflect on the tremendous resistance he encountered among his peers when attempting to study subjective well-being and its implications for economics (de Neve, 2021).

And, if this was the situation within the prevailing mainstream, it cannot be said that consumer society continued to occupy an important role in the vision of those heterodox economists who managed to survive as such. In part understandably, these economists largely abandoned critiques of consumerism that, while pertinent during the post-war boom, now seemed less urgent. In an era of unemployment and painful social adjustments, the focus shifted to identifying a new "regime of accumulation" (or a new "social structure of accumulation") and fighting its controversial political correlate: the transition to a neoliberal economic order. The question of consumer society was absent, for instance, from the agenda of one of the most dynamic branches of heterodoxy that emerged in the late 1970s and 1980s: the so-called regulation school. Led by Michel Aglietta (1979) and especially Robert Boyer (1986), this school offered an original synthesis of Marxism, institutionalism, and Keynesianism. For the regulationists, the decline of Fordist production systems and the economic policies associated with them signalled the opening of a new phase in the history of capitalism. Their analysis was imbued with a profound historical sense, even opening doors to the incorporation of some form of economic sociology. In the specific realm of consumption, each phase of capitalist history would correspond with the social diffusion of a certain "consumption norm" to which individuals would converge when (and if) their economic possibilities allowed them to. Interestingly, this matched the transition that some economic sociologists were describing, and historians have explored in depth in retrospect, from a mass consumption society to one that was more diversified and fragmented (de Grazia, 2005; Francks, 2009).

However, there was not much room for the type of economic philosophy that would evaluate these "consumption norms", or their empirical manifestations, in terms of human well-being or social progress. In an era of economic slowdown, social crisis, and neoliberal policies, the capacity of the post-war "regime of accumulation" to enable the diffusion of a Fordist consumer basket among the masses almost inspired nostalgia. The doubts that Galbraith had once raised about whether this "consumption norm" could entail some form of deviation went ignored among this new generation of heterodox economists, just as they were among their mainstream counterparts.

Even heterodox economists from a previous generation were beginning to question whether the type of conversation that Galbraith had initiated in the post-war decades was truly worth pursuing. By the end of our period, Albert Hirschman had become a cult social scientist after a truly idiosyncratic intellectual journey through development economics, social theory, and the history of ideas (Adelman, 2013). During the years when Galbraith's popularity peaked, Hirschman had been his colleague at Harvard, and he had not participated in the hostility with which mainstream economists received Galbraith's work. On the contrary, he had congratulated him on the publication of *The New Industrial State* (Chirat, 2021, p. 729). Hirschman had also aligned himself with Galbraith in the departmental struggles of the early 1970s, and in fact, he ended up leaving Harvard for the more open atmosphere offered by the Institute for Advanced Study at Princeton. From there, Hirschman devoted much of his later efforts to combating the uncritical defence of the free market, the critique of collective action, and the "rhetoric of reaction" that had come to dominate the intellectual and political landscape of the 1980s. Yet, this late-career Hirschman was not sure that consumer society was an object of study as relevant or appropriate as had been assumed on both sides of the post-war clash.

On paper, Hirschman (1977, 1984) had the tools necessary to produce some kind of synthesis between the progress thesis and the deviation thesis. In a manner more akin to a sociologist than to a mainstream economist, his view of individual behaviour did not take preferences as exogenous. In his eyes, Stigler and Becker's attempt to "endogenise" preferences had not fully succeeded because it still left out the value structures that led individuals to behave as they did. Furthermore, the one-dimensional conception of well-being favoured by the mainstream seemed overly restrictive to Hirschman, and, in the end, as tautological as the very notion of interest that had become tied to it. Was it not sensible for the *Contemporary Sociology* journal to ask him to review *The Market Experience*, the book by political scientist Robert Lane? Lane was arguing that the premises of mainstream economics were flawed, in particular the idea that more income led to more well-being. Market society should not be judged by its results in terms of production or material rewards but by its capacity to promote happiness and personal development, areas in which it seemed to perform poorly. At this point, the book was essentially a reformulation of the deviation thesis, supported by a multidimensional philosophy of well-being and an emerging psychology of subjective well-being.

However, Hirschman (1992) was not enthusiastic about Lane's argument that the market ended up deviating people from happiness. It is inevitable to wonder whether Hirschman's review was influenced by the fact that a few years earlier, his *Shifting Involvements* had been the subject of a harsh editorial review by Lane (Adelman, 2013, p. 512). In that very book, Hirschman (1982, p. 28n.) had praised a prior work by Lane in this direction as an "excellent essay", though he had distanced himself from the research programme in which it was embedded. Regardless, Hirschman now began by expressing his doubts about how operational said research programme was. One had to be cautious when focusing on explanatory variables that, by their very nature, were subject to cognitive biases that were difficult to correct. These biases could lead people, including the very researchers studying subjective well-being, to cling to opinions and arguments that confirmed themselves within a cognitive framework that excluded the possibility of refutation. At that point, "one almost wonders whether it might not be advisable to go along with the naïve economist": subscribing to the concept of revealed preference and "[leaving] matters at that" (Hirschman, 1992, p. 743).

But, even more strikingly, Hirschman ended up suggesting that market society might be intrinsically tied to democracy. In this case, beyond its impact on the subjective well-being declared by individuals, consumer society would be making a first-order instrumental contribution to their objective well-being: promoting the consolidation of a political order based on pluralism, deliberation, and respect for civil liberties. In a manner that surely made his followers raise their eyebrows and wait for a characteristic twist in the argumentation, Hirschman (1992, p. 743) supported these arguments with Milton Friedman. But there would be no twist: before an audience of sociologists and political scientists, the ever-subversive Hirschman adhered to a portion of the "conventional wisdom" of economists. In a way that was faithful to the *zeitgeist* of the time, the failed Soviet experience seemed to inspire a benign view of Western consumer society. The freedom of the sovereign consumer seemed like an additional element in the package of freedoms associated with market democracies: who would risk giving it up, even if some dubious indicators of subjective well-being were perhaps not behaving too well? In doing so, of course, Hirschman was mobilising what he himself had called the "jeopardy thesis" just a year earlier in *The Rhetoric of Reaction*: the idea that the problem with some reforms is that they could put valuable achievements of the past at risk (Hirschman, 1991).

Consumer society faded from the economic conversation, even among heterodox economists. Its flourishing during the post-war decades had generated anxieties that, at the very least, had favoured its visibility as an object of study. But the opening of a distinct historical phase in the 1970s and 1980s led fewer and fewer economists to hold this view. More than a progress or a deviation, consumer society began to look like a mirage.

Conclusion: The Great Clash

During the post-war decades, there were clear advances towards the kind of synthesis view that Marshall and Keynes had begun to outline during the first half of the twentieth century. John Kenneth Galbraith, in particular, articulated the theses of progress and deviation in a diachronic manner. In his view, the increase in private consumption had been a driving force of well-being during a long period of deprivation and scarcity. However, American society had reached a point where a reorientation was necessary. Continuing to emphasise new rounds of private consumption, largely promoted by the advertising manoeuvres of the business community, would lead away from more urgent objectives, including the provision of public services by the state. Galbraith was far from being the only intellectual to question consumer society, and in fact, he was part of a larger group that included sociologists, philosophers, and other social researchers. This group also included a varied range of economists from Marxists like Paul Baran and Paul Sweezy to mainstream dissidents like Tibor Scitovsky, E. J. Mishan, Fred Hirsch, and Richard Easterlin.

However, the deviation thesis struggled to survive in the economic conversation. Economists interested in it never became more than a minority, and in fact, the thesis was fiercely contested by the core of the profession. Under the eventual leadership of Milton Friedman, who ended up acquiring a public status as recognised as Galbraith's, most economists continued to identify with the progress thesis. The neoclassical tradition had always tended towards it: its economic theory revolved around the notion of equilibrium understood as a static optimal point, it showed no interest in the social origin of individual preferences, and it conceptualised well-being as a one-dimensional variable related to subjective utility and proxied by income and expenditure. During the Cold War, these underlying tendencies manifested with a force that far surpassed what had been their gradual development during the pluralist interwar period. The very way in which this intellectual battle unfolded contributed to the eventual disappearance of the conversation about consumer society.

We do not wish to convey the impression that the synthesis view was formulated in a perfectly satisfactory way during the post-war decades. History played a role in the narrative of economists interested in the deviation thesis, but their history was what Gareth Austin (2008) would call a "compressed" history. It was little more than a sequence contrasting the "now" of the affluent society with the "before" of a society marked by scarcity. There was no clear criterion for delimiting the boundary that supposedly separated these two moments. There was no explicit identification of the consumption pattern that defined such a boundary. In the hands of someone like Galbraith, the deviation thesis suggested the existence of a certain order of priorities among the different goods and services that could enter consumers' lives, as well as a certain notion of balance between the different dimensions that made up human well-being. But while this broke with the economic philosophy associated with neoclassical economics, it did not replace it with another, comparably nitid philosophy.

We do not intend to deny that these limitations contributed to the difficulties the deviation thesis faced in remaining a part of the conversation once the post-war boom had passed and once the moment of maximum personal influence of charismatic communicators like Galbraith had passed as well. However, on the other hand, these limitations alone are not enough to explain the decline of the deviation thesis and the subsequent fading of the path towards the synthesis view. After all, how many concepts and arguments with initial limitations of this kind (if not more serious ones) have managed to persist in the economic conversation thanks to all sorts of elaborations and reformulations! In this case, however, there was a deeper battle about the nature of economics. The favourable ground for the cultivation of the synthesis view was one in which it was professionally accepted that "pure economics" should be combined with elements of sociology and philosophy. As became evident during this period, perhaps that ground could also be nourished by psychology. However, during the Cold War, the space for that approach to flourish contracted greatly. Galbraith was not, in this sense, so different from Mill, Marshall, or Keynes. What was truly different was his era, as economics was gradually becoming "the unsocial social science" (Backhouse & Fontaine, 2010). During the Cold War, the neoclassical school achieved a hegemonic position, and from that position, it ensured that more and more economists adhered to the professional red lines drawn by Lionel Robbins before the war. These lines involved a preference for "pure economics" and an increasing disinterest in its potential connections with other social sciences and the humanities. Far from being seen as potentially enriching complements, these connections were increasingly viewed as contaminating elements that distorted the work of a rigorous economist.

On the other hand, during the Cold War, more and more economists felt that the connection Mises had proposed and which economists like Friedman were now developing was basically correct: not only market economies, but democracy itself, rested on the premise that consumers had to be sovereign in making the decisions they deemed appropriate, regardless of what rulers, religious authorities, or (for that matter) intellectuals thought about them. Any step backward in this regard could be a step towards Hayek's "road to serfdom". Using consumer sovereignty as a major tool, mainstream economists were contributing to the making of the neoliberal order that the events of the later part of the period, from the socio-economic crisis starting in 1973 to the collapse of the Soviet bloc, would eventually configure. This new political atmosphere reinforced the effects of purely academic dynamics and contributed to the disappearance of the deviation thesis from the conversation, even among heterodox economists. The progress thesis seemed so evident that consumer society ended up becoming an intellectual mirage. It had drawn the attention of post-war generations, but it now disappeared from the economists' field of vision. As we examine in the following chapter, this would have a profound impact on the conversation moving into the present.

References

Adelman, J. (2013). *Worldly philosopher: The Odyssey of Albert O. Hirschman*. Princeton University Press. [Spanish edition: *El idealista pragmático: la odisea de Albert O. Hirschman*. Universidad de los Andes, 2017.]

Aglietta, M. (1979). *A theory of capitalist regulation: The U.S. experience*. Verso.

Alonso, L. E., & Conde, F. (1994). *Historia del consumo en España: una aproximación a sus orígenes y primer desarrollo*. Debate.

Arrow, K. J. (1951). *Social choice and individual values*. Wiley.

Austin, G. (2008). The 'reversal of fortune' thesis and the compression of history: Perspectives from African and comparative economic history. *Journal of International Development, 20*(8), 996-1027.

Backhouse, R. E. (2021). Individualism and ethics: Samuelson's welfare economics. In R. E. Backhouse, A. Baujard, & T. Nishizawa (Eds.), *Welfare theory, public action, and ethical values: Revisiting the history of welfare economics.* Cambridge University Press.

Backhouse, R. E., & Cherrier, B. (2017). The age of the applied economist: The transformation of economics since the 1970s. *History of Political Economy, 49*(supplement), 1-33.

Backhouse, R. E., & Fontaine, P. (2010). Introduction: History of economics as history of social science. *History of Political Economy, 42*(supplement), 1-21.

Bairoch, P. (1993). *Economics and world history: Myths and paradoxes.* University of Chicago Press.

Baran, P. A., & Sweezy, P. M. (1966). *Monopoly capital.* Monthly Review Press. [Spanish edition: *El capital monopolista.* Fondo de Cultura Económica, 1968.]

Becker, G. S. (1965). A theory of the allocation of time. *Economic Journal, 75*(299), 493-517.

Boltanski, L., & Chiapello, È. (1999). *Le nouvel esprit du capitalisme.* Gallimard.

Boyer, R. (1986). *La théorie de la régulation: une analyse critique.* La Decouverte.

Brassley, P. (2009). Food production and food processing in Western Europe, 1850-1990: Some conclusions. In Y. Segers, J. Bieleman, & E. Buyst (Eds.), *Exploring the food chain: Food production and food processing in Western Europe, 1850-1990.* Brepols.

Brenner, R. (2006). *The economics of global turbulence: The advanced capitalist economies from long boom to long downturn, 1945-2005.* Verso.

Burgin, A. (2012). *The great persuasion. Reinventing free markets since the Great Depression.* Harvard University Press.

Burgin, A. (2013). Age of certainty: Galbraith, Friedman, and the public life of economic ideas. *History of Political Economy, 45*(supplement), 191-219.

Burns, J. (2023). *Milton Friedman: The last conservative.* Farrar, Straus and Giroux.

Chirat, A. (2021). *L'Économie intégral de John Kenneth Galbraith (1933-1983).* Garnier.

Coase, R. H. (1960). The problem of social cost. *Journal of Law & Economics, 3*(October), 1-44.

Cross, G. (2000). *An all-consuming century: Why commercialism won in modern America.* Columbia University Press.

de Grazia, V. (2005). *Irresistible empire: America's advance through twentieth-century Europe.* Harvard University Press.

de Neve, J.-E. (2021). The economics of happiness: A conversation with Richard Easterlin. Retrieved 27 November 2024, from https://www.youtube.com/watch?v=8PDK9R3QZfg

Deaton, A., & Muellbauer, J. (1980). *Economics and consumer behavior.* Cambridge University Press.

Di Giovinazzo, V. (2019). A tale of two critics: Erich Fromm and Tibor Scitovsky on the consumer society. *History of Political Economy, 51*(2), 329-359.

Di Giovinazzo, V. (2025). Taming tyrants: Tibor Scitovsky's understanding of the mass market. *History of Social Science, 1*(1), 54-90.
Duesenberry, J. (1949). *Income, saving, and the theory of consumer behavior.* Harvard University Press.
Easterlin, R. A. (1974). Does economic growth improve the human lot? Some empirical evidence. In P. A. David & M. W. Reder (Eds.), *Nations and households in economic growth: Essays in honor of Moses Abramovitz.* Academic Press.
Eichengreen, B. (2007). *The European economy since 1945: Coordinated capitalism and beyond.* Princeton University Press.
Francks, P. (2009). *The Japanese consumer: An alternative economic history of modern Japan.* Cambridge University Press.
Freeman, C., & Louçã, F. (2001). *As time goes by: From the industrial revolutions to the information revolution.* Oxford University Press.
Frieden, J. A. (2006). *Global capitalism: Its fall and rise in the twentieth century.* W. W Norton.
Friedman, M. (1953). *Essays in positive economics.* University of Chicago Press.
Friedman, M. (1957). *A theory of the consumption function.* Princeton University Press.
Friedman, M. (1962). *Capitalism and freedom.* University of Chicago Press.
Friedman, M. (1977). From Galbraith to economic freedom. IEA Occasional Paper no. 49.
Friedman, M. (1980). *Free to choose.* PBS television series.
Friedman, M. (1994). Introducción. In F. Hayek, *Camino de servidumbre.* Unión Editorial, 2007.
Friedman, M. & Friedman, R. (1979). *Free to choose.* Harcourt Brace Jovanovich. [Spanish edition: *Libertad de elegir: hacia un nuevo liberalismo económico.* Grijalbo, 1980.]
Fromm, E. (1955). *The sane society.* Rinehart & Company.
Fromm, E. (1976). *To have or to be?* Harper & Row.
Galbraith, J. K. (1958). *The affluent society.* Houghton Mifflin. [Spanish edition: *La sociedad opulenta.* Ariel, 1984.]
Galbraith, J. K. (1967). *The new industrial state.* Houghton Mifflin.
Galbraith, J. K. (1983). *The anatomy of power.* Houghton Mifflin.
Galbraith, J. K. (1999). The unfinished business of the century. In J. K. Galbraith, *The essential Galbraith.* Houghton Mifflin (2001).
Gerstle, G. (2022). *The rise and fall of the neoliberal order: America and the world in the free market era.* Oxford University Press.
Gordon, R. J. (2017). *The rise and fall of American growth: the U.S. standard of living since the Civil War.* Princeton University Press.
Hands, D. W. (2010). Economics, psychology and the history of consumer choice theory. *Cambridge Journal of Economics, 34*(4), 633-648.

Hirsch, F. (1976). *Social limits to growth.* Harvard University Press.
Hirschman, A. O. (1977). *The passions and the interests: Political arguments for capitalism before its triumph.* Princeton University Press, 1997.
Hirschman, A. O. (1982). *Shifting involvements: Private interest and public action.* Princeton University Press. [Spanish edition: *Interés privado y acción pública.* Fondo de Cultura Económica, 1986.]
Hirschman, A. O. (1984). Against parsimony: Three easy ways of complicating some categories of economic discourse. *American Economic Review, 74*(2), 89-96.
Hirschman, A. O. (1991). *The rhetoric of reaction: Perversity, futility, jeopardy.* Harvard University Press.
Hirschman, A. O. (1992). Does the market keep us out of mischief or out of happiness? *Contemporary Sociology, 26*(6), 741-744.
Hobsbawm, E. (1994). *Age of extremes: The short twentieth century, 1914-1991.* Michael Joseph.
Hodgson, G. (2001). *How economics forgot history: The problem of historical specificity in social science.* Routledge.
Hodgson, G. (2004). *The evolution of institutional economics: Agency, structure, and Darwinism in American institutionalism.* Routledge.
Horowitz, D. (2004). *The anxieties of affluence: Critiques of American consumer culture, 1939-1979.* University of Massachusetts Press.
Lancaster, K. (1971). *Consumer demand: A new approach.* Columbia University Press.
Lee, F (2009). *A history of heterodox economics: Challenging the mainstream in the twentieth century.* Routledge.
Lerner, A. P. (1972). The economics and politics of consumer sovereignty. *American Economic Review, 62*(1/2), 258-266.
Levy, J. (2021). *Ages of American capitalism: A history of the United States.* Random House.
Lindert, P. H. (2004). *Growing public: Social spending and economic growth since the eighteenth century.* Cambridge University Press.
Maddison, A. (2001). *The world economy: A millennial perspective.* OECD.
Malassis, L. (1997). *Les trois âges de l'alimentaire: essai sur une historie sociale de l'alimentation et de l'agriculture.* Cujas.
Marcuse, H. (1964). *One-dimensional man: Studies in the ideology of advanced industrial society.* Beacon Press.
Medema, S. G. (2020). 'Exceptional and unimportant'? Externalities, competitive equilibrium, and the myth of a Pigovian tradition. *History of Political Economy, 52*(1), 135-170.
Mirowski, P., & Hands, D. W. (1998). A paradox of budgets: The postwar stabilization of American neoclassical demand theory. *History of Political Economy, 30*(supplement), 260-292.

Mirowski, P., & Hands, D. W. (2006). Introduction to 'Agreement on demand: Consumer theory in the twentieth century. *History of Political Economy, 38*(supplement), 1-6.

Mishan, E. J. (1967). *The costs of economic growth.* Staples Press.

Nordhaus, W. D., & Tobin, J. (1972). Is growth obsolete? In *Economic growth.* National Bureau of Economic Research.

Oddy, D. J., & Drouard, A. (Eds.). (2013). *The food industries of Europe in the nineteenth and twentieth centuries.* Ashgate.

Olsen, N. (2019). *The sovereign consumer: A new intellectual history of neoliberalism.* Palgrave Macmillan.

Packard, V. (1957). *The hidden persuaders.* David McKay Co.

Piketty, T. (2014). *Capital in the twenty-first century.* Harvard University Press.

Piore, M. J., & Sabel, C. F. (1984). *The second industrial divide: Possibilities for prosperity.* Basic Books.

Popkin, B. M. (1993). Nutritional patterns and transitions. *Population and Development Review, 19*(1), 138-157.

Prados de la Escosura, L. (2008). Inequality, poverty, and the Kuznets curve in Spain, 1850-2000. *European Review of Economic History, 12*(3), 287-324.

Riesman, D. (1950). *The lonely crowd: A study of the changing American character.* Yale University Press.

Riesman, D. (1964). *Abundance for what? and other essays.* Chatto & Windus.

Robbins, L. (1932). *An essay on the nature and significance of economic science.* Macmillan.

Roncaglia, A. (2005). *The wealth of ideas: A history of economic thought.* Cambridge University Press.

Roncaglia, A. (2019). *The age of fragmentation: A history of contemporary economic thought.* Cambridge University Press.

Schmelzer, M. (2016). *The hegemony of growth: The OECD and the making of the economic growth paradigm.* Cambridge University Press.

Schumacher, E. F. (1973). *Small is beautiful: Economics as if people mattered.* Harper & Row.

Scitovsky, T. (1976). *The joyless economy: An inquiry into human satisfaction and consumer dissatisfaction.* Oxford University Press. [Spanish edition: *Frustraciones de la riqueza: la satisfacción humana y la insatisfacción del consumidor.* Fondo de Cultura Económica, 1986.]

Solow, R. M. (1967). The new industrial state or son of affluence. *The Public Interest*, 9.

Stigler, G. J., & Becker, G. S. (1977). De gustibus non est disputandum. *American Economic Review, 67*(2), 76-90.

Tobin, J. (1974). Galbraith redux. *Yale Law Journal, 83*(6), 1291-1303.

Trezzini, A. (2012). Relative income vs. permanent income: The crisis of the theory of the social significance of consumption. *Journal of the History of Economic Thought, 34*(3), 355-377.
Wallerstein, I. (1996). *Open the social sciences: Report of the Gulbenkian Commission on the restructuring of the social sciences.* Stanford University Press.
Wapshott, N. (2021). *Samuelson Friedman: The battle over the free market.* W. W. Norton.
Weber, I. M. (2021). *How China escaped shock therapy: The market reform debate.* Routledge.

CHAPTER 6

The Aftermath (1990 to the Present)

The great clash of the period 1945–1990 left a profound mark on the economic conversation about consumer society. If, in any periodisation of history, there are reasons to speak of "path dependencies", this is particularly evident in the case at hand. There is much in the last thirty years that can be read as an extension of the intellectual dynamics that gained momentum during the 1945–1990 period. On the other hand, and at the same time, we do not wish to convey an image of sequential determinism. Path dependencies have adopted an open-ended character, and some ruptures have taken place. If we project these elements forward in time, we could very well imagine a future in which the period 1945–1990 is regarded as an exceptional period, rather than the narrative focal point we have made of it in this book. For the moment, however, we must stick to history as it really happened over the past thirty years.

The chapter is organised into five sections. As usual, the first section is dedicated to reconstructing the socioeconomic and intellectual context of the period: a new wave of consumer society and the consolidation of the gap between mainstream and heterodox approaches to economics. Yet, there was some internal pluralism in the mainstream, and the second section addresses what it meant for the debate on consumer society. Next, the third section reviews the contributions of various heterodox schools. The fourth section examines the dominant view among most economists,

F. Collantes, *Consumer Society and the Economists*, Palgrave Studies in the History of Economic Thought,
https://doi.org/10.1007/978-3-031-96645-3_6

emphasising its continuity with the 1945–1990 period. The fifth section presents another significant continuity: the limited presence of consumer society in the contemporary economic mind. The conclusions reflect on these developments from a long-term perspective.

Fragmentation

Few would dispute that the history of capitalism entered a new phase from the final stretch of the twentieth century. Innovation took a different path, with electronics, information, and communications driving a third technological revolution. Business organisation was rearranged: Fordism gave way to flexible specialisation, just-in-time production, and global value chains. In part as a consequence of the political success of neoliberalism, the state began to retreat from economic life. A new pattern of economic growth, based on digitalisation and "financialization", began to take shape. Moreover, the collapse of the Soviet Union and China's gradual shift towards the market meant that a large majority of the world's population was participating in a global capitalist system for the first time. With growing international flows of commodities, capital, and labour, global capitalism fostered a degree of international economic integration far superior to that of any previous moment in history. Finally, globalisation was accompanied by a restructuring of the world's economic geography, with China and a number of peripheral economies growing at a faster rate than developed countries (Arrighi, 1994, 2007; Freeman & Louçã, 2001; Frieden, 2006; Harvey, 2005; Levy, 2021).

Meanwhile, a new wave of changes in consumption unfolded. The traditional centres of consumer society, namely the United States, Western Europe, and Japan, witnessed a new cycle of transformation in consumption patterns. A large majority of households gained purchasing power greater than that of the post-war decades, with all the possibilities this entailed. In some cases, particularly among the upper and middle classes, this was the result of their successful insertion into the new economy of the period. In other cases, particularly among a new lower class composed of unskilled manual workers, it could be more difficult to gather the resources and skills necessary to participate in a deindustrialising economy. However, even in these cases, households' consumption possibilities improved more than the modest growth in their income level would suggest. There were substantial falls in the relative price of most basic goods, beginning with food. The rampant financialisation of economic life enabled a level of household debt that would have been unthinkable in previous periods. Finally, the household economy of all social strata was transformed by the increasing incorporation of women into the labour market. In an era of modest reductions in working hours, this amounted to a sizeable expansion of the labour supply. Some historians have seen this as a replica of the so-called industrious revolution of the early modern period, when households increased their labour supply in order to access a more abundant and varied consumer basket than the traditional one (Barba & Pivetti, 2009; Behringer et al., 2024; Crouch, 2009; de Vries, 2008, 2023; Piketty, 2014).

An enthusiastic consumer culture gave people reasons to transform their growing purchasing power into the acquisition of more goods and services. This included commodities that did not even exist at the beginning of the period. While cars and household appliances had been the great symbol of the post-war consumption pattern, the new cycle of consumer society found its great icon in consumer electronics, from computers to mobile phones. There were, however, all kinds of "qualitative substitutions" in the basic categories of household budgets, such as food and housing (Collantes, 2017; de Grazia, 2016; Gordon, 2017; Malassis, 1997).

Nonetheless, the new wave of consumer society was more than just a simple déjà vu of post-war dynamics. Massification gave way to the diversification and fragmentation of consumption styles. Alternatives proliferated within each consumption niche, around which cultural structures were woven that vertically linked social strata, but also cohesively bound them horizontally and intertwined them fluidly with other segmentations derived from gender, race, or age. Although none of this was entirely new, and although the mass consumer culture of the post-war decades had not been as monolithic as is sometimes assumed, diversification and fragmentation reached an unprecedented scale (de Grazia, 2005; Francks, 2009).

Diversification even had a territorial dimension as Western-style consumer society began to spread across more and more regions in the world. During the post-war decades, the economic and social development of what was then called the "Third World" had left some room for the transformation of the world of consumption, but not much. It was mainly from the late twentieth century onwards that significant proportions of the population in Asia, Latin America, and Africa experienced a revolution in material life. Given its size and geopolitical relevance, the case of China is particularly striking. Although it was an export-driven economy, the accumulation of several decades of accelerated growth had some trickle-down effect on domestic demand. A middle class emerged whose consumption pattern broke with the rudimentary standards that had prevailed in the country well into the twentieth century. The traditional territorial limits of consumer society, initially a creature of the Cold War's US bloc, began to crumble (Trentmann, 2016).

Meanwhile, academia was changing too. Although the teaching of economics remained firmly aligned with the traditional agenda of the neoclassical school, considerable fragmentation in research efforts occurred. This partly reflected the increasing specialisation of economists in specific fields but also some deeper movements. The research programme focused on general equilibrium, in a sense the crown jewel of the neoclassical tradition, declined as more and more economists saw logical inconsistencies in what had previously been seen as transitory anomalies. In part related to this, more and more economists turned their attention to empirical aspects. While theory had held a privileged status in the post-war decades, now an "empirical turn" re-established the situation of the late nineteenth and early twentieth centuries. The empirical testing of alternative theoretical hypotheses became the primary occupation of most economists, supported by computers and software that vastly expanded the possibilities for constructing large databases and applying sophisticated statistical techniques to them. As faith in a grand unifying theory deteriorated, concern for empirical credibility grew. In this new context, more and more researchers became interested in behavioural economics to explore the empirics of individual behaviour. This represented a break away from assuming that behaviour could be axiomatically reconstructed from the premises informing *homo economicus*. Was this, as some suggested, a Copernican paradigm shift? At the very least, it must be acknowledged that the mainstream was becoming more pluralistic than it had been in the post-war decades (Ambrosino et al., 2024; Backhouse & Cherrier, 2017; Hamermesh, 2013; Offer & Söderberg, 2016; Thaler, 2015).

This internal pluralism, however, coexisted with persistent marginalisation of heterodox schools of thought. Heterodox schools faced more difficulties in coalescing around shared theoretical foundations and, even more so, around a shared methodology for empirical research. Furthermore, the dynamics of the academic labour market continued to push their supporters out of economics departments. The period witnessed the rise of a bibliometric culture for research evaluation that tended to favour mainstream economists, if only because of the scale bias involved in the calculations. Consequently, the figure of the economist remained associated with that of the "pure" economist, perhaps now more closely aligned with psychology as a related discipline, but still uninterested in history, sociology, or philosophy (Lee, 2009; Martins, 2014).

It could even be argued that neoclassical economics was not as dead as some of the enthusiasts of behavioural economics and internal pluralism sometimes claimed. After all, the utility-maximising *homo economicus* continued to thrive in various subfields. And, in a manner very consistent with the neoclassical tradition, most economists remained fundamentally confident in the market as a mechanism for social coordination. Beneath the changes at other levels of economic thinking, the underlying political discourse continued to move in terrain very similar to that of the past. It is likely that this contributed more than anything else to the student protest movement that, during the Great Recession, spread across the major developed countries, demanding a reform of the economics curricula. Although, at the time of writing, its flame has not been extinguished, it seems clear that the protest has not succeeded in erasing most of the red lines that had previously defined the mainstream region of economic education (D'Ippoliti, 2021; Hodgson, 2019).

Belle Époque Cracks

The Cold War mainstream had firmly adhered to the progress thesis and had been notably successful in creating an epistemological, methodological, and political terrain in which the deviation thesis could hardly take root. Nevertheless, and as we saw in the previous chapter, since at least the 1970s dissident research lines had begun to emerge, opening cracks in the mainstream conviction that consumer society represented the best of all possible worlds. Although none of these lines had received much attention in their early stages, all managed to thrive during the capitalist *belle époque* between the fall of the Berlin Wall and the outbreak of the Great Recession. Today, they form an established part of the movement towards a more plural mainstream.

Let us begin with a development originating at the very heart of the post-war mainstream: the models of endogenous preferences first imagined by Chicago economists George Stigler and Gary Becker. Certainly, these models did not change the way economists thought overnight, and in fact, the black box of exogenous preferences remained very much present in the conversation. But over time, an increasing number of economists sought to produce extensions of conventional models by incorporating some endogenous specification of preferences. By the 1990s, the first book Becker published after receiving the Nobel Prize, beyond an updated edition of his famous *Human Capital*, was *Accounting for Tastes*, a book that synthesised the neoclassical strategy for the endogenisation of preferences. In Becker's (1996) hands, the task of making preferences endogenous did not require the economist to incorporate dense sociological context. Tastes could be explained without abandoning methodological individualism and without having to resort to a notion of society as anything else than an aggregation of individuals. In fact, we agree with readers who, while reading this paragraph, were thinking that the endogenous preferences approach, like all of Becker's work, should not be seen as an expression of dissent, but rather as a conventional extension of the mainstream.

But what would happen if this device fell into the hands of dissident economists? In that case, the deviation thesis might reappear in the conversation. Stigler and Becker's intent does not seem to have been that at all, but it was an approach with potentially devastating implications for the kind of defence of consumer society that mainstream economists had been making. This could have become evident from the outset, inasmuch as some of Becker's protagonists were "rational" drug addicts that had little chance of carrying Panglossian connotations. While it was a bold attempt to conquer new territory for the field of rational choice, it was difficult to engage with this argument without at least glancing at the ethical field that Robbins had wished to leave beyond the boundaries of true economics. Obvious to most readers, the fact that drug addiction could be rational in the way economists used the term could hardly be taken as equivalent to it leading to better lives for the consumers involved, or to a better society.

The suspicion that the performance of the sovereign consumer did not have to be optimal began to spread among a faction of mainstream economists. This was so especially among those more inclined to drop restrictive assumptions and discover the impact that this had on the conclusions of analysis, generally with a political agenda more aligned with some version of social democracy than with Becker's market liberalism. This was the case, for example, with Joseph Stiglitz, whose career originally focused on researching the profound implications of discarding a traditional assumption in neoclassical microeconomics: that individuals had perfect information. In macroeconomics, Stiglitz was aligned with what (albeit at risk of some confusion) we would call the Keynesian faction of the neoclassical school, that is, those economists working within the "neoclassical synthesis" of the post-war decades. When Stiglitz was presented with the opportunity to retrospectively evaluate Keynes' "Economic Possibilities", the result was, in fact, an exercise in "neoclassical synthesis". Dropping the traditional assumption of exogenous preferences in favour of an endogenous specification, Stiglitz (2008) presented a formalised model in which the representative agent finds themselves on a suboptimal path characterised by a high level of consumption, long working hours, and little time for leisure and personal relationships. Stiglitz, in a way that was quite empathetic with Keynes' argument, called this "excessive consumerism". In a sense, Becker's rational drug addict had ended up opening the door to a consumer that was addicted to buying all sorts of goods and services.

A second fissure was "happiness economics". As we saw in the previous chapter, the premise here was not the relaxation of some traditional assumption, but the attempt to empirically approach a key concept that had until then been assumed to be unobservable: utility. While endogenous preferences affected the variables of the neoclassical consumer's maximisation programme, happiness economics directly targeted the object of the programme. Happiness economists were using self-reported subjective well-being to empirically scrutinise the theoretical assumption that had governed neoclassical thought until then: that consumers knew what they were doing and that their decisions led them to attain the highest possible level of utility. Slowly but relentlessly, the seed planted by Easterlin in the 1970s gave rise to a new field of empirical research, led by figures such as Richard Layard (2005) and Bruno Frey (2008). This was a field whose alignment with traditional neoclassical economics was not particularly strong. Certainly, it shared more than a few theoretical and methodological foundations, but these remained largely implicit and, more importantly, became somewhat diluted as the "empirical turn" took place, putting the emphasis on credible econometric testing. This, of course, did much to restore a more balanced field in which the theses of progress and deviation could thrive according to their respective empirical merits.

By the early twenty-first century, about a generation after Easterlin's seminal contribution, the state of the art was complex. Not everyone agreed with the way in which the Easterlin paradox seemed to relativise the role of income and consumption in people's happiness. Disaggregated data by social status had revealed that high-income groups did tend to report higher levels of subjective well-being than low-income groups. International comparisons also showed that countries with the lowest levels of life satisfaction tended to be low-income countries. This led some to propose a restoration of the simple message that had long underpinned, and still fundamentally underpinned, mainstream economics: more was better (Ortiz-Ospina & Roser, 2024). Others, however, including Easterlin himself (1998, 2001), remained convinced that this simple message was misleading. After all, these direct connections between income and happiness seemed to be confined to the empirical space of low-income levels: above a certain income threshold, whether by social status groups or by countries, the connections seemed to fade or, at the very least, become confused with other influences and interactions between variables. Through a very different route from Mill in 1848 or Keynes in 1930, this was not far away from a notion of sufficiency. At least, it was further away from the restless insatiability traditionally attributed to the neoclassical consumer. According to Easterlin (1998, pp. 153–154), the historical balance did not consist in humanity triumphing over material desires, but rather the opposite:

> [Real] income is being deflated by rising material aspirations, in this case to yield essentially constant subjective economic well-being. While it would be pleasant to envisage a world free from the pressure of material want, a more realistic projection, based on the evidence, is of a world in which generation after generation thinks it needs only another ten or twenty percent more income to be happy. Thus, the epoch of modern economic growth is leading to a world stuck on a "hedonic treadmill" in which wants and real income grow commensurately.

In a related way, Scitovksy's followers argued that the same forces that drove growth in GDP or consumption were having a negative impact upon the development of those capacities and skills necessary to lead a creative, vibrant life (Pugno, 2016). Others located the crucial negative impact in the quality of social relationships (Layard, 2005).

All happiness economists seemed to agree, in any case, that subjective well-being had components that were difficult to reduce to a single dimension. Time and again, econometric models showed that people who reported being happier tended to be embedded in dense social networks that presumably provided them with connection, affection, and love. A healthy, stable partnership, for example, was common among the happy, while marital breakups were more common among those who were less happy. Again and again, econometric models also supported what, from another methodological world, Veblen had proposed long ago: that people attached great importance to comparisons with others. The absolute endowment of income or material goods was not as important for subjective well-being as the relative endowment. The same consumer basket could provide higher levels of happiness in an equitable society than in an unequal one. Finally, econometric models also tended to identify as important other variables related to something resembling the meaning of life, ranging from participation in community life to religious beliefs. The overall picture was that of an empirical portrait of subjective well-being that clashed with the traditional neoclassical image of well-being as a one-dimensional variable. Rather, well-being would have diverse sources, and synergies could be established among them, but also conflicts.

This fit well with other findings by behavioural economists who were engaging with psychology. For Robert Frank (1999), in particular, it was clear that there was an element of deviation in the evolution of consumer society. Consumers may not have been as manipulable as (allegedly) Galbraith had thought, but they were still subject to psychological and social tendencies that led to an "arms race" in the world of consumption. A "luxury fever" had broken out, as more and more purchases were motivated by the desire to demonstrate status. As in Veblen, this positional race had no intrinsic value for society as a whole, although each individual could find reasons to partake in it. The political implications of this view could be far-reaching. Traditionally, from the mainstream perspective, any behaviour that did not have a negative impact on others was exempt from policy scrutiny. But was private consumption truly that sort of unproblematic behaviour? When private decisions about consumption began to be seen as contributions to the reproduction of a culture that eventually influenced the decisions of other consumers, the political implications became more complex.

While happiness and behavioural economists approached psychology, others turned towards a "post-utilitarian" philosophy. This would be the origin of a third crack through which the deviation thesis would have the chance to re-enter economic conversations of the 1990s and 2000s. The figure who made the most systematic and influential challenge to the subjective theory of value and the theory of utility and demand based on it was Amartya Sen. Sen was a dissident who had trained at Cambridge in the 1950s, when it was the undisputed centre of heterodox economics, but whose interest lay less in post-Keynesianism or neo-Marxism than in the theory of social choice by mainstream economists like Kenneth Arrow.

Throughout the 1970s and 1980s, Sen had already gained a notable reputation in this subfield, searching for the political and philosophical foundations of the collective decision-making process that would make well-being possible. Sen had managed to walk a narrow path where economics combined with philosophy in a way that resonated in fields like welfare economics and development economics. But it was especially during our period when his influence soared.

Sen's work spread across numerous fields and directions, but for our purposes, a fundamental influence was his call to reconsider the indicators used to measure human well-being. Sen did not start from utilitarian philosophical premises. He was sceptical about the connection that economists often established between income and consumption, on the one hand, and well-being and quality of life, on the other. For Sen, income and the goods consumed with it could not be taken as the ends of economic life: they were means by which individuals could develop the capabilities and functionalities that could truly be understood as constitutive of well-being. Human development had non-monetary dimensions, such as health, education, and the enjoyment of basic civil and political rights, which also had to be considered. When, to take one of Sen's favourite examples, life expectancy in the Indian state of Kerala was higher than among the Black population in the United States (with a much higher income level), the possibility that human well-being could be adjusted to a one-dimensional axis became implausible. The neoclassical premise that there was a single dimension in which income, utility, and well-being overlapped was excessive. More income could mean more health or more education, or maybe not: well-being was multidimensional (Sen, 1985, 1987, 1999).

At a time when mainstream economists were diving into their "empirical turn", the path forward for those sensitive to this line of reasoning was clear: alongside conventional monetary variables, non-monetary variables that were also constitutive of well-being should be collected. The result would be synthetic indicators like the Human Development Index. Along the way, the multidimensional conception of well-being would be sidelined once again in favour of a single variable, albeit now defined as a weighted sum of different sub-variables. All in all, it was clear that the one-dimensionality that had returned through the back door was no longer dominated by subjective utility or personal income.

Through any of these paths, the traditional propensity of mainstream economists towards the progress thesis mitigated somewhat. At least among the dissident groups, there was a return to terrain more akin to that which had prevailed during the pluralist interwar period: a terrain more conducive than the Cold War era for cultivating what we have called a "synthesis view". This tendency would be reinforced by developments that were taking place among heterodox economists.

The Advent of Keynes' Grandchildren

Keynes did not have children, so he had no grandchildren to experience the economic possibilities of the future. Had he had any, they might have been born at the end of the Second World War or perhaps in the immediate post-war years. If they had been interested in economics, they would have witnessed the rise and fall of the post-war debate about the affluent society. This is more or less the perspective that the British Robert Skidelsky, born in 1939, found himself in. By the time Keynes died at the premature age of 61, Skidelsky was a child about to turn seven. Skidelsky trained as a historian and later became a professor of economics at the University of Warwick. By the time of the Great Recession in 2007, already nearing 70, he had made a name for himself primarily as a biographer of Keynes, whose life and work he analysed from various angles in influential and award-winning publications (Skidelsky, 1983–2000, 1996). In parallel, like Galbraith, he had been an active intellectual in the public sphere and in the political life of the country.

When the Great Recession erupted, Skidelsky oriented his academic work in the direction that the events suggested most urgently. As an accredited expert on Keynes and his work, he embarked on a Keynesian reading of what was happening. Once the fantasy of self-regulating markets had been swept away by events, the stage was set for the "return of the master", to borrow the title of his book (Skidelsky, 2009). For Skidelsky, mainstream economics had placed excessive trust in mathematical formalisation and free markets. The time had come to return to a type of economic analysis more closely connected to social and human reality, as well as to more active public policies. If neoclassical economists had seen the crisis of the 1970s as a call to question the Keynesian idea of a mixed economy, how could post-Keynesian economists not see the Great Recession as a call to question the doctrine and practice of neoliberalism?

There was, however, something that was different about Skidelsky. As someone deeply familiar with Keynes' intellectual life, Skidelsky (1996) placed more emphasis than other Keynesians on the philosophical substrate that should accompany the return of the master. Although "Economic Possibilities for Our Grandchildren" could be read as a lightweight utopia, there was no doubt that it formed part of Keynes' "deep religion": the belief that solving the "economic problem" was not an end in itself, but rather a means to enhance the good life and the good society. For Skidelsky, this philosophical framework became crucial when it came to reorienting economic analysis and public policies in a genuinely Keynesian direction.

While Galbraith felt that he had started with the "window" of *The Affluent Society* and later incorporated it into the "house" of *The New Industrial State*, Skidelsky proceeded in the opposite direction. After the "house" of *The Return of the Master*, he embarked on a more detailed elaboration of the philosophical "window" of Keynesian economics and its implications. As Western economies were plunged into the biggest economic crisis since the Great Depression, Skidelsky set out to do the same thing that Keynes had done in the midst of that storm: reflect on the relationship between capitalism and the good life. He teamed up with his son Edward, a philosopher specialising in the history of ideas, and together they published *How Much Is Enough? The Love of Money and the Case for the Good Life* (Skidelsky & Skidelsky, 2012).

The Skidelskys' starting point was a retrospective view of the predictions made by Keynes in 1930. When the historical moment had finally arrived to pose the question, how accurate had the master been? Not much, was the conclusion. Keynes had been quite correct regarding the magnitude of economic growth that Western societies would experience once the Great Depression was overcome. However, he had spectacularly failed in the other part of his argument. His portrayal of populations liberated from the harsh economic struggle, who could then focus on cultivating personal relationships or enjoying art and nature, seemed in 2012 almost as distant as it must have seemed in 1930. Instead of solving their economic problem, what people had actually done was define new rounds of consumer goals. And to satisfy these new "relative needs" (to return to the term used by Keynes), they had found it necessary to continue working long hours. According to the Skidelskys, a central feature of traditional philosophical and religious systems had been their caution about the danger of orienting life towards the unlimited pursuit of material wealth. An essential component of what was understood as the good life was then the notion of sufficiency. The point was not maximising the consumption of goods. The point was satisfying basic needs. But now, capitalism and consumer society had torn down this caution, giving rise to a horizon of perpetual improvement in consumption patterns.

The final result of the positional race would be paradoxical. The reproduction of consumer society was based on the creation of new "relative needs" that implicitly or explicitly defined as improvable the level of well-being the consumer had reached up until that moment. The notion of sufficiency, key in the traditional definition of what constituted a good life, was openly challenged by consumerist culture. The Skidelskys concluded that, while capitalism had allowed for unprecedented levels of wealth, it had also made people less capable of directing that wealth towards achieving the good life. In a related vein, some post-Keynesian economists have encouraged us to read Stephen King's novel *Needful Things* as a dystopian illustration of how consumer society—with its emphasis on the pursuit of self-fulfilment and identity through the acquisition of goods—can lead to a deterioration of social relations with serious consequences for well-being (Cedrini et al., 2021). All of this can be seen as a new iteration of an argument that, albeit in different guises, has been familiar to us since we reviewed the classical political economists: if well-being is multidimensional, there may be reason to worry that material progress evidenced in the realm of consumption is being achieved at the expense of regress in other dimensions.

By the time the post-Keynesians revisited the economic realities of the master's grandchildren, the deviation thesis was being revitalised, largely autonomously, by a growing group of researchers who adopted the label of ecological economists. While the roots of ecological economic thinking can be traced back to the Renaissance, this perspective had taken some shape in the 1960s and 1970s with pioneering contributions from researchers like Herman Daly (1972, 1991), and it flourished vigorously from the 1990s onwards, resulting in an avalanche of publications and alternative indicators of development (Vianna Franco & Missemer, 2022; Spash, 2020). For ecological economists, mainstream economics presented a distorted view of the economic system because it relied on valuations and measurements made in monetary units, disregarding the biophysical realities in which the activities of businesses, consumers, and governments were embedded. Said biophysical realities were often worrisome. GDP was growing, but humanity was destroying the planet. The depletion of non-renewable resources and the rise in pollution meant that the prosperity achieved by developed societies was actually less than it appeared to be according to conventional monetary measurement. Furthermore, its maintenance over time faced bleak prospects, compromising the possibilities of future generations.

Ecological economics had a distinctive identity, but it could easily converge with the type of critique of consumer society that we had seen emerge in other heterodox schools, and even among some classical and neoclassical economists. One of its philosophical pillars was after all that some things, in this case natural resources, had an intrinsic value that should be recognised, regardless of whether the market economy's pricing system acknowledged it. The price system could assign some goods a lower value than they actually had, as well as overvalue others. Along with business strategies and government policies, consumer behaviour was then one of the vectors contributing to the systematic over-exploitation of the planet's natural resources. The diffusion of alternative consumption patterns, more moderate and focused on meeting genuine needs, was a necessary piece of the socioeconomic transformation programme advocated by ecological economists.

Tim Jackson's work is particularly representative of this convergence between ecological concerns and the critical tradition of consumer society. Jackson, born in 1957 and thus a sort of late grandchild of Keynes, initially studied mathematics and philosophy before earning a doctorate in physics. His interest in the world of energy quickly led him to the emerging field of ecological economics. Within this field, his research on sustainability and environmental management also developed strong ties to the analysis of lifestyles, social values, and consumer cultures from an early stage. His public profile included participation in the United Kingdom's Commission on Sustainable Development, created by Tony Blair's Labour government in 2004 and dismantled after the 2011 electoral shift that brought David Cameron's Conservatives to power. It was during these years, and within this framework, that he published his influential *Prosperity Without Growth*. In it, Jackson (2009) argued that economic growth was subject to notable social and environmental limits. Therefore, its ability to genuinely improve people's lives was less than commonly assumed. One piece of his argument concerned what Jackson, adopting a metaphor coined by Max Weber, called the "iron cage" of consumerism.

According to Jackson (2009, pp. 209 and 211), "Consumer society seems bent on heading toward disaster": it induced "material waste" that depleted essential natural resources and exerted unsustainable pressure on ecosystems. As in Aristotle, prosperity consisted in people having the capacity to flourish, which ultimately depended on their participation in social life:

> [Living] well on a finite planet cannot simply consist of consuming more and more things. [...] Prosperity, in any meaningful sense of the term, is related to the quality of our lives and our relationships, to the resilience of our communities, and to a sense of individual and collective purpose. (Jackson, 2011, p. 11)

However, consumer society would have transferred a disproportionate responsibility to material goods in sustaining the psychological functions related to social inclusion. This positioned Jackson before what he referred to as the "complex social logic" of consumerism, which, alongside mere positional consumption, also included elements of sociability and self-expression. This social logic was reinforced by the relentless tendency of capitalism to stimulate novelty through the development of product innovations. The result was a path of economic change that hindered, rather than promoted, human flourishing:

> [It] is tempting to ask what the connection is between this vision of self-perpetuating creative capitalism [...] and the needs and desires of ordinary human beings. At some point, the circular flow of production and consumption may have been a useful way to organise human society to ensure that people's basic needs were met. But what does this continuous cycle of creative destruction have to do with human flourishing? (Jackson, 2009, p. 128)

In other words, in the terms we have been using in this book, there had been progress first and deviation later. According to Jackson, the recovery of the path to prosperity would involve not only an ecological macroeconomics attentive to the environmental limits of growth but also public investment aimed at improving people's ability to seek their flourishing in a less materialistic manner.

More recently, in his *Post-growth: Life After Capitalism*, Jackson (2021a) continued to problematise consumerism, arguing that, in addition to contributing to the reproduction of an environmentally unsustainable system of production, it faced difficulties in inducing significant improvements in human well-being. In an approach that (as we know) harkens back to Aristotle, Jackson's vision of prosperity entailed finding a healthy balance between the various dimensions that informed human well-being. Rather than maximising one of these dimensions (income growth), it was necessary to organise the economy in such a way that everyone could have a good life, taking into account distributive, environmental, and psychological dimensions. In an interview about *Post-growth*, Jackson (2021b) asserted that the COVID-19 pandemic, by forcing societies to find a balance between health and wealth, provided a short-term metaphor for the general problem that affluent societies were facing in the long term.

Critiques of consumerism were also a substantial part of other proposals aligned with ecological economics. The French scholar Serge Latouche (2010, 2019), in particular, led an intellectual movement with a remarkable public profile grouped under the label of *décroissance* ("degrowth"). For Latouche, it was necessary to decolonise the collective imagination to set it free from the emphasis on economic growth as the supreme societal goal. This had implications for governments and businesses, but also for consumers and their lifestyles. It was necessary to exit consumer society and embrace values and practices closer to the notion of "voluntary simplicity". In a related fashion, Ulrich Brand and Markus Wissen (2021) referred to an "imperial mode of living" in the Global North, arguing that it represented a pattern of consumption reliant on the maintenance of unfair, asymmetrical relations with poorer countries, and that it was driving capitalism into a severe ecological crisis. As was typical in this intellectual tradition, what was good for the planet also turned out to be beneficial for humans from the perspective of personal and social flourishing.

Thus far, we have presented the post-Keynesian and ecological versions of the deviation thesis sequentially, focusing on their most prominent representatives. This may have had its advantages, but it has prevented us from doing justice to the eclectic economist who more persistently and earlier sought to keep the conversation about consumer society alive. This is Juliet Schor, whose work initially focused on labour economics but soon shifted to investigate the links between the evolution of consumption patterns and the dynamics of the labour market. Schor trained in the 1970s, influenced by the new currents of heterodox economics emerging in the United States. However, by the 1980s, for Schor (as for many others of her generation), it was clear that her initial expectations of a paradigm shift in academic economics had been inflated (Schor, 2014). Nevertheless,

Schor managed to develop an original research programme that led to the publication of influential books such as *The Overworked American*.

In that work, Schor (1991) documented how, far from being reduced, the American workday had tended to increase during the 1980s, driven in part by the desire of a large portion of the population to acquire a more distinguished consumption pattern. Considering the resulting reduction in leisure time and its implications, the balance of these intense cycles of "getting and spending" was dismal. In other critical publications on consumer society, Schor (1998, 2004, 2005) would later analyse how consumer pressure was leading to an increased demand for consumer credit (from the overworked American, Schor moved, in the title of a later book, to the overspent American) or how this pressure was spreading among the youngest through the growing commercialisation of childhood. In a related way, other empirical studies carried out by Schor and her co-authors found a connection between the length of the workday and environmental impact.

Armed with this empirical background, Schor (2007, 2010) would also intervene on the theoretical side of the debate. In her view, it was necessary to vindicate the critical tradition regarding consumer society. This was a path not taken in the history of economic thought and, as such, could now be useful in rethinking the very conception of wealth and prosperity upon which developed societies were based. Prosperity should not be seen as an endless increase in consumption, but rather as a shift towards a more environmentally sustainable consumption pattern and a lifestyle characterised by greater availability of free time and stronger social connections.

As had occurred during the post-war decades, these critical voices from the field of economics were accompanied by others from different fields. Sociologist Zygmunt Bauman (1998, 2007, 2008) offered an unflattering view of the consuming lives characteristic of "liquid modernity". Psychologists such as Barry Schwartz (2004) and Tim Kasser (2002) raised alarms about the mental costs that consumerism and materialism seemed to have, according to their empirical experiments. For Schwartz in particular, consumer societies offered such an excessive range of choices that the pressure to make the right decisions took a notable toll on consumers' well-being. This was especially true among those who, instead of limiting themselves to securing a certain level of satisfaction (i.e., those following what the Skidelskys would call a sufficiency criterion), behaved as maximisers (i.e., those who behaved in the way neoclassical economists presumed everyone behaved). Schwartz's practical conclusion was clear: it was necessary to foster a culture that allowed individuals to live more wisely with the abundance and the choices this opened up. Finally, journalists also converged in this critical space regarding consumer society. Carl Honoré (2004), for example, argued that a hurried consumerist culture was conspiring against satisfaction and well-being. While the roots of a social movement in praise of slowness can be traced back to food activist Carlo Petrini's "slow food", Honoré quickly became its global guru.

The deviation thesis had returned. But would it manage to attract the interest of orthodox economists?

A Lampedusa Mainstream

Unlike what had occurred during the post-war decades, mainstream economists did not feel strongly interpellated by the arguments that heterodox economists were raising regarding consumer society. Back in the post-war decades, Galbraith had been a prominent figure in academia, public debate, and (at times) in the Democratic Party. His arguments, made from within the field of economics and successfully disseminated to the general public, could not be ignored: they had to be responded to. However, the reopening of the debate by Keynes' grandchildren did not have a comparable influence because none of them reached a comparable stature as public intellectuals.

Additionally, it must be considered that more and more heterodox economists were affiliated with the periphery of the academic system, if not entirely outside economics departments. Galbraith had been able to develop his entire academic career as an economics professor at a very prestigious university. But by the late twentieth and early twenty-first centuries, the scope for the development of this type of academic career was much narrower. The evaluations of individual research careers, as well as the collective performance of departments, became more formalised than in the past, accompanied by standards and criteria that were aligned with mainstream economics (Lee, 2009). In retrospect, heterodox economists trained in the 1970s and 1980s have argued that, compared to the overwhelming homogenisation that followed, the Cambridge or the Harvard of their time had been relatively pluralistic after all (Chang & Lari, 2024; Lazonick et al., 2024).

If the heterodox economists of Schor's generation had once dreamed of provoking a Copernican paradigm shift, by the end of the twentieth century the goal was simply to keep their intellectual traditions alive. Robert Skidelsky was an atypical example of a historian-turned academic economist, but many of the other critics of consumer society no longer held positions in economics departments. In a particularly symbolic way, Schor not only left the Harvard where Galbraith had spent his career but also left the world of economics departments altogether to become a professor in the field of sociology. Her research agenda remained unchanged, but her position within the research system was obviously different, especially given the persistent sense of superiority that economists maintained over supposedly "softer" social sciences (Fourcade et al., 2015). In France, which was more belatedly influenced by these changes, Serge Latouche managed to finish his career as an economist, but his younger followers were feeling more pressure to reform and adapt to mainstream standards (Parrique, 2024).

None of these scholars critical of consumer society worked in economics departments that, by their prestige, could be compared with Keynes' Cambridge or Galbraith's Harvard. Consequently, mainstream economists could safely apply the same strategy that their post-war predecessors had used to deal with such a publicly influential figure, yet so far removed from economics departments, as Marcuse: ignore them. If economists like Veblen and Galbraith were retrospectively re-labelled as sociologists by historians aligned with orthodox economics (Blaug, 1968, pp. 828–832; Ekelund & Hébert, 1990, pp. 480–506), what would not happen to someone like Juliet Schor, who had left the Econ tribe to join a sociology department? There was a "penumbra of non-economists", to use the apt expression that James K. Galbraith (2022, p. 50), son of John Kenneth, proposed in an unintended echo of Robbins' "sociological penumbra". And that penumbra was expanding over time.

The case of internal dissidents was different, and each of the cracks we identified at the beginning of the chapter attracted increasing attention. However, none of them led to a revolution of such magnitude that it threatened the terms of the conversations in which most mainstream economists participated. In general, it remained acceptable to work within a framework where preferences were exogenous, consumers maximised an unobservable utility, and researchers could be income-based utilitarians. In fact, it is interesting to note that, although we have described these three dissenting lines in their area of convergence (their ability to house the deviation thesis alongside the progress thesis), there were tensions between them that hindered potential synergies. There was no substantial feedback between the cracks, and some even seemed to clash with one another.

The clearest example was the tension between happiness economics and post-utilitarianism. The former was fundamentally empirical, focused on measuring variables of subjective well-being that could fill the theoretical space traditionally covered by the notion of utility. The latter, however, was primarily theoretical and questioned the role that had been attributed to subjective utility. Sen (1987), for example, was a vocal critic of the attempts by happiness economists to equate well-being with the subjective sensations of individuals. After all, humans could adapt to situations of oppression and deprivation, transforming their lives into relatively happy ones despite the circumstances. Conversely, they could become capricious beings, prisoners of unrealistic expectations that prevented them from being happy even in the most benign of circumstances. However, for happiness economists, the real danger was that post-utilitarianism would focus solely on objective contexts, thus blocking once again the study of mental states. If the expansion of objective capabilities did not lead to more subjective well-being, should one not think that something was going wrong after all?

The fact that these dissenting trends grew amid points of friction made it difficult for them to join forces in some sort of alternative paradigm. As a result, most mainstream economists were able to remain politely aloof while continuing to work within their respective fields. The general conversation was moderately permeated by these developments, especially with the incorporation of the Human Development Index into the common lexicon of economists and the interest sparked in some circles by the Stiglitz-Sen-Fitoussi report on the measurement of economic and social progress (Stiglitz et al., 2010). However, not everyone agreed that income per capita should be so easily dethroned (Leunig, 2011). For most economists, more was simply better, and the rest remained modest footnotes dealt with by niche literatures.

It is also interesting to note that, when the dissenting trends did manage to permeate the broader conversation, they did so in a way that did not restore the vision (in Schumpeter's sense) of a consumer society or the deviation thesis. The recognition of this shift can be illustrated by looking at Angus Deaton. The Deaton who won the Nobel Prize in the 2010s was no longer an economist so aligned with the neoclassical theory of utility and demand as the one we met at the start of his career in the previous chapter. He now worked with a multidimensional notion of well-being and was keen to highlight the potential conflicts between different dimensions. In this book *The great escape*, Deaton (2013) worked with a bidimensional framework: on one side, there was income, which was a means to purchase goods that provided utility, but on the other side, there was health, which did not have to correlate monotonically with income. Both dimensions of well-being were connected, but one of the central arguments in the book was that neither of them could be subsumed into the other. In particular, it was impossible to assume that the health outcomes of a society would follow a trajectory tightly linked to its economic growth outcomes. Health thus became something intrinsically valuable—one of those things that made life worthwhile—regardless of whether it could be valued through the pricing system and national accounting (Case & Deaton, 2020).

What we observe here is the influence of Sen, vaguely referenced in secondary passages of his earlier book, in action. Deaton was so convinced by Sen's objective conception of well-being that his review of happiness economics was not at all enthusiastic. Furthermore, when descending into empirical observation, there were few reasons to view subjective well-being as an additional dimension of human well-being. The Easterlin paradox only existed if you misinterpreted the data. By applying appropriate logarithmic transformations, happiness and income actually went hand in hand. There was no need to worry too much about happiness because, after all, it was capturing something that was already quite well represented by the conventional metric of economic growth. It was the health dimension that could not be subsumed into the income dimension; the happiness dimension, however, could.

Even if one accepted that happiness economics allowed for the measurement of performance along the traditional neoclassical axis of subjective well-being, it turned out that the no less traditional convention that income reliably captured this subjective well-being was not so misguided after all. In fact, when Deaton explored potential discrepancies between monetary metrics and the value that certain goods and services truly had in promoting better lives, he joined those economists who emphasised discrepancies with a direction opposite to that pointed out by critics of consumer society. Rather than addressing cases in which (like Galbraith) consumers spent large sums of money on possibly superfluous goods, Deaton addressed cases in which consumers had access to incredibly useful things, such as electricity or an Internet search engine, at very low prices.

Some product innovations and qualitative improvements in consumer goods were not well captured by monetary metrics, especially when there was an underlying trend of falling relative prices. The resulting image was of consumer society as a vehicle of progress, and even more so than the money metric would have it. For Deaton, who was born in 1945 to a mining family, there was no doubt that progress existed, and thus, his grandchildren, according to him, were incredibly fortunate to live in a world full of opportunities, so different from the one he had known as a child (Deaton, 2013, p. 13).

Ultimately, beneath the waves of dissidence and internal pluralism, there remained a fundamental continuity among mainstream economists. The famous phrase uttered by Tancredi Falconeri in *The Leopard*, the novel by Giuseppe Tomasi di Lampedusa, comes to mind: "If we want things to stay as they are, things will have to change". The element of continuity here has less to do with "pure economics" or its possible intersections with other disciplines, and more with the political discourse surrounding the economic conversation. The core idea, as in the past, is that the market economy generally works well and that public intervention in its decentralised mechanism should be limited to cases that can be convincingly characterised as market failures (D'Ippoliti, 2021). Within this political discourse, the principle of consumer sovereignty plays a central role. Even though today's economics may differ significantly from the Austrian views of Mises and Hayek, or (for that matter) the type of neoclassical economics promoted by Robbins, the legacy of these economists in defining the political playing field is evident. Consumer society is portrayed as a vehicle for progress, both in itself and because freedom of choice would be one of the core principles that underpin a healthy market democracy.

The persistence of this political discourse is especially illustrative in the case of those dissidents whose research showed that consumer behaviour could not be expected to validate the traditional neoclassical notion of rationality. A prime example is behavioural economists like Richard Thaler, who, after having reached this result, proposed a political solution that would prove influential both within academia and beyond. What governments should do in the face of potential misalignments arising from sovereign consumer behaviour was not to intervene with large-scale regulations that distorted market signals, much less restrict the freedom of consumer choice (Thaler, 2015; Thaler & Sunstein, 2008). Clearly, governments should not remain idle either. However, there was an intermediate solution: a "real third way" of "libertarian paternalism" (Thaler & Sunstein, 2008, pp. 253–254). Governments could adjust small details that psychological research revealed had a significant impact on individual decision-making. This included, for example, details about how options were presented to consumers. In this way, behavioural dissidents aimed to correct deviations in consumer society in a way that left the principle of consumer sovereignty intact. The role of power in consumer society remained as unexplored as in traditional neoclassical economics.

The extent to which this political alignment has been crucial to the success of behavioural economists can be illustrated by the contrast between Thaler and his colleague Richard Frank. As we have described earlier in the chapter, Frank turned to economic psychology to denounce the existence of a positional consumerist race that contributed nothing to overall well-being. What was his political recommendation to correct this deviation? Implement a consumption tax that discourages people from behaving that way. The result would be a lower level of consumption, but society's well-being would remain unchanged because, after all, the consumption that would be cut back would be that which served merely a positional function. However, as Frank (2022) himself reflected towards the end of his career, it cannot be said that his recommendation had been influential. How much better Thaler had fared, both in academia and beyond, with what he himself defined as "gentle nudges"!

Who Cares About Consumer Society Anymore?

So far, we have examined contemporary formulations of the progress and deviation theses, along with their synergies and tensions. Almost all of these, from adherence to consumer sovereignty to the depiction of consumerism as a senseless positional race, have clear roots in preceding periods. However, if there is one aspect in which the legacy of that period remains particularly alive, it is in the fading of consumer society as a relevant object of study among economists. After all, this had been the outcome of the intellectual battle fought during the Cold War: the full deployment of consumer society had occurred, and some economists had focused their attention on it, but by the end of the period the topic seemed to have become a mirage upon which most economists found little reason to continue reflecting. This has largely remained the situation into the present day.

Let us jump thirty years after the collapse of the Soviet Union and listen to Robert Gordon (2021, p. 823) present us with the following mental game:

> Gather a group of economists together and ask what most concerns them, and a wide variety of topics would soon emerge: slowing economic growth in the rich nations, the inability of many poor nations to converge toward the rich, rising income and wealth inequality, the increasing dominance of superstar firms, growing profit margins and the decline in labor's income share, globalization and the human costs of outsourcing, deaths of despair, and the threat of climate change.

It is only fair to recognise that this list of topics, each of which has a substantial body of specialised literature behind it, is extensive. Perhaps it could be expanded, but few would suggest that Gordon is committing a significant omission by not mentioning consumer society. The conversation among economists continued to be primarily a discussion about the production of wealth and its distribution. Once wealth had been produced and distributed, the question of how individuals made use of it fell outside of the conversation, or at least outside the most vibrant niches of it. At best, the topic could reappear in some related discussion. Gordon (2017) himself illustrates this: he contributed a remarkable reconstruction of the material life of Americans from the mid-nineteenth century onwards, but his interest was on the macroeconomic implications rather than on well-being per se.

The lack of importance attached to the issue of consumer society is particularly well illustrated when a prestigious economist discovers it almost by accident and, upon confronting it, apologises for having been irrelevant. This was the case of Paul Krugman in the late 1990s. Krugman was a neoclassical economist who had little praise for Galbraith's institutionalism. In fact, his image of Galbraith was quite similar to that propagated by Friedman and other post-war mainstream economists to their readers and young students: more than a scientifically relevant economist, he had been a popular policy entrepreneur (Levinson, 2007). Krugman was a dissident, but his dissent was internal in the way Stiglitz's was: he was a mainstream economist unwilling to accept the restrictive assumptions of post-war neoclassical economics. Just as Stiglitz renounced perfect information, Krugman renounced constant returns to scale. And the impact of this on economic theory and policy recommendations was no less notable. Add generous doses of neoclassical Keynesianism, and the result was an economist for whom mainstream tools did not lead as unequivocally as often claimed by heterodox economists to the recommendation that the state withdraw and markets function freely.

Like Stiglitz, Krugman (1998) encountered the deviation thesis through one of the dissenting cracks presented at the beginning of this chapter: the approach of endogenous preferences. He did so in a brief opinion piece in which he questioned the evolution of British cuisine and diet by looking at the French case. It was a decidedly minor piece, but highly significant for our purposes. Very reminiscent of his work on path dependence, Krugman pointed out that, since British consumers had not had the opportunity to develop preferences for quality food, the free interplay of supply and demand was generating a self-reinforcing path in which producers and consumers were meeting in low-quality spaces. In his remarks on the causes of preference formation, Krugman resorted more to the social context than a Gary Becker would have, but he still managed to rely on objective and measurable variables: for example, he blamed early British urbanisation for the development of overly crude culinary habits. But, although his approach to endogenous preferences was somewhat more eclectic, his point of arrival could be summarised in terms of Becker: consumers developed a kind of rational addiction to low-quality food. And if this was the case, it seemed difficult to view with favour the way in which consumer society reproduced this trap.

But at this point, Krugman decided to downplay the issue: he closed the article by admitting that such problems were "small potatoes" and paled in comparison to the pressing issues of the time: ethnic cleansing in the Balkans, the devaluation of the yen. In the following years, especially after the outbreak of the Great Recession, Krugman's public profile would become increasingly prominent. Together with Stiglitz, he would become one of the most recognisable voices in the economic culture of the Democratic Party. However, consumer society and its possible deviations were not mobilised in his formulation of alternatives to the neoliberal proposals of the time.

This is illustrative of the true scope of the dissenting cracks, but we would not want to give the impression that the argument applies to mainstream economists only. In fact, the lack of interest in consumer society was even more striking in the heterodox schools of economic thought. Heterodox economists quickly accepted the forensic report issued by the mainstream of a previous generation about Galbraith: he had been a writer for non-economists who did not even seem to deserve a place in new histories of institutionalism (Chirat, 2021, pp. 909–947; Hodgson, 2004). Let us clarify that this lack of interest was not total, and that alternative syntheses such as Chang's (2014, pp. 272–273) illustrate the niche that the deviation thesis seemed to have reserved within the heterodox field of vision. But the niche was far from vibrant. In fact, consumer society had disappeared from the main conversations being opened up by the most prominent heterodox economists. Take, for example, the debate initiated by the neo-Schumpeterian economist Mariana Mazzucato (2013, 2021) on the public sector, innovation, and value creation. During the Great Recession and its aftermath, Mazzucato, bolstered by the success of her book *The Entrepreneurial State*, strongly advocated for a vision of economic growth in which, through public-private collaboration focused on major societal challenges, growth would be smart, inclusive, and sustainable. These three dimensions captured the concerns of many heterodox economists at the time: restoring economic growth (and avoiding its fluctuations), promoting social equity in the distribution of income and wealth, and doing so in a way that respected the environment and future generations (Jacobs & Mazzucato, 2016). In other words, the focus was on the production of wealth and its distribution, but not truly on its utilisation.

For Mazzucato (2018, 2021), however, it made sense to reflect on a topic closely linked to the use of wealth: the direction of economic change. Economic growth, in her view, was not just a rate: it was also a direction. In the terms we have been employing in this book, the appropriate framework for assessing economic growth was not a one-dimensional scale to measure the distance between two points, but a multidimensional matrix. In such a matrix, the same growth rate could be achieved through different combinations of activities, each with its own implications in terms of social utility, capacity building, equality, environmental impact, or long-term growth potential. Consequently, for Mazzucato, it was essential to revive the notion of "economic mission". The state had to define relevant societal goals and develop structures for public-private collaboration that would direct investment accordingly, instead of merely letting short-term market signals do the guidance. However, Mazzucato's analysis, while bridging the creation and use of wealth, has not delved into the perspective of the consumer as an agent who also participates in shaping a particular direction for economic change.

If this was the case in the conversation on innovation, what about the even more vibrant discussion on inequality? The explosion of *Capital in the Twenty-First Century* as an unlikely bestseller during the aftermath of the Great Recession allowed Thomas Piketty (2014) to play a leading role in that conversation. Piketty, whose influences were eclectic and who could perhaps be framed most fittingly within the tradition of the historical school, argued based on a profound and painstakingly constructed database that the dynamics of capitalism generally favoured increases in inequality, and that this was precisely what had been happening since the late twentieth century. Piketty's approach was, of course, a direct attack on much of the economic culture that had triumphed during the *belle époque* between the Berlin Wall and the outbreak of the Great Recession. The concentration of wealth in the upper classes had reached notable proportions and, unless policies were implemented to prevent it, it would not take long for the peaks of social polarisation reached by the First World War to come back.

Piketty, however, did not build any bridge (even secondary or marginal) between the issue of wealth distribution and the issue of how individuals made use of it. The criterion of evaluation that seemed to permeate his work was that inequality was bad, at least insofar as it was not justified by some social function. It must be conceded that in a later work Piketty (2019) studied in depth the discourses in various societies that have legitimised inequality. However, even if we accept without much objection that inequality is bad and that most of these discourses are unconvincing, the question remains open: can we assess the severity of inequality without examining how different social classes use their income and wealth?

In this regard, consumption was strikingly absent from Piketty's work, as were the notions of quality of life and well-being. For Piketty, as for Marx before him, more seemed to be better, and the key question was *cui bono*: more was better, but for whom? If we were returning to the levels of inequality of the long nineteenth century, did that mean we were returning to a situation equally problematic from a social standpoint? Did it make a difference that inequality coexisted now with widespread basic comforts for a large majority of the population? Or, on the contrary, was it assumed that income and wealth differences inevitably translated into situations of relative deprivation just as serious, even though they now materialised in different consumer goods? Could it be taken for granted that the formidable concentration of wealth and income in the hands of high-status groups contributed to them leading a better life? Or perhaps part of their consumption pattern served little more than, for example, signalling status?

These questions were not addressed by Piketty, who merely noted in passing that, if we set aside "artificial" needs based on social or environmental exploitation, most of the diversity of aspirations and preferences found among consumers had to be considered "legitimate" (Piketty, 2019, pp. 707–712). In fact, Piketty seemed to feel comfortable within the philosophical reductionism championed by the neoclassical economists of the mid-twentieth century and adopted a one-dimensional monetary scale to assess the results of socioeconomic change. This was also the case with other authors who brought inequality back to the economic conversation (Rogan, 2017, pp. 1–15). In a conversation in which it was implicitly assumed that more was better, consumer society remained out of the frame.

This was a tendency shared by a substantial fraction of contemporary heterodox thought, particularly those economists connected to Marx. The most significant contribution in this regard was perhaps that of Ben Fine (2002), who proposed framing the analysis of consumption within a "systems of provision" approach. For Fine, the key rupture with neoclassical theory was that, instead of a horizontal theory extending to all consumer decisions, a vertical theory was needed that would explain each consumer decision based on the developments occurring in the production chain. Once embedded in this "system of provision", the material and cultural dimensions of consumption could be integrated, recognising that firms not only produced goods but also social images of them. The result was a perspective in which, in contrast to the narrative of the sovereign consumer, business power structured consumer decisions and induced inequalities among consumers. There were no bridges to the issue of affluence, not even in the version of it that, as shown by heterodox Marxists like the psychologist Erich Fromm during the Cold War, could be derived from a humanist reading of the young Marx. It was implicitly assumed that more was better, and the issue was simply that some consumed much more than others. Only in very recent times has a Marxist reflection on "degrowth" (Saito, 2023, 2024) emerged, and its capacity to change the conversation remains uncertain.

There is no doubt that some heterodox economists from other affiliations sought to open alternative conceptual routes. Evolutionary economists like Ulrich Witt (2001, 2017), for example, proposed a "learning to consume" approach to capture the role of personal trajectories and social influences on consumer decisions, which led to an ambivalent view of their welfare effects (Chai, 2017). Some radical political economists proposed an approach influenced by postmodernism and feminism (Pietrykowski, 2007). However, their influence has been small, even among other heterodox economists. When these economists looked at the world of consumption, they preferred to focus on power asymmetrics between producers and consumers, as well as the segmentation and hierarchies among consumers (Todorova, 2014). After all, the suspicion that there was a mainstream bias in focusing too narrowly on consumption floated in the air. When Chang (2014, pp. 155–158) attempts to identify the domain of economics that various traditions of thought consider the most important, consumption only appears in the neoclassical tradition. For all others (classical, Marxist, developmental, Schumpeterian, and, with nuance, institutionalist, behavioural, and Keynesian), the most important domain is that of production. Perhaps the history of economic thought could have taken other routes, but Chang does a good job at suggesting the structural limits that the question of consumer society faces within the very heterodox approaches in which it flourished in the past.

The political context has also not been the most favourable for reorienting the conversation of heterodox economists in this direction. During the *belle époque* of 1989–2007, neoliberalism found few reasons to worry about the issue, but the "third way" with which social democracy tried to fight it back also accepted the figure of the sovereign consumer as an essential element of the economic and political order (Olsen, 2019, p. 227–258). The doubts about consumer society, which had not been absent in the early days of social democracy, became lost causes, quickly acquiring a status like public enterprises or big regulation. The Great Recession, for its part, did little to rehabilitate the question of consumer society. On the contrary, much like the 1970s crisis, it contributed to the sense that Galbraith's concerns about the affluent society belonged to a very different historical era—one in which economic growth was expected to be fast and social inequality decreasing (Berry, 2013; Tooze, 2018).

It is true that the recent rise of the ecological transition in political agendas has created a new space for reflection on the role of consumption patterns in environmental degradation and its correction. But, in practical terms, there is little sign of a new generation of consumption policies aimed at correcting this or other potential deviations. Adherence to consumer sovereignty, perhaps supplemented by a renewed emphasis on the need for consumers to have the right information, continues to dominate the public policy landscape. Even in fields like food, where it is possible to speak of deviations backed by nutritional science, corrective policies have been few, unsystematic, and, where they have conflicted with business interests, hotly contested (Collantes, 2024, pp. 207–224). This political atmosphere has done little to reintegrate consumer society into the field of vision of economists, even for those who were seeking to connect their academic work to the renewal of left-wing political agendas.

Conclusion: The Aftermath

Over the past thirty years, most economists have continued to lack a vision (in Schumpeter's sense) of consumer society. This is a legacy of the intellectual battle waged during the Cold War. Although during this period some heterodox and dissenting economists had suggested in various ways that consumer society could be both a vehicle for progress and a source of deviation, cultivating what we have referred to as the "synthesis view", the outcome was that the majority of economists adhered to the progress thesis and, over time, consumer society faded away as a topic for serious economic research. This situation has largely persisted into the present day because its causes have persisted as well.

The cultivation of the "synthesis view" required that the deviation thesis could flourish somewhere, and this was much more feasible if economists understood that their "pure economics" had to maintain "close relations" (to once again use Schumpeter's expression) with other disciplines such as history, sociology, and philosophy. Despite some signs of change, and despite the renewal brought about by the beginning of such close relations with psychology, this is still far from the case. In an honest reflection on the way in which he has been forced to "rethink his economics", Angus Deaton (2024) has recently offered us a remarkable confession of all that, beneath the waves of renewal that are triumphally announced from time to time, has not changed within the profession:

> [We] have largely stopped thinking about ethics and about what constitutes human well-being. We are technocrats who focus on efficiency. We get little training about the ends of economics, on the meaning of well-being—welfare economics has long since vanished from the curriculum—or on what philosophers say about equality. When pressed, we usually fall back on an income-based utilitarianism. We often equate well-being with money or consumption, missing much of what matters to people.

And, regarding history, Deaton asserts that, given the importance in the real world of "slow-acting mechanisms that operate with long and variable lags",

> Historians, who understand about contingency and about multiple and multidirectional causality, often do a better job than economists of identifying important mechanisms that are plausible, interesting, and worth thinking about, even if they do not meet the inferential standards of contemporary applied economics.

Deaton concludes with a telling suggestion that does not have anything to do with "pure economics": "Economists could benefit by greater engagement with the ideas of philosophers, historians, and sociologists, just as Adam Smith once did".

This intellectual isolation has significantly hindered economists from visualising consumer society. There has also been a political factor at play: the adherence of most economists to the principle of consumer sovereignty as the cornerstone of market democracies. During the Cold War era, the figure of the sovereign consumer had become firmly established within the political atmosphere of the profession, once heterodox protests like those from Galbraith were vigorously repelled. In the present day, generational turnover has meant that an increasing proportion of economists have been educated in that atmosphere. Additionally, it must be noted that this alignment has been very congruent with the political dynamics of the period: especially during the *belle époque* of 1989–2007, but even up to the present day, both neoliberalism and social democracy ceased to question the direction of socioeconomic change, the origins of consumer preferences, or the potential conflicts between consumption and other dimensions of the good life.

The intellectual isolation of economists and their political adherence to the principle of consumer sovereignty had an even more pronounced effect because of the dynamics prevailing in the academic labour market. Controversial mechanisms for evaluating and ranking research have permeated every corner of academic life, pushing even further than before the tendency to expel dissidents and heterodox economists who do not share the mainstream's assumptions about the nature of economics. The academic system does not provide good opportunities for young economists to emulate Deaton's Adam Smith, at least if they want to retain their affiliation to an economics department.

Yet, our era has also given rise to dynamics suggesting that the question of consumer society may make a return or, at the very least, survive. It is true that even among heterodox economists who persist in the profession, there is no automatic tendency to visualise consumer society. However, some heterodox currents, especially followers of Keynes and ecological economists, have done so. Furthermore, dissenting circles have emerged in the mainstream that, by focusing on endogenous preferences, happiness, or post-utilitarianism, have expanded the analytical space for cultivating the "synthesis view". Through largely autonomous routes, though not without tensions between them, these dynamics have kept alive the suspicion that consumer society may harbour elements of deviation.

The path towards articulating the theses of progress and deviation remains largely to be paved. Beyond the academic inertia we have discussed above, there are purely intellectual obstacles that still await confrontation. The question about consumer society survives, but it is not evident that the available answers have been incorporated into a cycle of cumulative progress in knowledge. The problem is, in part, empirical. There is no doubt that the new combinations of the progress and deviation theses are based on a more solid empirical foundation than those of previous generations. But has this "empirical turn" been sufficient, considering the magnitude of the historical change that has occurred between the consumption patterns of Galbraith's era (let alone Mill's or Keynes' eras) and those of the present day? Historical sense strongly suggests that the combination of the progress and deviation theses cannot be limited to a diachronic view: first one thing, then the other. This leads us to an unresolved theoretical issue. Can the good life be a finished outcome once and for all? Or is it rather a process that will always be ongoing? In the final chapter of the book, we revisit these questions in the context of a longer-term analysis of consumer society in the history of economic thought.

References

Ambrosino, A., Cedrini, M., & Davis, J. B. (2024). Today's economics: One, no one and one hundred thousand. *European Journal of the History of Economic Thought, 31*(1), 59-76.

Arrighi, G. (1994). *The long twentieth century: Money, power, and the origins of our times.* Verso.

Arrighi, G. (2007). *Adam Smith in Beijing: Lineages of the twenty-first century.* Verso.

Backhouse, R. E., & Cherrier, B. (2017). The age of the applied economist: The transformation of economics since the 1970s. *History of Political Economy, 49*(supplement), 1-33.

Barba, A., & Pivetti, M. (2009). Rising household debt: Its causes and macroeconomic implications – a long-period analysis. *Cambridge Journal of Economics, 33*(1), 113-137.

Bauman, Z. (1998). *Work, consumerism and the new poor*. Open University Press.

Bauman, Z. (2007). *Consuming life*. Polity.

Bauman, Z. (2008). *Does ethics have a chance in a world of consumers?* Harvard University Press.

Becker, G. S. (1996). *Accounting for tastes*. Harvard University Press.

Behringer, J., González-Granda, M., & van Treeck, T. (2024). Varieties of the rat race: Working hours in the age of abundance. *Socio-Economic Review, 22*(1), 141-168.

Berry, M. (2013). *The affluent society revisited*. Oxford University Press.

Blaug, M. (1968). *Economic theory in retrospect*. R. D. Irwin.

Brand, U., & Wissen, M. (2021). *The imperial mode of living: Everyday life and the ecological crisis of capitalism*. Verso.

Case, A., & Deaton, A. (2020). *Deaths of despair and the future of capitalism*. Princeton University Press.

Cedrini, M., Dagnes, J., & Akdere, Ç. (2021). Stephen King's 'Needful things': A dystopian vision of capitalism during its triumph. *Journal of Post-Keynesian Economics, 44*(3), 341-364.

Chai, A. (2017). Rethinking the economic possibilities of our grandchildren: What is the future of consumption? *Journal of Evolutionary Economics, 27*(2), 215-219.

Chang, H.-J. (2014). *Economics: The user's guide*. Penguin.

Chang, H.-J., & Lari, T. (2024). Economics, pluralism and democracy: An interview with Ha-Joon Chang. *Erasmus Journal for Philosophy and Economics, 17*(2), 201-238.

Chirat, A. (2021). *L'Économie intégral de John Kenneth Galbraith (1933-1983)*. Garnier.

Collantes, F. (2017). *La economía española en 3D: oferta, demanda y largo plazo*. Pirámide.

Collantes, F. (2024). *Milk in Spain and the history of diet change: The political economy of dairy consumption since 1950*. Bloomsbury.

Crouch, C. (2009). Privatised Keynesianism: An unacknowledged policy regime. *British Journal of Politics and International Relations, 11*(3), 382-399.

D'Ippoliti, C. (2021). *Democratizing the economics debate: Pluralism and research evaluation*. Routledge.

Daly, H. E. (1972). *The steady state economy*. W. H. Freeman and Co.

Daly, H. E. (1991). *Steady-state economics*. Island Press.

de Grazia, V. (2005). *Irresistible empire: America's advance through twentieth-century Europe*. Harvard University Press.
de Grazia, V. (2016). The crisis of hyper-consumerism: Capitalism's latest forward lurch. In J. Kocka & M. van der Linden (Eds.), *Capitalism: The reemergence of a historical concept*. Bloomsbury.
de Vries, J. (2008). *The industrious revolution: Consumer behavior and the household economy*. Cambridge University Press.
de Vries, J. (2023). Whatever happened to the affluent society? Or, the dynamics of consumer-driven capitalism revealed. *Capitalism, 4*(2), 215-257.
Deaton, A. (2013). *The great escape: Health, wealth, and the origins of inequality*. Princeton University Press.
Deaton, A. (2024). Questioning one's views as circumstances evolve can be a good thing. *Finance & Development*, March.
Easterlin, R. A. (1998). *Growth triumphant: The twenty-first century in historical perspective*. University of Michigan Press.
Easterlin, R. A. (2001). Income and happiness: Towards a unified theory. *Economic Journal, 111*(473), 465-484.
Ekelund, R. B., & Hébert, R. F. (1990). *A history of economic theory and method*. McGraw-Hill. [Spanish edition: *Historia de la teoría económica y de su método*. McGraw Hill, 1997.]
Fine, B. (2002). *The world of consumption: The material and cultural revisited*. Routledge.
Fourcade, M., Ollion, E., & Algan, Y. (2015). The superiority of economists. *Journal of Economic Perspectives, 29*(1), 89-114.
Francks, P. (2009). *The Japanese consumer: An alternative economic history of modern Japan*. Cambridge University Press.
Frank, R. H. (1999). *Luxury fever: Why money fails to satisfy in an era of excess*. Free Press.
Frank, R. H. (2022). Success, luck, and luxury. Interview at the *Rational reminder* podcast. https://rationalreminder.ca/podcast/230
Freeman, C., & Louçã, F. (2001). *As time goes by: From the industrial revolutions to the information revolution*. Oxford University Press.
Frey, B. (2008). *Happiness: A revolution in economics*. MIT Press.
Frieden, J. A. (2006). *Global capitalism: Its fall and rise in the twentieth century*. W. W Norton. [Spanish edition: *Capitalismo global: el trasfondo económico de la historia del siglo XX*. Crítica, 2007.]
Galbraith, J. K. (2022). Review of "L'économie intégrale de John Kenneth Galbraith (1933-1983)" by Alexandre Chirat. *Iberian Journal of the History of Economic Thought, 9*(1), 49-50.
Gordon, R. J. (2017). *The rise and fall of American growth: The U.S. standard of living since the Civil War*. Princeton University Press.

Gordon, R. J. (2021). How to boost the payoff from innovation while shrinking its destructive side effects. *Business History Review, 95*(4), 823-840.

Hamermesh, D. S. (2013). Six decades of top economics publishing: Who and how? *Journal of Economic Literature, 51*(1), 162-172.

Harvey, D. (2005). *A brief history of neoliberalism*. Oxford University Press.

Hodgson, G. (2004). *The evolution of institutional economics: Agency, structure, and Darwinism in American institutionalism*. Routledge.

Hodgson, G. (2019). *Is there a future for heterodox economics? Institutions, ideology and a scientific community*. Edward Elgar.

Honoré, C. (2004). *In praise of slow*. Harper.

Jackson, T. (2009). *Prosperity without growth: Economics for a finite planet*. Earthscan. [Spanish edition: *Prosperidad sin crecimiento: economía para un planeta finito*. Icaria, 2011.]

Jackson, T. (2011). Prólogo a la edición en castellano. en *Prosperidad sin crecimiento: economía para un planeta finito*. Icaria.

Jackson, T. (2021a). *Post growth: Life after capitalism*. Polity Books.

Jackson, T. (2021b). Post growth: Life after capitalism. Interview at *New Books Network*. newbooksnetwork.com.

Jacobs, M., & Mazzucato, M. (2016). Rethinking capitalism: An introduction. In M. Jacobs & M. Mazzucato (Eds.), *Rethinking capitalism: Economics and policy for sustainable and inclusive growth*. Wiley-Blackwell.

Kasser, T. (2002). *The high price of materialism*. MIT Press.

Krugman, P. (1998). Supply, demand, and English food. *Fortune*, 20 July. [Spanish edition: La oferta, la demanda y la comida inglesa. In P. Krugman, *El gran engaño*. Crítica, 2004].

Latouche, S. (2010). *Pour sortir de la société de consommation: voix et voies de la décroissance*. Les Liens qui Libèrent.

Latouche, S. (2019). *La décroissance*. Que sais-je?.

Layard, R. (2005). *Happiness: Lessons from a new science*. Penguin.

Lazonick, W., Carpenter, M., & Sakinç, M. E. (2024). An economist for our times: Innovative enterprise, changing industrial leadership, and the looting of the US business corporation. An interview with William Lazonick. *Revue de la Régulation* (online), 36, http://journalsopenedition.org/regulation/24232.

Lee, F. (2009). *A history of heterodox economics: Challenging the mainstream in the twentieth century*. Routledge.

Leunig, T. (2011). Measuring economic performance and social progress. *European Review of Economic History, 15*(2), 357-363.

Levinson, M. (2007). The 'usefully dangerous' economist. *Dissent, 54*(2), www.dissentmagazine.org

Levy, J. (2021). *Ages of American capitalism: A history of the United States*. Random House.

Malassis, L. (1997). *Les trois âges de l'alimentaire: essai sur une historie sociale de l'alimentation et de l'agriculture*. Cujas.
Martins, N. O. (2014). *The Cambridge revival of political economy*. Routledge.
Mazzucato, M. (2013). *The entrepreneurial state: Debunking public vs. private myths in innovation*. Anthem.
Mazzucato, M. (2018). *The value of everything: Makers and takers in the global economy*. Allen Lane.
Mazzucato, M. (2021). *Mission economy: A moonshot guide to changing capitalism*. Allen Lane.
Offer, A., & Söderberg, G. (2016). *The Nobel factor: The prize in economics, social democracy, and the market turn*. Princeton University Press.
Olsen, N. (2019). *The sovereign consumer: A new intellectual history of neoliberalism*. Palgrave Macmillan.
Ortiz-Ospina, E., & Roser, E. (2024). Happiness and life satisfaction. Retrieved 5 February 2025, from www.ourworldindata.org
Parrique, T. (2024, September 2). About degrowth, breaking rules, writing and other things. *Ceteris Never Paribus*, podcast episode no. 42.
Pietrykowski, B. (2007). Exploring new directions for research in the radical political economy of consumption. *Review of Radical Political Economics, 39*(2), 257-283.
Piketty, T. (2014). *Capital in the twenty-first century*. Harvard University Press.
Piketty, T. (2019). *Capital and ideology*. Harvard University Press. [Spanish edition: *Capital e ideología*. Planeta, 2019.]
Pugno, M. (2016). *On the foundations of happiness in economics: Reinterpreting Tibor Scitovksy*. Routledge.
Rogan, T. (2017). *The moral economists: R. H. Tawney, Karl Polanyi, and E. P. Thompson*. Princeton University Press.
Saito, K. (2023). *Marx in the Anthropocene: Towards the idea of degrowth communism*. Cambridge University Press.
Saito, K. (2024). *Slow down: The degrowth manifesto*. Astra House.
Schor, J. (1991). *The overworked American: The unexpected decline of leisure*. Basic Books.
Schor, J. (1998). *The overspent American: Upscaling, downshifting, and the new consumer*. Basic Books.
Schor, J. (2004). *Born to buy: The commercialized child and the new consumer culture*. Scribner.
Schor, J. (2005). Sustainable consumption and worktime reduction. *Journal of Industrial Ecology, 9*(1–2), 37-50.
Schor, J. (2007). In defense of consumer critique: Revisiting the consumption debates of the twentieth century. *Annals of the American Academy of Political and Social Science, 611*, 16-30.
Schor, J. (2010). *Plenitude: The new economics of true wealth*. Penguin.

Schor, J. (2014). Reflections on popular economics: An interview with Juliet Schor. www.populareconomics.org

Schwartz, B. (2004). *The paradox of choice: Why more is less.* Harper.

Sen, A. (1985). *Commodities and capabilities.* Oxford University Press.

Sen, A. (1987). *On ethics and economics.* Basil Blackwell.

Sen, A. (1999). *Development as freedom.* Oxford University Press.

Skidelsky, R. (1983–2000). *John Maynard Keynes: A biography.* Macmillan.

Skidelsky, R. (1996). *Keynes.* Oxford University Press. [Spanish edition: *Keynes.* Alianza, 1998.]

Skidelsky, R. (2009). *Keynes: The return of the master.* Allen Lane.

Skidelsky, R., & Skidelsky, E. (2012). *How much is enough? The love of money and the case for the good life.* Allen Lane.

Spash, C. L. (2020). A tale of three paradigms: Realising the revolutionary potential of ecological economics. *Ecological Economics, 169*, 106518.

Stiglitz, J. E. (2008). Toward a general theory of consumerism: Reflections on Keynes's *Economic possibilities for our grandchildren.* In L. Pecchi & G. Piga (Eds.), *Revisiting Keynes: Economic possibilities for our grandchildren.* MIT Press.

Stiglitz, J. E., Sen, A., & Fitoussi, J.-P. (2010). *Mismeasuring our lives: Why GDP does not add.* The New Press.

Thaler, R. (2015). *Misbehaving: The making of behavioral economics.* W. W. Norton.

Thaler, R. H., & Sunstein, C. R. (2008). *Nudge: Improving decisions about health, wealth, and happiness.* Yale University Press.

Todorova, Z. (2014). Consumption as a social process within social provisioning and capitalism: Implications for heterodox economics. *Journal of Economic Issues, 48*(3), 663-678.

Tooze, A. (2018). *Crashed: How a decade of financial crises changed the world.* Penguin.

Trentmann, F. (2016). *Empire of things: How we became a world of consumers, from the fifteenth century to the twenty-first.* HarperCollins.

Vianna Franco, M. P., & Missemer, A. (2022). *A history of ecological economic thought.* Routledge.

Witt, U. (2001). Learning to consume: A theory of wants and the growth of demand. *Journal of Evolutionary Economics, 11*(1), 23-36.

Witt, U. (2017). The evolution of consumption and its welfare effects. *Journal of Evolutionary Economics, 27*, 273-293.

CHAPTER 7

Conclusion: Consumer Society and the Economists

Faced with the question about consumer society, economists have struggled to develop a "synthesis view". Throughout the history of modern economic thought, we have encountered presentations of the progress thesis, which asserts that access to a more abundant and diverse basket of consumer goods makes it possible to improve people's well-being. At the same time, we have also seen various presentations of the deviation thesis, which warns about the capacity of consumerism to divert individuals from the good life and societies from the true path to progress. Historians, with the advantage of hindsight, teach us that both theses are plausible. It is possible that each thesis could claim a distinct temporal province in which to reign: the progress thesis at the start of the modern era and the deviation thesis in more recent periods. Even more plausibly, both theses could be simultaneously correct: in a given period, the dynamics of consumer society could encompass elements of both progress and deviation. Consequently, one might expect that economists would have ventured into the territory of a "synthesis view" that combines both perspectives and that their dialogue would have revolved around different modes and styles of combining the progress and deviation theses. However, this has not been the case. To begin with, the deviation thesis has struggled to find a place within mainstream economic discourse. Moreover, even among

F. Collantes, *Consumer Society and the Economists*, Palgrave Studies in the History of Economic Thought,
https://doi.org/10.1007/978-3-031-96645-3_7

economists who have remained open to this thesis, there has been little cumulative progress towards a "synthesis view".

In this concluding chapter, we address both problems in turn, before introducing a third: the limited presence of consumer society in the field of vision of most economists. This book attests to the fact that reflections on consumer society, or reflections that can retrospectively be interpreted under that light, are far from absent in the history of economic thought. Nevertheless, considering the profound historical transformation represented by the formation and development of consumer societies in various parts of the world during the modern era, economists have responded weakly—or, at best, intermittently.

The chapter is structured as follows. The first section traces the forging of two intellectual genealogies, whose primary distinction lies in their differing degrees of receptivity to the deviation thesis. The following two sections examine each of these genealogies in turn. The second section focuses on the difficulties faced by the deviation thesis in taking root within the field cultivated by the first genealogy. The third section addresses the challenges encountered by members of the second genealogy in articulating a synthesis between the progress and deviation theses. Finally, the fourth section analyses the reasons why the question about consumer society has not featured prominently on the agenda of most economists.

Two Genealogies

Throughout this book, we have found it useful to employ the labels traditionally used to group individual authors in schools of thought. Accordingly, we have referred to classical political economy, Marxism, institutionalism, the neoclassical school, Keynesianism, or ecological economics. At the same time, we have avoided treating these schools as monolithic entities, trying to capture different currents and nuances within them. Precisely for this reason, we have sought to combine the identification of orthodoxies and heterodoxies, intellectual cores and peripheries, with a sensitivity to how the lines separating them were drawn, shifted, and redrawn as time went by. We have been determined to avoid the ahistorical approach of presenting our narrative in terms of a long-term opposition between a mainstream allegedly committed to the progress thesis and a heterodoxy committed to the deviation thesis.

When it comes to analysing the overall picture composed of our four periods—spanning from the late eighteenth century to the present—it is nonetheless useful to recognise the existence of two distinct intellectual genealogies. The dividing factor between them is not any of the usual suspects in general histories of economic thought: not the theory of value (objective versus subjective), the conceptual core of economic analysis (surplus versus scarcity), or the language used (common language versus mathematical models). Instead, the key factor has proved to be more specific: the degree of openness to the deviation thesis. Despite nuances in emphasis and implication, the idea of consumption as progress has been recurrent among economists. It is the possibility of consumption as deviation that has divided them.

From this perspective, we can distinguish between two intellectual genealogies. The first, in the sense that it emerged earlier in chronological terms, is open to exploring the deviation thesis. This does not mean it unreservedly endorses the thesis or excludes the possibility of articulating it alongside the progress thesis. It simply means that, according to this first genealogy, the development of consumer society might indeed involve elements of deviation, and these elements deserve consideration. The second genealogy, by contrast, gravitates around the progress thesis and remains decidedly sceptical about the possibility of deviation.

In the first of our periods, the classical political economists and Marx laid out ambivalent analytical lines that we can read as contributions to the first of these genealogies. Until well into the nineteenth century, the consumption patterns of most of the population were so rudimentary that it is unsurprising the classics and Marx viewed a more abundant and diverse basket of consumer goods as a path to a better life and a better society. At a time when many basic needs were still inadequately met, the prospect of material prosperity was a horizon of progress. Furthermore, one could even speculate that an enlarged consumer basket might have positive effects beyond the strictly material domain, making the possibility of fuller human self-realisation more attainable. However, this line of analysis—focused on the interaction between the material and immaterial dimensions of the good life—soon encountered the possibility that the interaction could also generate negative feedback loops. Once basic needs were comfortably met, doubts began to arise, especially in John Stuart Mill: might the persistence of materialistic priorities prevent individuals from developing their full human faculties? In the field of classical political economy and Marx, both the progress and the deviation thesis could emerge.

This cautious ambivalence continued to inform a significant portion of economic discourse during the second of our periods. Between 1870 and

1945, an embryonic consumer society emerged in Western countries, and increasingly professionalised economists began to reflect more systematically on it. The deviation thesis not only remained alive within these reflections but tended to develop and become more systematic. In the most forceful formulation of the deviation thesis up to that point, the institutionalist Thorstein Veblen depicted the emerging consumer society as an absurd positional race driven by the instinct of emulation and conspicuous consumption. Veblen emphasised the argument so strongly that he practically left it to the reader to imagine that, at some earlier point in time, the progress thesis might have had its share of validity.

Other authors belonging to what we have identified as the first genealogy—such as Alfred Marshall and John Maynard Keynes—did attempt to develop something resembling a "synthesis view". Both proposed a sequence in which the progress thesis reigned at the beginning and the deviation thesis could have a chance of reigning later. The progress thesis prevailed while most of the population lacked the means to adequately satisfy their basic needs. Once that threshold was crossed, however, the danger arose that a persistent focus on consumerism might impact the non-material dimensions of the good life, such as the ability to appreciate art, nature, and personal relationships. Although neither Marshall nor Keynes fully integrated these reflections into the core of their economic thought, their search for a "synthesis view" clearly places them within the first of our two genealogies.

This period also witnessed the birth of the second genealogy, which revolved around the progress thesis and was largely unreceptive to the deviation thesis. A key turning point was the marginalist revolution and its success in transforming political economy into what became simply economics. The marginalist *homo economicus* could be expected to make rational decisions and maximise the utility derived from their basket of consumer goods. Therefore, consumer society was seen as reflecting a set of equilibria in which consumers obtained the highest possible level of well-being given their personal economic circumstances. However, as the case of Marshall shows, the school that later became known as neoclassical was not necessarily aligned with this second genealogy from the outset. The alignment took shape gradually over time, particularly during the interwar period. Against the backdrop of the Bolshevik Revolution and the crisis of classical liberalism, the Austrian school added an indirect argument in favour of consumer society: the sovereign consumer was not only the *primum mobile* of the market economy, compelling producers to meet their desires, but also the embodiment of the basic liberties that defined democratic systems. By the end of this period, neoclassical economists, accompanied by the Austrians, had shifted to a framework that left little room for the coexistence of the progress thesis and the deviation thesis.

This framework became the dominant terrain for economists during the Cold War, when the second genealogy clearly overshadowed the first. The period was highly significant for the historical development of consumer society. In the decades following the Second World War, a fully developed version of mass consumer society emerged in the United States and eventually spread to Western Europe and Japan. Although notable changes also occurred in the consumption patterns of the Soviet Union and its Eastern European satellites, these were less profound and unfolded in a radically different political context. If, as has been convincingly argued, American consumer society acted as an "irresistible empire" for Western Europeans (de Grazia, 2005), it also served as a point of contrast between the two sides of the Cold War divide.

The Cold War was an important period for the history of economic thought too. The neoclassical school rose to a position of hegemony that it had not enjoyed during the pluralistic interwar years, while other schools of thought were pushed to the periphery. It was in this context that the second genealogy became the dominant orthodoxy among economists. Neoclassical consumers were portrayed as optimisers of their own well-being—a variable they presumably understood far better than any government or intellectual could hope to. Consequently, if post-war consumers were increasing their expenditure to purchase more and better goods than in the past, the sequence of events that was moving them from their former equilibria to new ones seemed to be a self-evident vehicle of progress. Furthermore, during the Cold War era, the political argument that the Austrian school had introduced was more relevant than ever. Consumer sovereignty was not only the foundation for a flourishing market economy but also one of the political pillars of a free world threatened by what Milton Friedman (1962, p. 201) called "the evil men of the Kremlin".

The dominance achieved by the second genealogy was vividly illustrated by the difficulties encountered by economists who were swimming against the tide and adhered to the first genealogy. The most prominent of these was the institutionalist John Kenneth Galbraith, who placed at the centre of his thought what had been a peripheral element in the work of Mill, Marshall, and Keynes: a "synthesis view" in which each of the two rival views of consumer society was given a specific temporal province in which to reign. For Galbraith, the progress thesis reigned in a past characterised by scarcity and deprivation, but the deviation thesis took over in the affluent society created by the post-war boom of American capitalism. In this new context, consumers—strongly influenced by corporate advertising and a culture of emulation—were channelling their expenditure towards satisfying relatively trivial desires, while the provision of essential public goods was neglected.

However, this flirtation with the deviation thesis—reinforcing arguments made by other prominent public intellectuals, such as the philosopher Herbert Marcuse—was severely condemned by mainstream economists. Their objections ranged from concerns related to economic theory or empirical evidence to those tied to political implications. Although other heterodox economists, such as Paul Baran and Paul Sweezy on the Marxist side, and mainstream dissidents like Tibor Scitovsky and Richard Easterlin, found reasons to question that consumer society was truly a vehicle for progress, the deviation thesis struggled to survive in the conversation of most economists. Towards the end of the period, the success of Friedman as a public intellectual opposing Galbraith was the end of a cycle: a few decades during which the first of our genealogies, despite experiencing more vigorous internal development than in the past, was ultimately reduced to a marginal position.

The Cold War period thus emerges as a key chapter in our story. It was then that the tension between rival views—prefigured from the late nineteenth century through the Second World War—culminated in a head-on confrontation. The outcome of this clash left a legacy that extended beyond the Cold War era and into the present day. Although every chapter in the history of economic thought contains threads that link different periods and vectors, in our case it is undoubtedly this period where we find the strongest connections. The intellectual dominance of the neoclassical school during the Cold War, along with its control over the academic labour market, left an enduring mark on how future generations would view consumer society. Over the past three decades, the default stance for most economists has been to adhere to the progress thesis and, in the terms we have been using in this chapter, to join the second of our genealogies. Interestingly, this has been true not only for those economists who have placed their trust in free markets in the style of Friedman but also for most of those mainstream economists who have found reasons to advocate for significant public intervention in economic life. Beneath the important debates in which they were engaged, there was a prevailing consensus about the way in which the question about consumer society had been resolved during the Cold War.

Let us understand this path dependence in a weak sense: as a kind of inertia from the past that conditioned but did not predetermine what would happen next. In the present time, the second genealogy has continued to dominate, but the first has shown far more vitality than one might have expected. If there had been a strong kind of path dependence, the wounds inflicted on the first genealogy during the Cold War would surely have led to its demise. And yet, the first genealogy has remained alive. It has done so partly through the work of economists who have rediscovered and updated the arguments of predecessors like Keynes. But new lines of heterodox thought have also flourished, such as ecological economics. Moreover, the mainstream has become less monolithic. Some of its dissenting strands have now turned into niches in which, alongside the progress thesis, there is also room to consider the possibility of deviation. The most relevant case is probably that of happiness economics, subjective well-being studies, and, more generally, the mainstream turn towards some sort of synthesis between neoclassical and behavioural economics.

Through these various channels—often poorly interconnected—economic thought might eventually recover its capacity to work towards a "synthesis view" of consumer society. If that were to happen, the Cold War period might come to be seen as a strange parenthesis during which, just as consumer societies were flourishing in an unprecedented way, economists lost touch with the ambivalence that had permeated the thought of their predecessors—an ambivalence that may well return in the future. The path towards this "synthesis view", however, remains blocked by three significant obstacles, which we will consider in turn.

The first obstacle is that many of the underlying causes for the rise of the second genealogy are still in operation. The second is that the ambivalence characteristic of the first genealogy does not guarantee a satisfactory articulation of the progress and deviation theses. The third is that consumer society may fall outside the field of vision of economists so that the kind of conversation we have been reviewing in this book might end up becoming a mirage in the history of economic thought. In the following sections, we examine each of these three obstacles separately, seeking to understand what history can teach us about them.

Deviation… What Deviation?

When we reflect on the reasons why the deviation thesis has struggled so hard to emerge among the authors of our second genealogy—which ultimately became dominant—it is tempting to attribute some role to what many regard as the main rupture in the history of economic thought: the replacement, beginning in the late nineteenth century, of an economic theory centred on the concepts of surplus and reproduction with one focused on scarcity and equilibrium. When it comes to the world of consumption, this rupture may have had less immediate and far-reaching implications than in other areas, but it certainly had some. The notion of surplus lent itself well to economists drawing distinctions between those consumer goods that were necessary for workers to perform their tasks effectively and those that served other purposes. The former could be seen as one of the many requirements necessary for the reproduction of the interwoven network of production chains that made up the economy. In that sense it could be labelled "productive consumption". The latter consumption, by contrast, could be viewed as "unproductive".

How classical economists or Marx himself drew this dividing line is another matter. Should the basic consumer basket be limited to goods necessary for the biological survival of the population? Or, as most of these thinkers argued, was it a basket that included goods considered essential for cultural reasons? What the classics or Marx decided to do with this dividing line is also another matter. After all, the widespread use of concepts like "productive consumption" and "unproductive consumption" concealed profound differences in the implications that were attributed to them (Perrotta, 2018). Did unproductive consumption represent a diversion of resources from the stream of economic life that most contributed to the wealth of nations? Or, on the contrary, was it a gateway to the full realisation of human faculties hitherto dormant due to poverty and deprivation? In any case, the distinction between two types of consumption—productive versus unproductive—made it more plausible for economists to consider the possibility of deviation.

The marginalist revolution and the subsequent rise of the neoclassical school erased this distinction. The new theory of utility and demand could be applied equally to all kinds of goods. What mattered was not the role that consumer goods played in the reproduction of the economic system but, more modestly, the role they played in enabling individuals to increase their utility. Utility was decidedly subjective. Researchers could not aspire to measure it directly and instead had to infer it from the decisions they observed consumers making. It was expected that consumers would start with basic goods that made a significant contribution to their utility level and only later begin to set other goals. But the space in which the marginalist consumer made these decisions was elegantly continuous rather than discrete. The consumer basket was supposed to reflect the equilibrium point at which the respective marginal utilities of various goods balanced out. In this new analytical framework, it was more likely that consumer society would be conceptualised in terms of progress rather than deviation. After all, empirically observable consumption patterns could be seen as a set of individual equilibrium points to which consumers had arrived after rejecting other possibilities they believed would yield lower levels of utility. The neoclassical consumer was attributed a kind of rationality that made the possibility of deviation difficult to consider.

It is true, however, that between 1870 and 1945 there were relevant neoclassical economists who, while accepting the transition to a marginalist-rooted economic theory, still found it necessary to make room for the deviation thesis. Alfred Marshall, for example, dispensed with the classical dichotomy between productive and unproductive consumption but retained an analytical framework similar to Mill's. For him, it remained to be seen whether increasingly prosperous societies would be able to use their wealth wisely and thrive in the immaterial dimensions of life. His disciple Arthur Pigou founded a welfare economics that provided analytical space for the possibility that the private utility individuals derived from their consumer goods could differ from social utility. The equilibrium points reached by marginalist consumers did not necessarily represent the best of all possible worlds. Could the neoclassical toolkit accommodate not only the progress thesis but also the deviation thesis? Probably yes, but little progress was made in that direction. After all, Marshall encountered insurmountable difficulties in integrating static marginalist analysis with the kind of dynamic analysis that framed his views on progress. Pigou's welfare economics, meanwhile, fell far short of generating anything resembling a cohesive tradition.

Throughout this book, however, we have emphasised that the difficulties faced by the deviation thesis in taking root within the second of our intellectual genealogies had less to do with what Schumpeter calls "pure economics" than with the gradual vanishing of other social sciences and humanities from the economic mind. In our reconstruction, these other disciplines include two of those highlighted by Schumpeter: history and sociology. But we have also found it necessary to add a third: philosophy. When it comes to views on consumer society, the transition from political economy to pure economics was significant primarily due to its impact on these accompanying disciplines. For the classical economists and Marx, it was common to complement pure economics with elements of history, sociology, and philosophy. This became far less common among new generations of economists, who were engaged in an ambitious project to institutionalise their scientific discipline as an autonomous field. Still during the time of early neoclassical figures like Alfred Marshall, traces of the traditional links with history, sociology, and philosophy remained. But especially after the Second World War, mainstream economists increasingly isolated themselves from the other social sciences. This isolation was not devoid of connotations of superiority and played a key role in shaping the professional identity of the modern economist. The result was the destruction of the space in which, even within the framework of neoclassical "pure economics", the deviation thesis could emerge.

History was crucial because it conferred a temporal dimension on the economists' vision. History could encourage economists to reflect on the direction of economic change. "Divorced from history, economics is a rudderless ship", wrote the great historian Eric Hobsbawm (1997, p. 116), "and economists without history have not much idea of where it is sailing to". Without history, how can we know where the ship is headed? The progress thesis had better chances of surviving in an ahistorical framework. It aligned with the kind of common sense one would expect to find in societies trying to overcome scarcity. Moreover, its positive connotations fit well with the tendency of marginalist and neoclassical discourse to conceptualise time as a transition between successive equilibrium points, each representing a local optimum. The deviation thesis, however, required a more explicit reflection on historical time because it challenged the direction of economic and social change.

Sociology, on the other hand, was important because it created space to investigate the causes of consumer preferences. Some form of economic sociology was required to explore why consumers desired what they desired. Rather than treating preferences as an exogenous given, sociology could turn them into an endogenous variable. It could do so in a way different from what would later be known as endogenous preferences among mainstream economists. A sociology of consumption could identify how social and cultural structures influenced individual behaviours. These structures would pre-exist any individual considered in isolation, while at the same time depending on the aggregation of countless individual behaviours for their reproduction and transformation over time.

Thorstein Veblen emphasised with particular force that what individuals perceived as rational could be the result of how they were influenced by absurd social and cultural structures. More generally, wherever we find formulations of the deviation thesis, we often find some kind of economic sociology suggesting social and cultural influences on individual behaviour. Such was the case in the flashes by Mill, Marshall, or Keynes and certainly in Galbraith's broader treatment of the subject. Conversely, this is what we do not find in the Austrian school or in later versions of the neoclassical school, which explains why it was difficult for the deviation thesis to take root in such environments. If the factors explaining individual behaviour no longer included those that shaped preferences, all that remained were those that allowed people to get what they wanted. Under such circumstances, a narrative of progress was far more natural than one of deviation.

Finally, philosophy was important because it provided criteria for evaluating whether a given transformation in consumption patterns promoted human flourishing and social progress. The deviation thesis could take root more easily to the extent that economists worked with criteria of evaluation that did not have to coincide with those that motivated consumers to make their decisions. If, on the other hand, economists accepted consumers' own criteria, they would be far more likely to align themselves with the progress thesis. Since the time of classical political economy, the profession had flirted with utilitarian philosophy, which took consumers' individual criteria as valid. The alliance between economics and utilitarianism was not without its tensions and counterweights and, in fact, did not fully crystallise until the mid-twentieth century when neoclassical economists like Lionel Robbins proposed that the profession should avoid making ethical judgements altogether. Whether this truly banished philosophy from the economist's desk is debatable. Economists could dispense entirely with history or sociology, but they could never completely avoid philosophy. The difference was that economists in the second of our genealogies began to work with a very thin layer of philosophy. This was what Schumpeter (1954, p. 173) criticised as "the shallowest of all conceivable philosophies of life"—a thin layer of utilitarianism that became implicit in the discourse, like an addendum to the common sense of professionals. According to this addendum, human well-being was seen as a one-dimensional, subjective variable.

The economists of the first of our genealogies, however, often worked with a different notion. For them, human well-being was a multidimensional variable. The subjective dimension mattered, but so did others that were objective in nature or related to the contexts in which individuals made their subjective evaluations. Yet, economic philosophies of this kind came under suspicion of paternalism. The Austrian school and the version of mainstream economics cultivated by Milton Friedman were particularly influential in this regard. Aligning with consumers' own criteria not only made scientific sense—since it could be assumed that individuals were motivated by a rational desire to maximise their utility, while researchers lacked the necessary information to reconstruct their individual utility maps—but also protected the economist from accusations of ethical paternalism.

What was at stake was not merely a scientific issue—it was also a political one. In an era of increasing state intervention in economic life, the goal was to keep the world of consumption depoliticised. Aligning with consumers' own criteria was equivalent to respecting consumer preferences, avoiding the temptation to redirect them based on allegedly more enlightened ideas from researchers or policymakers. Economists of the second genealogy thus found themselves caught in a loop. Having adopted utilitarianism as the default philosophy of the profession, any attempt to work with a different economic philosophy required making that philosophy explicitly articulated. However, since mainstream economists believed they worked without any underlying philosophy, any such attempt to change the conversation was inevitably labelled as paternalistic. Within this loop, the world of consumption remained insulated from collective deliberation and, therefore, from politics.

These dynamics began to unfold in the late nineteenth century and gained considerable momentum by the 1930s, but it was above all during the Cold War that they fully developed, freed from the counterweights they had previously faced. This was partly due to the institutionalisation of economics as an autonomous discipline and the rise of the neoclassical school to a position of hegemony. This factor, in turn, activated a powerful feedback mechanism: the growing capacity of neoclassical economists to control the academic labour market. During the Cold War, institutional mechanisms for reproducing a particular kind of economist—one who worked in isolation from history, sociology, or philosophy—became more effective. Other profiles in the profession were increasingly marginalised. The real-world context also conspired against the chances of the deviation thesis gaining traction among economists. The full emergence of mass consumer societies after the Second World War coincided with a political environment marked by the tension between the United States and the Soviet Union. In this context, many economists viewed consumer sovereignty as an analytical and normative pillar that represented a crucial difference from the unappealing Soviet world. And when, starting in the 1970s, economic growth slowed down and unemployment rose, many economists felt that the deviation thesis was a deviation (if we may play on words) from the real problems.

Nonetheless, real-world circumstances began to shift in the 1990s with the end of the Cold War and the start of a new wave of economic growth. Yet most economists continued working in a field where the deviation thesis could hardly take root. This was largely a consequence of the feedback loops that had emerged in previous decades. Economists remained largely isolated from historians, sociologists, and philosophers. Internal dissent did arise, but its ripple effects barely touched the question about consumer society. Arguably, the closest this movement came was through the work of the so-called happiness economists. Since most economists had adopted a utilitarian philosophy, the only opening through which the deviation thesis could reappear was the combination of "pure economics" with psychology. An empirical examination of the subjective notion of well-being could open the door for researchers to find gaps between the expected satisfaction that informed consumers' decisions and the actual satisfaction they ended up achieving.

Even so, the overall landscape of the profession remained deeply influenced by the legacy of the Cold War. It was very difficult for anything resembling a "synthesis view" to emerge, for the simple reason that one of the two key elements of such a synthesis—the deviation thesis—was conspicuously absent from most analyses. Of course, articulating such a synthesis would not have been an easy task, as demonstrated by what we have been calling the first of our intellectual genealogies.

Obstacles in the Way Towards a "Synthesis View"

The economists of our first genealogy have been open to considering the deviation thesis, but not all of them have shown the same interest in cultivating some kind of "synthesis view". The deviation thesis has often carried iconoclastic connotations that favoured sharp formulations—vigorous wake-up calls meant to radically shake the foundations of the conversation. This was, in part, an unfortunate by-product of the way the marginalist revolution and the rise of the neoclassical school led that conversation to gravitate around the progress thesis. It was precisely then that the deviation thesis began to appear less as an ambivalent counterpoint to the progress thesis and more like what Hirschman would call an exalted generalisation.

The most evident case is that of Veblen. Veblen was by no means the first economist to develop some kind of sociology of consumption to formulate a version of the deviation thesis. Nor was he the only one to mobilise themes such as emulation and conspicuous consumption within that sociology, which in fact had appeared sporadically yet quite naturally in the intellectual line connecting Smith, Mill, Marshall, and later Keynes. But Veblen was the first to make the deviation thesis a central element of his economic thought. Moreover, he realised that this perspective was bound to clash head-on with marginalist and neoclassical economics. It was also destined to collide with the social and cultural atmosphere that Veblen perceived as dominant in the United States of his time. As a result, Veblen showed little interest in articulating the deviation thesis with the progress thesis. Beyond a few isolated references to a vague past requiring a different type of analysis, Veblen's present was that of an emerging consumer society in which an absurd positional race was taking place. The deviation thesis dominated his argument, leaving almost no room for the progress thesis, just as subsequent generations of orthodox economists would leave little room for the deviation thesis.

It is fair to acknowledge that, once they identified the deviation thesis as plausible, many economists from the first genealogy sought to prevent it from becoming an exalted generalisation. Instead, they tried to find a way to articulate the possibility of deviation with the possibility of progress. This is at least how we have interpreted the British line connecting Mill, Marshall, and Keynes throughout this book. We also believe this is the best way to read Galbraith, an institutionalist more interested than Veblen in giving some space to the progress thesis. Even some of the recent work on happiness economics could be read in a similar way. Nevertheless, combining the progress and deviation theses has proven to be a difficult task.

It is (once again) tempting to attribute some of the obstacles to the decline of concepts such as surplus and reproduction in economic thought. In the era of classical political economy, these concepts opened the door to differentiating between productive and unproductive consumption. In

John Stuart Mill's mature formulation, there even seemed to be an orderly way to combine the progress and deviation theses. Progress would consist, first, in ensuring the necessities and basic comforts of productive consumption. Second, it would consist of incorporating increasing amounts of unproductive consumption aimed at human flourishing, including activities related to enjoying nature, culture, and art. In contrast, there would be deviation when unproductive consumption was oriented towards other types of goals, particularly new rounds of crudely materialistic objectives. Although Mill, like other economists of his time, could not reflect on a consumer society that did not yet exist, he did offer an analytical framework within which such reflections would be possible. More importantly for our argument here, that framework was solidly connected to the main body of his economic thought.

One of the problems with later attempts to develop a "synthesis view" is that they tended to take place in analytical frameworks that had a less relevant epistemological status. This is particularly evident in the cases of Marshall and Keynes. Both were updating Mill's argument when they warned their readers that once basic needs were met, it was time to shift priorities: one should abandon materialism and focus on other dimensions of the good life. However, despite how dear this idea was to them, they did not integrate it into their major works and central messages with the same clarity that can be found in Mill. There may have been several reasons for this, but the shift in economic thought away from reproduction and surplus is likely one of them. It was much more difficult for a neoclassical economist like Marshall or a heterodox macroeconomist like Keynes to find suitable hangers in their main intellectual frameworks on which to hang these cherished reflections. This would have required reintroducing the reproductive perspective through the back door and finding reasons to blame consumerist deviation for potential economic problems in a subsequent round of value creation. However, as became particularly evident in the case of Keynes, the macroeconomic dangers of alleged underconsumption could prove more pressing.

The argument cannot be extended to Galbraith, whose reflection on consumer society was indeed incorporated into the core of his thinking about American capitalism and economic life. Moreover, the institutionalist tradition to which Galbraith belonged did not explicitly theorise about reproduction and surplus, but it certainly maintained a closer connection to these concepts than, say, the neoclassical school. Even so, we can still ask whether this distance contributed to shaping the main blind spot of

Galbraith's analysis of consumer society: the absence of clear criteria for distinguishing between consumption that satisfied urgent, important needs and consumption that should rather be considered part of an absurd consumerist race.

In any case, once we recognise the role that these developments in the field of "pure economics" may have played in articulating the progress and deviation theses, our argument throughout the book has leaned more on the accompaniment provided by history, sociology, and philosophy. If the lack of such accompaniment prevented economists from the second genealogy from recognising the deviation thesis, the difficulty in establishing solid ties with these accompanying disciplines proved to be a significant obstacle for the economists of the first genealogy who sought a "synthesis view".

To begin with, there was the issue of how to treat historical time. Thinking historically is one thing. Ensuring that such thinking remains historically consistent as time goes by is quite another. Mill, Marshall, Keynes, Galbraith, and some contemporary economists of the first genealogy, such as the Skidelskys, think in historical terms. Their notions of progress and deviation are anchored in the evaluation of a temporal trajectory. Their "synthesis view" is built by assigning each thesis its own temporal province. The more distant province—marked by poverty and deprivation—belongs to the progress thesis. The present (or, in Keynes' case, perhaps the future), marked by abundance, corresponds to the deviation thesis. By the mid-nineteenth century, Mill was already working with this type of historical theory: the average British consumer was probably at the border between these two provinces. The only remaining life left for the progress thesis would consist of ensuring that all social classes, including the lower ones, reached that point. Marshall was saying something very similar at the beginning of the twentieth century, and in 1930 Keynes retained the argument, only with the caution of projecting the boundary between the two provinces a couple of generations into the future. In the decades after the Second World War, Galbraith was announcing that the moment had arrived: a very large portion of the population had crossed the threshold. The Skidelskys, in turn, recycle this argument, placing the boundary at the late twentieth and early twenty-first centuries.

But how consistent are these various formulations of a "synthesis view" with each other? The continuity of the argument is so strong that the discrepancies between their suggested chronologies are rather unsettling. If, for example, Galbraith's affluent society had already fully arrived in the United States by 1958, does that mean Mill was wrong to consider the far more rudimentary consumption patterns of the average British household in 1848 sufficiently good? Or does it mean that Galbraith was accepting the novelties that had been added to the consumer basket over the previous century, thus delaying the moment when the deviation thesis would come into play? To put it in his own terms, did these new additions help furnish the room, or did they just continue to crowd in furniture? What to make of (say) household appliances such as the washing machine? We can pose the same questions for what we have called Keynes' grandchildren in the present. If a good enough consumption pattern had already materialised in Galbraith's America—or a couple of generations after Keynes wrote his 1930 essay—what does that imply for everything that followed, including (for example) personal computers and mobile phones?

It seems fair to attribute to the spirit of most of these economists a cautious and ambiguous response to this last question. But this only reveals their difficulties in crafting a historically consistent argument. The problem is similar to that which Cosimo Perrotta (2004, p. 7) expresses with admirable clarity in his study of the "fear of goods" in economic thought prior to Adam Smith:

> [Criticism] of the new consumption is quite divorced from any idea of development over time. These critics always refer only to the new consumption of that moment, which they consider unnecessary and unnatural. But they ignore the fact that the traditional commodities, which they themselves are used to consuming and which they find necessary, were in turn considered new, that is "unnecessary" and "unnatural", in the past.

A not insignificant part of the problem is, of course, empirical. Only a careful empirical study of consumer society could clarify the contours of the province in which each thesis would be called to reign or perhaps even identify dynamics in which both theses could be valid simultaneously. However, the gap between the lofty generalisations of the economists in our first genealogy and their empirical foundation has at times been colossal. In the interwar period, a reviewer of R. H. Tawney's *The Acquisitive Society* wrote something that actually applies more generally to the bulk of our first genealogy: "[This] book remains a contrast between two societies with no hint of how the bridge is built between them" (cf. Rogan, 2017, p. 49).

It is possible that, as we saw in the final section of this book, this gap is narrowing as these economists participate in the so-called empirical turn that has affected the entire profession. Nevertheless, it remains a large gap. Long-term statistical reconstructions of consumption patterns have had a modest presence, mostly limited to aggregate views that serve to generalise and illustrate, rather than to advance interpretation. Not much progress has been made in exploring the qualitative sociology of consumption either. As we have seen in the previous section, these economists have mobilised sociological elements to reflect on the origins and causes of consumer preferences. Veblen's instinct of emulation and Galbraith's dependency effect are clear examples, but Mill, Marshall, Keynes, and the Skidelskys also work with similar notions. However, little progress has been made in documenting these notions empirically so that such findings can feed into a more elaborated theoretical conceptualisation. Many intellectual opponents have easily attacked these ideas by pointing out empirical anomalies. The most famous and still used in debates today: if consumers are mere puppets of advertising, how could the Ford Edsel fail in the late 1950s? Only a solid sociology of consumption can accommodate this empirical material within a convincing theoretical framework. At the moment, however, the volume of qualitative research necessary to ground it has yet to emerge among the economists of our first genealogy.

In fact, the absence of reflections on different versions of consumer society across time and space is highly revealing. This perspective has proven very fertile for analysing capitalism, starting with the dichotomy between liberal market economies and coordinated market economies, and continuing with the subsequent dissolution of this dichotomy into a more complex tree of possibilities and alternatives (Hall & Soskice, 2001; Boyer, 2005). None of this has made its way into the conversation about consumer society, despite the fact that there is no shortage of evidence suggesting that it too exists in different varieties. It seems clear, for example, that although there are strong links between Americanisation and consumer society in the post-1945 world, European and Japanese dynamics retain certain distinctive features in comparison to the American model (de Grazia, 2005; Francks, 2009). Nevertheless, theoretical reflections have tended to revolve around an object of study assumed to be essentially uniform across contexts and have not engaged with the existence of different "varieties of consumer society". Had this been the case, following recommendations such as those by Hirschman (1992), it is more likely that the problems of assigning a temporal province to each thesis had been subjected to closer scrutiny.

Another part of the problem, however, is less empirical than theoretical. We are not thinking now of economic theory in the strict sense, but of the type of relations that economists develop with philosophy. Among the economists of the first genealogy, we find a philosophical tension, almost always implicit, between two visions of the good life. Both share a rejection of the one-dimensional, subjective view of human well-being. Both advocate for a multidimensional conceptualisation in which, alongside the mental states of individuals, the objective contexts and their different components matter. However, is the good life a result or a process? Is it something that can be achieved once and for all? Or, on the contrary, is it rather an abstract ideal that will never be fully attained in an imperfect world, and whose main function is to allow us to decide whether one path of change is more desirable than another? This tension closely resembles the one identified by Amartya Sen (2009) in his exploration of the concept of justice. Consequently, we will identify its two poles using the same labels proposed by him. The first notion of the good life, which associates it with an absolute state in which sufficiently satisfactory outcomes in all dimensions of well-being are achieved once and for all, is a transcendentalist notion. The second notion, which sees it as a relative reference subject to periodic redefinitions as the context changes, is a pragmatist notion.

Although it would be unfair to classify Keynes's economic mind as transcendentalist, the way in which he reflects on "the economic problem" in "Economic Possibilities for Our Grandchildren" is perhaps the best-known illustration of a transcendentalist approach to the world of consumption. Since there are immutable absolute needs, it is feasible to aspire to resolve the "economic problem" as a precondition for progress in the non-material dimensions of human flourishing. At its core, Keynes' view is simply the most explicit exposition of an economic philosophy that had been underlying in the first of our genealogies. It is also a philosophy that has been resurrected in our time by the "degrowth" wing of ecological economics: since infinite growth is not possible in a finite world, a consumption pattern that satisfies the material needs involved in the good life must be retained. Once this satisfactory state is achieved once and for all, it makes no sense to pursue a allegedly superior consumption pattern.

The pragmatist notion of the good life has on the other hand been more present among institutional economists. Much has been written about the links between Veblen and the philosophy of John Dewey, but in our topic, we find Galbraith's pragmatism especially illustrative (Berry, 2013, pp. 176–177; Hodgson, 2004). While there are undoubtedly lines of kinship between Galbraith's *The Affluent Society* and Keynes' "Economic Possibilities", their respective points of reference are different. Galbraith never speaks of resolving the "economic problem" once and for all, nor does he devote much space to the immaterial dimensions of the good life. Instead, Galbraith is proposing that the affluent society is not capable of adequately addressing the most urgent economic problems. What in Keynes is a problem of balance between the economic dimension and the other dimensions of the good life, in Galbraith it is a problem of balance between different economic dimensions. It has rightly been pointed out that Galbraith denies his readers a clear definition of what is urgent and what is superfluous: for him, these are not absolute categories, designed to stubbornly resist transplantation to other places and times, but rather simply relative categories that allow comparisons between alternative paths of change in a given context.

The long shadow of transcendentalism has conditioned the attempts of our first genealogy of economists to produce a "synthesis view". Transcendentalism is bound to produce synthesis views in the weak sense of the term. If it is possible to identify a sufficiently satisfactory state once and for all at a specific moment in time, it is tempting to assign the progress thesis to the period prior to that moment and the deviation thesis to the period afterwards. The pragmatist notion of the good life has more chances of leading us towards a stronger version of the "synthesis view". Even once a reasonably satisfactory state has been achieved in a given historical context, there may be scope for innovative consumer goods that embed progress. Said goods may or may not coexist with others that entail a consumerist deviation. If we do not know what the future may hold, how can we be sure that a given consumption pattern today is the one that will most contribute to the good life? But could we not also make the same argument looking back in time? After having heard economists from different periods place the separation between the temporal provinces of progress and deviation at different points in time, it seems reasonable to imagine that there are actually numerous provinces characterised by the coexistence of both theses. This could be a good starting point for a new generation of "synthesis views".

A Mirage?

Consumer society has had difficulties in establishing itself as a relevant object of analysis for economists. Following Schumpeter, economists (like other researchers) start from a certain "vision" as a prior basis from which to conceptualise and analyse reality. In the reconstruction we have provided in this book, the presence of consumer society in that vision has proven to be intermittent and unstable, leaving us with a sense not dissimilar to that of a mirage, which only seemed to gain clarity during a brief period after the Second World War.

It is fair to concede that the path leading us to that brief period reflects the typical, inevitably gradual process through which researchers become aware of the emergence of new socio-economic realities. We cannot expect the classical economists or Marx to have had a vision of consumer society because, after all, consumer society had not yet emerged in their time. The consumption patterns of most households were rudimentary and showed no clear trend towards expansion or diversification. We can look back to that pre-1870 period in search of analyses of the world of consumption and read them through the lens of what would later become the conversation about consumer society, but that is all.

In contrast, between 1870 and 1945, an emerging consumer society began to carve out a space in the field of vision of economists. Considering the significant limitations still present in this embryonic consumer society, economists became reasonably aware of the transition to a more comfortable material life. The neoclassical school built upon this base its vision of an economic life driven by the desires of consumers seeking to maximise their utility. The Austrian school placed this emerging consumer society—and what would come to be called consumer sovereignty—at the forefront of their defence of capitalist order and democracy. The institutionalist school, on the other hand, critiqued what it perceived as the dark side of this society, in which individuals eagerly threw themselves into the task of emulating the consumption patterns of those above them in the social hierarchy. There were even attempts, such as those by Marshall and Keynes, to synthesise the progress thesis and the deviation thesis.

These dynamics led to the rise of the debate on consumer society in the decades following the Second World War, just as consumer society itself was fully flourishing in the real world. The fact that society had transitioned to one in which most households were spending more and more money on an increasing variety of consumer goods did not go unnoticed by contemporaries, and economists were no exception. By means of the institutionalism of a high-profile economist like Galbraith, the question about consumer society took on an important space within the economic conversation of the decades following the Second World War. Galbraith can be seen (as he himself did) as a link in an intellectual tradition stemming from Veblen, but also (as we have argued in this book) as a culmination of the efforts made by Mill, Marshall, and Keynes in pursuit of a "synthesis view" and, more broadly (we now add), as the culmination of the process through which economists were discovering consumer society. The fragmentary efforts of the preceding period, focused on an emerging consumer society, now transformed into systematic analyses of a fully formed consumer society.

As we have stated, there is nothing particularly remarkable about this gradual process of discovery. What is remarkable is that once consumer society had been discovered, economists quickly forgot about it. The debate on consumer society boomed in the decades after the Second World War, but it soon became relegated to the status of an intellectual mirage. This was already perceptible in the final stage of the Cold War and, up to some extent, has continued to be the case to this day. The dynamics of consumer society have continued to unfold, with more and more countries recording an ongoing revolution in material life and more and more households transitioning to ever more abundant and diverse baskets. Yet, the debate of the decades after the Second World War has not been continued with much vigour.

This is partly related to the internal dynamics of the profession. Galbraith's contribution was met with great scepticism, if not outright hostility, from most of his colleagues. The institutionalism to which Galbraith adhered was no longer what it had been in the first half of the twentieth century. It had become a marginal current. The way the clash between Galbraith and his mainstream critics was resolved did much to turn the question about consumer society into an intellectual mirage. If the field in which the deviation thesis could sprout was disappearing, the debate on consumer society that Galbraith had opened was, in fact, a non-debate. Was there any sense in participating in a non-debate?

When we add to these intellectual developments the professional developments with which they intertwined, the response becomes obviously negative. The Cold War mainstream was more powerful than the groups that could deserve the label in earlier periods. Its capacity to set quality standards for the entire profession was remarkable. This is, in part, a story of cultural hegemony, based on the power of ideas and of internal cohesion around methodological principles that gave the profession of economics a decidedly "scientific" identity. But it is also, to a considerable extent, a story of growing power over the academic labour market, restricting the viability of the spaces in which alternative schools of economic thought had been flourishing.

These internal dynamics were important in keeping the question of consumer society in the background because, in addition to their impact during the Cold War, they have left a notable trace to this day. After all, these were forces that fed back into one another as time went by. It should not surprise us that recent attempts to revitalise the question about consumer society have come not only from the heterodox fringes of the profession, but also from researchers who, despite participating in the secular conversation we call the history of economic thought, do not have a professional affiliation as economists.

A key factor was the intertwining of these internal dynamics of the profession with a largely autonomous development occurring in the political realm. During the Cold War, the sovereign consumer was firmly established as one of the cornerstones of political thought across the broad spectrum of dominant centre-right and centre-left parties. Heated debates could take place on issues such as macroeconomic management, the welfare state, or labour market regulation, but not on the politics of the sovereign consumer, which became a point of internal cohesion against the authoritarianism of the Soviet bloc. The sovereign consumer had not played such a prominent role in political discourse in the preceding period and, in fact, the nascent social democracy of the time had distanced itself somewhat from it. By the time of the Cold War, and with that distance absorbed by the system in the form of policies for consumer protection (availability of reliable information, implementation of complaint and guarantee systems), the sovereign consumer became part of the discourse of social democracy in the same way it was part of the discourse of both moderate conservatism and neoliberalism. There were even social democratic governments that applied the logic of the sovereign consumer to reform their own public administrations. These trends accelerated after the end of the Cold War, as social democracy sought to reconstruct its electoral basis by redefining itself as a market-friendly "third way".

We do not intend to deny that economists were among the actors who inserted the sovereign consumer into the political culture of the Cold War and beyond. However, we now find it more interesting to highlight the other side of the equation: how the consolidation of this political culture permeated the work of economists. The eclipse of consumer society as a possible item of political debate did not help the topic stay alive in an academic debate that, for the reasons we have examined earlier, already showed a tendency to push it aside. This especially applies to economists whose political leanings were left of centre: from mainstream economists who saw numerous market failures in economic life to heterodox economists who had never believed in the first place that market coordination was so very good as a general rule. These economists were more numerous than is sometimes assumed, but the question about consumer society was outside their field of vision. Many of them accepted the mainstream narrative that the prior conversation about consumer society had lacked scientific rigour. Only a political climate in which consumer society had been the subject of a more heated public debate could have changed this dynamic.

The question about consumer society was historically unlucky. Its object of study, consumer society, emerged precisely at the moment when the most extreme version of the "pure economist" was triumphing in academia, happily isolated from historians, sociologists, and philosophers, and at the very moment when the Cold War and its neoliberal aftermath turned the sovereign consumer into a non-partisan element of democratic life. These two forces fed back into each other up to the present day, and the question about consumer society tended to blur, almost like an intellectual mirage.

Conclusion: The Next Stepping Stone

At the beginning, I mentioned that the ambition of this book was to reach one of those stepping stones referred to by Alexander Gerschenkron (1962): results that, far from answering all the questions and even further from offering a definitive treatment, could serve as a starting point for new research. There are many aspects in which our analysis may have fallen short for some readers, and I hope this will inspire future researchers. Why not, after all, go much further back in time and delve into economic thought prior to the late eighteenth century, beyond the brief glimpses offered here? As the work of Cosimo Perrotta (2004) powerfully suggests, we could subject these authors to the kind of backtracking exercise we applied to classical political economists and Marx, and this would likely give us a more complete picture of the origins of the rival views of consumer society. Why not focus more on the conjunctural time, or even the time of events, at the expense of the structural time emphasised in this book? Our four periods have been very long, and while we believe this has allowed us to capture the main threads of the narrative, a more detailed consideration of the different phases involved in its development would provide a wealth of nuances and analytical insights. Why not study more thoroughly authors and works that may sit in the second tier of relevance, but precisely for that reason may help us gain a more complete picture of the evolution of discourse within each school of thought? Or analyse in depth the diffusion of arguments beyond the focal points where they were generated? Or, to give one last example from a list that could be longer, reconstruct the link between economic thought on consumer society and the intellectual history of the concept of consumer society itself?

I would be more than satisfied if the reader considers that this first journey towards a stepping stone has been worthwhile and could serve as a starting point for others. Since the onset of the Great Recession, and even more so following the COVID-19 crisis and its aftermath, there has been much talk of rethinking capitalism. Much is debated about the A-side of the system, in search of ways to combine its potential for economic growth, on the one hand, with social cohesion and environmental sustainability, on the other. But beyond these broad themes related to the production of wealth and its distribution, the question of how we use that wealth is also crucial. The B-side of capitalism may also need rethinking in order to ensure that economic and social change leads to genuine progress in human well-being. At no point have we claimed that reflecting on consumer society is a simple task. In fact, one of the main difficulties involved has been its multidimensional character and the resulting challenge of synthesising different perspectives. I have simply asserted this reflection as necessary for the debates on capitalism.

At the start of the book, we heard Albert Hirschman conclude his classic *The Passions and the Interests* by arguing that this type of history of ideas helps to "raise the level of debate". Having reached now the end of this book, it may be worth emphasising that it is not just about the debate on consumer society or capitalism. It is also about the debate on the nature of economics. What makes a good economist? A century ago, at the death of Marshall, Keynes wrote that a great economist must possess "a rare combination of gifts":

> He must reach a high standard in several different directions and must combine talents not often found together. He must be a mathematician, historian, statesman, philosopher—in some degree [....] He must study the present in the light of the past for the purposes of the future. No part of man's nature or his institutions must lie entirely outside his regard. (Keynes, 1924, p. 322)

What is one to think of these words a century later? It has to be admitted that the book has shown sympathy for this position, and in doing so, it has taken a critical (though not hopeless) stance on what economists have more often been in reality. But I would like to think that even those readers who do not share this perspective will agree that (as the book has hopefully shown) the "many-sidedness" that Keynes speaks of matters: for better or worse, the fact that it is present or absent among participants in the economic debate shapes the terms in which that debate is framed and the paths it will take.

The same applies to the political debate in which we are all called to participate, including social science researchers. Half a century ago, the great economic historian Paul Bairoch (1971), a pioneer in the reconstruction of long statistical series of GDP, assured his readers that if abundance did not exist already in the developed countries, it never would. What he meant was that, after two centuries of sustained economic growth, the time had come for public policies to confront the fact that societies were no longer characterised by widespread deprivation. Bairoch did not present himself as a market liberal or as a communist: he advocated for "a certain form of planning" which, within the framework of a market economy, would not emphasise maximising economic growth, but rather a more equitable distribution of wealth, a "reorientation of the *structure of consumption*", and a reorientation of technological change "strictly subordinated to the *real interests* of societies" (Bairoch, 1971, pp. 316, 321 and 324; emphasis added). Bairoch was essentially calling for a renewal of the economic agenda of social democracy, the historical origins of which had understandably been tied to a narrower conception of economic progress and social justice. Today, we know that this renewal did not materialise.

Thomas Piketty (2019) rightly points out that this failure to adapt to changing conditions was an important reason why social democracy was displaced by market liberalism at the end of the twentieth century and into the twenty-first. Piketty has in mind the neglected issue of the international framing of social justice, and he is not without reason. But social democracy also neglected, and continues to neglect, a domestic issue: the fact that most households had gained access to a comfortable and diversified consumption pattern and that, as a result, their well-being was beginning to be exposed to what Avner Offer (2006) calls the "challenge of affluence". During its heyday in the post-war decades, social democracy failed to develop a politics of the good life. That would be a politics that departed from the "more is better" logic and invested in creating the collective capacity needed for the "reorientation of the structure of consumption" that Bairoch deemed necessary (Offer, 2007). When economic growth slowed down in the 1970s, or (for that matter) during the Great Recession, the social democratic response was greatly conditioned by its adherence to the "hegemony of growth" (Schmelzer, 2016). Today, social democracy is seeking its place among the various "countermovements" that, in Polanyi's (1944) fashion, have been eroding what, after the fall of the Berlin Wall, had been a triumphant neoliberalism. In this new historical juncture, will social democracy be able to give consumer society, its dynamics and its problems, the attention they deserve? Even those readers who do not identify with the social democratic cause, to whom I apologise for burdening them with the content of this last pair of paragraphs, will agree that (as this book has shown) the researchers and activists who today fight to revitalise the debate on consumer society are not alone: they are accompanied by a long history of economic thought

References

Bairoch, P. (1971). *Le Tiers-Monde dans l'impasse: le démarrage économique du XVIIIe au XXe siècle*. Gallimard. [Spanish edition: *El Tercer Mundo en la encrucijada: el despegue económico desde el siglo XVIII al XX*. Alianza, 1973.]

Berry, M. (2013). *The affluent society revisited*. Oxford University Press.

Boyer, R. (2005). How and why capitalisms differ. *Economy and Society, 34*(4), 509–557.

de Grazia, V. (2005). *Irresistible empire: America's advance through twentieth-century Europe*. Harvard University Press.

Francks, P. (2009). *The Japanese consumer: An alternative economic history of modern Japan*. Cambridge University Press.

Friedman, M. (1962). *Capitalism and freedom*. University of Chicago Press.

Gerschenkron, A. (1962). *Economic backwardness in historical perspective: A book of essays*. Harvard University Press.

Hall, P. A., & Soskice, D. (2001). An introduction to varieties of capitalism. In P. A. Hall & D. Soskice (Eds.), *Varieties of capitalism: The institutional foundations of comparative advantage*. Oxford University Press.

Hirschman, A. O. (1992). Does the market keep us out of mischief or out of happiness? *Contemporary Sociology, 26*(6), 741–744.

Hobsbawm, E. (1997). *On history*. Weidenfeld and Nicolson. [Spanish edition: *Sobre la historia*. Crítica. 1998.]

Hodgson, G. (2004). *The evolution of institutional economics: agency, structure, and Darwinism in American institutionalism*. Routledge.

Keynes, J. M. (1924). Alfred Marshall, 1842-1924. *Economic Journal, 34*(135), 311–372.

Offer, A. (2006). *The challenge of affluence: Self-control and well-being in the United States and Britain since 1950*. Oxford University Press.

Offer, A. (2007). A vision of prosperity. Position paper for the Sustainable Development Commission, UK Department of Environment, Food and Rural Affairs.

Perrotta, C. (2004). *Consumption as an investment, I: The fear of goods from Hesiod to Adam Smith*. Routledge.

Perrotta, C. (2018). *Unproductive labour in political economy: the history of an idea*. Routledge.

Piketty, T. (2019). *Capital and ideology*. Harvard University Press.

Polanyi, K. (1944). *The great transformation: The political and economic origins of our time*. Farrar & Rinehart.

Rogan, T. (2017). *The moral economists: R. H. Tawney, Karl Polanyi, and E. P. Thompson*. Princeton University Press.

Schmelzer, M. (2016). *The hegemony of growth: The OECD and the making of the economic growth paradigm*. Cambridge University Press.

Schumpeter, J. A. (1954). *History of economic analysis*. Oxford University Press. [Spanish edition: *Historia del análisis económico*. Ariel, 1994.]

Sen, A. (2009). *The idea of justice*. Allen Lane.

Index

F. Collantes, *Consumer Society and the Economists*, Palgrave Studies in the History of Economic Thought,
https://doi.org/10.1007/978-3-031-96645-3

Kolibri 360 GmbH
Ferdinand-Jühlke-Straße 7
99095 Erfurt, Deutschland
produktsicherheit@kolibri360.de